PROBLEMS IN DEVELOPING ACADEMIC LIBRARY COLLECTIONS

. . . .

by Jasper G. Schad and Norman E. Tanis

R. R. Bowker Company
New York & London, 1974
A Xerox Education Company
XEROX

Published by R.R. Bowker Co. (A Xerox Education Company)
1180 Avenue of the Americas, New York, N.Y. 10036

Printed and bound in the United States of America.

Library of Congress Cataloging in Publication Data
Schad, Jasper G   1932–
    Problems in developing academic library collections.
    (Problem-centered approaches to librarianship)
    Includes bibliographical references.
    1. Acquisitions (Libraries)—Case studies.   2. Libraries,
University and college. I. Tanis, Norman E.,
1929–   joint author. II. Title.
Z689.S3   025.2'1   72-1944
ISBN 0-8352-0551-7

When a man does not know what harbor he is making for,
no wind is the right wind.

Seneca, Epistle LXXI

CONTENTS

· · · · · · · · · · ·

FOREWORD

· · · · · · · · · · ·

This seventh volume in Bowker's "Problem-Centered Approaches to Librarianship" series differs from its predecessors not only in subject matter, but in other significant respects as well. It is a collaboration of two experienced practicing academic librarians, and is, in addition, the first collection of problem case studies for instructional use to have been prepared by library administrators, rather than by teachers of librarianship. The latter should be regarded as an especially happy development by all in the library education fraternity who have sought the benefit of a closer and more constructive interchange between library schools and librarians in service. No more impressive example of the contribution that practitioners can make to library education can be found than in Jasper G. Schad and Norman E. Tanis's *Problems in Developing Academic Library Collections.*

The great strength of this case collection lies, I think, not merely in the fact that it is written out of the immediacy of the day-by-day problems of professional practice, but also in the range and variety of personal experience upon which its authors have been able to draw. Between them, they span most of the spectrum of American college and university libraries, from the two-year institution with a strong orientation toward vocational-technical programs to the large university where graduate study and research command the lion's share of resources and services. While both authors possess the perspective of top management, which permits them to present a problem in the context of its broad policy implications, their collective experience also encompasses the quite distinct points of view of the acquisitions librarian, the bibliographer, and the collection development specialist.

Like all of the volumes in this series, *Problems in Developing Academic Library Collections* is based on the notion that librarianship is not primarily a theoretical field, but rather, an applied discipline, requiring of those who practice it ability to modify, adapt, and alter general concepts to meet the varied demands of specific institutional environments and human situations. As this book illustrates so effectively, in no area of library practice are these capacities more needed than in academic library collection development, where the context for decision making is a unique set of institutional characteristics and instructional goals, the latter usually not even expressible as a single set of explicit aims, but most often instead an amorphous congeries of uncoordinated, conflicting individual aims and departmental aspirations. This is precisely what makes the case study, with its capacity for incorporating multiple complex variables into a single descriptive problem statement, such an eminently appropriate vehicle for presentation of the policy issues of academic library materials selection. It also accounts for the richness of detail that characterizes the case studies in this book.

Perhaps it is because of the very uniqueness and variety of academic acquisitions work that it has not, in the past, lent itself as well to consideration in the classroom as certain other specializations. In our effort to deal with this problem in library schools, we have sometimes tended to isolate the acquisitions function as a separate activity, and, as a consequence, usually succeeded only in trivializing it into a mere set of techniques, procedures, and skills. Similarly, when traditional teaching and learning approaches are employed, it is easy to foster the false notion that collection development is entirely a materials-oriented activity when, in point of fact, and as these case studies make abundantly clear, the more challenging problems in academic library acquisitions focus less on the characteristics of materials than on the characteristics of people—both the "choosers" and the "users." And, one must add, the nonusers as well, the great mass of members of the academic community who remain essentially unserved and untouched by the library.

While these problem case studies are primarily intended for classroom, continuing education, and in-service uses, they may profitably be read for their exemplary value as well. In many instances, they serve as effective and telling illustrations of the practical consequences of applying accepted principles or recommended procedures to real library situations. In this sense, they exemplify the real meaning of such concepts as cooperative acquisitions, decentralization of holdings, building to strength, or the balanced collection, by presenting them, not as abstract or generalized ideas, but clothed in the garments of operational reality. Especially striking in this respect, as one reads the case studies that follow, are the painful consequences for academic libraries of the present lack of satisfactory measures of adequacy or excellence in relation to collections. Before meaningful and useful standards can be formulated, however, it is first necessary that we be able to describe fully the kinds of environments in which they will need to be applied. In this last respect, over and beyond the very major contribution this volume makes to the improvement of instruction in the curricular area of collection development, it should prove valuable in its descriptive aspect as well.

The "Problem-Centered Approaches to Librarianship" series is designed to make case studies and related materials available for both formal and informal teaching purposes in the several subfields of librarianship, as well as to demonstrate the value of the case study as a vehicle for presentation and analysis of contemporary problems of professional practice. Future volumes in this series are planned to appear at regular intervals, and will be concerned with such areas as the simulation approach in the teaching of library administration, selection and utilization of the newer media in libraries, and public library services to children and youth. It is my hope that these will prove as useful and relevant to both the student and the practicing librarian as *Problems in Developing Academic Library Collections* surely must.

THOMAS J. GALVIN
Series Editor

PREFACE

· · · · · · · · · ·

All too often, library schools seem to have responded to the difficult question of how to teach acquisitions by not teaching it at all. In part, this is perhaps because acquisitions work is no longer viewed as fully professional. Training for the acquisitions librarian is now often seen as the responsibility of administration courses, while collection development is covered primarily in courses on the literatures of particular subject areas such as the sciences, social sciences, and humanities. This leaves students with a serious gap in their professional education, because collection building is an important element in any library program, and it profoundly affects the ability of a library to serve its clientele. The training of librarians for collection building is being approached primarily as a problem in knowing the resources used in particular disciplines. Certainly that is an essential element in the process, but others are just as important. What the curriculum all too often omits is a treatment of how to build a collection—strategies and techniques. Because of the particular nature of the collection development process, this is difficult to present using traditional teaching methods. The problems collection developers face have not been, or perhaps cannot be, reduced to a single set of guiding principles. Rather, they involve matters of judgment and the ability to work effectively with others—problems ideally suited to the case method.

Each of these cases originated from a real situation, although many now represent a synthesis of multiple sources, and considerable liberty has been taken in selecting and altering details to make the cases more useful instructionally. A number have been tested in the classroom at the School of Library Science, Simmons College. The cases attempt to cover neither all issues nor all kinds of libraries uniformly. That would require literally hundreds of cases. They do, however, seek to present a balanced range of some of the most significant problems typically found in academic libraries today. At first glance, several may appear to be limited to the organization and administration of the acquisitions department. However, these cases are designed to underscore the fact that collection building involves more than merely the individual librarian functioning in the isolated role of selector. In other words, the operation of an acquisitions department itself profoundly affects the development of the collection. Other cases were selected to illustrate broader problems. For instance, three cases deal with approval programs, but in each of these, the approval plan itself is only one of many issues and not necessarily the central issue.

These cases emphasize unresolved problems, and thus favor issues on which there is little agreement among academic librarians or uniformity from library to library. Methods of book selection and collection development vary, but not every method is as good as another. The size of the institution, the size of the book budget, the state of the existing collection, the subject capabilities of various personnel involved, and many other factors must be considered. Are approval programs suitable? Perhaps. Or, in a particular situation, are blanket orders better? Maybe, maybe not. Who should select retrospective materials? Faculty? Librarians? Sometimes faculty, sometimes librarians, sometimes both? How should material be selected? What criteria should be used? What is appropriate for the collection and what should be excluded? The questions appear endless, but they do have to be answered.

Many factors may intrude to deflect a library from its collecting goals. Individuals, administrative units, students, governmental agencies, the community, and other groups often pressure the library to further their own interests. Librarians find themselves in conflict with faculty members, administrators, legislators, students, and taxpayers. Sometimes pressures are internal, sometimes external. Battles are fought over the relative merits of disciplines, the share of available funding, questions of censorship, collecting goals and policies, and so on.

Such questions explain why these cases must contain so much detail. Enormous detail is required for effective decision making in collection development, often even in deciding the purchase of a particular title. Without detailed information, accurate decisions are impossible.

This collection of thirty problem case studies is designed primarily for use in the formal academic training of librarians at the graduate level. They may serve also in institutes and conferences, in-service training programs, and the self-education of those interested in and concerned with the problems of collection development in institutions of higher education.

To prepare realistically for work in collection development, it must be recognized that librarians operate in a variety of situations, often with limited resources. Equally important, librarians must understand the relationship of the collection development function to the library as a whole. The case method is ideally suited to this approach to a problem, as Thomas J. Galvin shows in *The Case Method in Library Education and In-Service Training* (Metuchen, N.J.: Scarecrow Press, 1973). It is important to note, that the case method differs greatly from traditional teaching and learning, which presents students with a body of material in the form of facts or data, principles or theories, and methodology or techniques that they are to master or memorize. Students are often judged or graded chiefly on their ability to recall this material, usually demonstrated through a test. The ability to memorize in no way guarantees the success of a student after graduation. Other factors, such as the ability to identify problems, and to select and organize the right information needed to solve them, are more important. Because there is often no single correct solution to a problem, the logic used to reach a solution takes on special importance. One of the prime responsibilities of graduate professional education must be to develop these skills. The case method can provide a better avenue for such training than the lecture-textbook method.

Because the case method is problem centered, it might seem that facts and principles are less important than in traditional learning. This is not true. While they are used differently, they are no less important. With the case method, students use information to develop solutions to problems. In so doing, they come to an understanding of course content, not as abstract or isolated facts or principles, but rather as something they need *now*, and will depend on in the future to function as effective members of the profession. The case method provides students, often unfamiliar with what to expect as professionals, with important insights into the kinds of problems librarians are actually facing today. This sense of immediacy and reality is something that is difficult, if not impossible, to convey with the traditional lecture-textbook method. Moreover, the case approach has the further benefit of improving both student motivation and retention.

This book offers, then, both a wholly new approach to describing the problems of academic library collection development, and a radical alternative to traditional ways of preparing librarians to deal effectively with these problems. It is the hope of the authors that it will provide those responsible for both formal and informal programs of preservice and in-service education of library personnel with the teaching materials needed to present this area of library operations as fully and as realistically as its importance merits.

JASPER G. SCHAD
Director of Libraries and Audiovisual Services
Wichita State University

NORMAN E. TANIS
Director of Libraries
California State University, Northbridge

INTRODUCTION

· · · · · · · · · · · · · · ·

A basic fact about the problems facing academic librarians in developing collections is that most of these problems have existed for many years. While a few such as system-wide cooperation and program budgeting are of recent origin, the rest have been around in one form or another for many years—some nearly a century. The same issues presented in "A Plan for Battle," and "But What about the Students, Professor Reid?" were matters of vital concern to academic librarians in the early years of the twentieth century.[1] In other words, to understand fully the problems presented in these cases, requires at least some knowledge of the historical development of collection building and acquisitions in academic libraries. Very little has been written on this subject, although J. Periam Danton's *Book Selection and Collections: A Comparison of German and American University Libraries*, published in 1963 by Columbia University Press, contains much valuable information, and David O. Lane's "The Selection of Academic Library Materials, A Literature Survey," which appeared in the September 1968 issue of *College and Research Libraries*, is a useful guide to other sources.

There were several key developments affecting the course of acquisitions and collection development in academic libraries. Most crucial, perhaps, was a fact noted by Roger Horn in an article in *College and Research Libraries* in January 1972: academic libraries began at a time when there was a much greater sense of community within institutions of higher education. Typically, the library was small and so was the number of its users. Indeed, there was generally a commonality of interest within academic institutions, which their libraries reflected. As the community and the library grew, the situation changed; there was no longer a true community of users. Departments proliferated, and many grew to the point that individual members of the faculty, each with a particular set of needs, worked in relative isolation from one another. The impact of this change on collection building was nothing short of revolutionary. The loss of community made imperative some agency or individual who could arbitrate the disparate needs and demands of faculty members. In some cases, it was a strong librarian, usually the director. In other institutions, the central administration allocated book funds directly to departments, but more frequently the responsibility fell to a faculty committee. However, committee members themselves often felt unable to evaluate the book requests of colleagues in other disciplines, and so they resorted to assigning or allocating specific amounts of the library's book funds to each department. Committees often developed formulas based on such factors as the total number of credit hours by department sometimes weighed by level (lower division, upper division, graduate), the number of courses in each department weighed on the basis of estimated library dependence, the rate of publication or the number of titles published annually relevant to a specific department, and their average cost. These and other methods were an attempt to allocate library funds objectively.

While imprecise, formulas did sometimes help to make the distribution of library funds more equitable. On the other hand, they posed a number of problems. Most serious was the fact that a common objective of formulas was to prevent over-ambitious faculty members and departments from getting more than their share of the book budget. Because control was a paramount consideration, librarians and teaching faculty were deflected from confronting questions relating to the real needs of the collection.[2] In addition, the responsibility for book selection was placed firmly in the hands of the teaching faculty rather than with the library where it belongs both philosophically and administratively.[3] Wide-spread abuses were reported within departments as chairmen or powerful senior members frequently used funds for their own needs or for those of favored colleagues. Finally, because of the complexity of informational resource requirements and many other variables connected with their acquisition, no entirely satisfactory formula has ever been developed.

With the responsibility for book selection firmly in the hands of the faculty, librarians focused their efforts on obtaining as large an unallocated segment of the budget as possible to provide a degree of flexibility to purchase books of a general nature, reference books, periodicals, and perhaps to fill in gaps, as well as to purchase special collections. This situation is still common at many colleges and universities as several cases, including "It's Not as Simple as You Think," illustrate.

As the amount of material published and library budgets increased, librarians, partly out of necessity, began to take a more active role in collection development. During the late forties and fifties, a number of librarians advocated acquisitions policies and developed such documents.[4] It was the sixties, however, that brought a dramatic rise in spending for higher education, which resulted in the second basic change in the way collections are built. For the first time, many libraries had budgets large enough to meet almost all of the institution's expressed book and journal needs. These schools found it no longer necessary to arbitrate. The problem became one of how to spend money wisely. By the mid-sixties, most large university libraries with area studies programs, as well as many new or rapidly growing institutions, had established formal collection development programs. The question of how to administer such programs arose, and this issue is presented in "The Question Is 'How?' " Typically, larger libraries established separate collection development departments with bibliographers or curators, or included bibliographers within the acquisitions department, while smaller libraries usually utilized reference librarians as subject specialists with the added responsibility of book selection.[5]

Yet at the same time, many other institutions continued to follow established procedures, changing not at all or only to a limited degree. Several cases, including "You've Wasted a Lot of Our Money!" and "I Just Don't Know What They Want," illustrate the kinds of problems such colleges and universities encounter as older attitudes and procedures conflict with the needs of the present. The important fact, however, is that the process of collection development is far from uniform, and anyone seeking to understand it is confronted with a myriad of policies and procedures. To recognize this fact is to understand a basic characteristic of the collection development function in academic libraries.

At the present time, two major issues have yet to be resolved by academic librarians. The first, and most difficult one, is, How important is the acquisitions program relative to other library program elements? It would be easy to answer this question if academic librarians agreed on what constitutes adequacy, but they do not. Various formulas[6] have been set forth, which attempt to provide models of adequacy, but no formula is uniformly accepted. Many contend that adequacy cannot be expressed in numbers alone, but that a large collection is essential to a good library. Others reject volume count as a valid measure of adequacy, preferring to define adequacy ". . .as the capability of the library to respond within a given time to a given percentage of book calls in general, and to given percentages of different types of materials (monographs, periodicals, etc.) and different levels of content (introductory, advanced, etc.) immediately."[7]

Determining how large the collection should be is only one aspect of this issue. Equally important is what it costs to acquire and process material. In other words, What percentage of total library resources should be allocated to the collection? Academic librarians do not agree on this issue. One position was expressed in the 1970 annual report of the Princeton University Library:

> While the effectiveness of a library is determined in part by the skill of the staff in putting it to work to meet the needs of users, the foundation factor is the collection itself—the size and quality of the library's portion of the record of society, and the quality of the permanent guide to the collection, the library catalogue.

Others suggest different priorities, feeling that collections have been developed at the expense of service. Robert S. Taylor, in his book *The Making of a Library: The Academic Library Transition* (New York: Becker and

Hayes, 1972), argues that, "Resources are not just rows of books, drawers full of art slides, or shelves of records. Resources are also the conscious exploitation of these inanimate things to challenge, to suggest, to explicate, to guide—in short, to educate. This is what libraries are all about. As with all the good and proper things compromise is required."

Paul Wasserman is somewhat more explicit, arguing that librarianship continues to stress traditional functions such as acquisitions and collection development or input rather than facing the broader and more important issues, or outputs. In *The New Librarianship: A Challenge for Change* (New York: R.R. Bowker Co., 1972) he contends that librarians place too much "emphasis on collection building and attendant record-keeping problems, rather than on innovative services."

The case "We've Got To Put Things in Perspective" illustrates that issue, and points out that the question is not theoretical but a practical one of how to provide the best possible program when there is not enough money to provide fully adequate resources and services.

Another part of the problem of the cost of purchasing and processing material is interinstitutional cooperation. Allen B. Veaner, in a 1972 report to the Colorado Academic Libraries Book Processing Center, gave a great deal of serious thought to this matter. He noted that in most libraries, collection building and processing has shown it lends itself better to cataloging, and that cooperative acquisitions has not yet and may never prove cost effective. Yet the question remains: can academic libraries continue to devote as large a percentage of their staffs to acquisitions as they have in the past? Veaner put it this way: "Perhaps it is time to inquire whether priorities of local technical processing need to be adjusted in the interest of directing more resources toward public service requirements." These issues are not well thought out in most libraries as two cases, "Maybe They'll Give Up Someday," and "Instant Deadwood!" make clear.

The second major concern deals with the selection process itself, an issue touched on in a number of cases, but particularly in "We've Got a Good Thing Going," and "It Looks Like We Need To Make Some Changes." Lawrence S. Thompson in a November 1960 article in *College and Research Libraries* argues that:

> Beyond the small college library, the problem of selecting individual titles from today's mass of publication is an unrewarding, well-nigh hopeless task for academic librarians. In universities the librarian should attempt to get away from the concept of selection of individual titles in most cases. In fields where there must be selection of individual titles, the teaching staff can handle the job and satisfy itself as best it may. If the teaching staff fails, it can stew in its own bibliographic juice; and it is a bitter juice of failure, whether concocted by professors or librarians.

Thompson goes on to state that American university library collections carefully selected a century ago are now essentially worthless. As evidence, he notes that many libraries are now paying high prices for books they did not order when originally published because they were not necessary for the curriculum at the time. Book selection, title-by-title, he concludes, has not produced collections of permanent value.

Margit Kraft vigorously challenged this position in a July 1967 article in *Library Quarterly*, arguing for careful selection and questioning whether the huge collections developed in American academic libraries are necessary and whether they contribute to scholarly progress as much as their defenders insist. She asserted that "librarians find satisfaction in the sheer size of their collection because size adds to their prestige [and] . . . because they do not trust their judgement in buying can neither trust it in eliminating." The solution, she argues, "requires the abandonment of the dogma of comprehensiveness and a serious attempt to distinguish between the explosion of knowledge and the explosion of printing presses. The only answer to indiscriminate publishing is increasingly selective buying."

Both arguments have validity, but ignore an important practical reality. Because book funds are almost always limited, collections are also limited, and unless the most needed basic material is acquired, students and faculty face the prospect of a library that, regardless of its size, contains material not essential to the educational and research objectives of the institution, but lacks other, more basic, titles. If the library is to satisfy the needs of its students and faculty, its collection must either be carefully selected or its budget large enough that any title can be acquired on demand. Careful selection, then, is for most libraries the only way to meet adequately the informational needs of the academic program.

This, then, is the context within which these cases are presented—the problems and issues facing academic librarians today.

NOTES

1. T. W. Koch, et al., "The Apportionment of Book Funds in College and University Libraries," *ALA Bulletin*, 2 (September 1908), pp. 341–347.
2. Jasper G. Schad, "Allocating Book Funds: Control of Planning?" *College and Research Libraries*, 31:3 (May 1970), pp. 155–156.
3. J. Periam Danton, *Book Selection and Collections: A Comparison of German and American University Libraries*. (New York and London: Columbia University Press, 1963), p. 69.
4. Robert Vosper, "Acquisitions Policy. A Symposium. Acquisitions Policy—Fact or Fancy?" *College and Research Libraries*, 14 (October 1953), pp. 367–370, and William T. Henderson, "Acquisitions Policies of Academic and Research Libraries" (unpublished M. A. thesis, University of Chicago, 1960).
5. Robert P. Haro, "Book Selection in Academic Libraries," *College and Research Libraries*, 28:2 (March 1967), pp.104–106, and Cecil K. Byrd,

"Subject Specialists in a University Library," *College and Research Libraries*, 27:3 (May 1966), pp. 191–193.

6. See, for example, Verner W. Clapp and Robert T. Jordan, "Quantitative Criteria for Adequacy for Academic Library Collection," *College and Research Libraries*, 25:5 (September 1965), pp. 371–380, and the California State Colleges Committee on Library Development, *Recommendations for the Support of California College Libraries* (Second report to the Chancellor), April 1966, pp. i–ii.

7. George J. Snowball, letter to the editor, *College and Research Libraries*, 33:6 (November 1972), p. 487.

1.
Orpha's on the Warpath!

- - - - - - - - - - - - - - - - - - -

Orpha Bosely was almost an institution at Aurora State College. She grew up with the school, where her father had taught for many years. She took her bachelor's degree in education at Aurora, and then taught third grade in a rural school for two years. One of her assignments there was the school library. This interested her particularly and she decided to return to Aurora to obtain a school library certificate. At the same time she completed her coursework, there was a vacancy on the library staff at Aurora, and she was appointed, partly as a result of her father's influence. That was nearly forty years ago. For the last eighteen, she had served as children's librarian in charge of the Ethel Caldwell Children's Room.

While most of the librarians respected her commitment to the Caldwell Room, Bosely irritated them because she had no interest in any other aspect of the library. No one was more troubled than Joseph Morvillo, who had been at Aurora just over a year as acquisitions librarian. At the same time he accepted the offer from the Director, John McEnroe, they talked at length about the problems of the collection. Established as a teacher's college, Aurora had dropped that designation and broadened its curriculum to include bachelor's and master's degrees in most disciplines. However, the library's holdings remained far from adequate in fields other than education. With a total book budget of only $104,000, it would be a long time before the library could ever expect to catch up. Morvillo explained that he would be interested in the position only if he could have an opportunity to work at developing a more balanced collection. McEnroe told him that he saw no reason why he could not give greater emphasis to acquiring retrospective titles, especially in the humanities, particularly in light of the fact that Aurora was fortunate in not having an allocated budget.

Soon after he arrived, Morvillo went through all of the prior-year orders to determine how book funds were being spent and what changes would be necessary. He assigned a subject to each book and prepared a summary report of spending for the director. It was this analysis that first revealed the fact that Orpha Bosely was one source of difficulty. He discovered that a total of $4,036 had been spent for children's books, and that as many as ten copies of some titles had been ordered. He made it a point to go up to the Caldwell Room to talk with Bosely and look over the collection.

She began by reciting the story of Ethel Caldwell, how she became interested in children's literature, and how her family had left money to construct and furnish the room as a memorial to her. Bosely then went on to talk about her work over the years with the children's book collection. After about half an hour of patiently listening to Bosely's narrative, Morvillo finally found out what he really wanted to know in the first place—how she had built the collection and what selection criteria she applied. She explained that she relied principally on *The Booklist, The Bulletin of the Center for Children's Books*, and *The Horn Book*. She checked the Newberry, Caldecott and other award winners and also received faculty requests, which were sometimes good. Next, Morvillo spent some time looking at the collection itself. He found that the vast majority of volumes had circulated only a few times, if at all, while a few titles were very heavily used.

Next, he met with McEnroe to discuss this aspect of the problem. The director agreed to talk with Bosely, and he reported afterward that he had impressed on her the significance of greater selectivity in the light of pressing needs to strengthen holdings in other disciplines. It was not long, however, before Morvillo realized that McEnroe had apparently made no impression on her. The stream of order cards continued without interruption. He took his problem back to the director, who suggested that this time Morvillo talk with Bosely. Each time a new group of cards arrived, he went up to the Caldwell Room to review the requests with her. After several meetings he realized that she simply wasn't listening. She didn't argue as they went over each book he reviewed, but she did comment on each one. For instance, "Oh, that's an important book. We must have several copies," "I just know that one will be used heavily," or "Dr. Kuhn in Education definitely will want this one."

Morvillo began to wonder what the people in Education really did want, especially in view of the fact that many volumes were not being used heavily. He concluded that the best thing to do would be to talk with those who actually taught children's literature. He was not surprised to learn that most of the collection was not useful to them at all. What did surprise him was the fact that while these instructors were upset, they had never complained to McEnroe. Lillian Kuhn, Associate Professor of Education, put it this way: "To be perfectly honest, Mr. Morvillo, we've sort of given up on the library for the time being. We're just waiting for Miss Bosely to retire. The way we teach our courses, we rely heavily on a limited number of books, but we need quite a few copies of those titles. The list changes some from year to year. We send in order cards, but if Miss Bosely doesn't like them, or if she thinks we don't need that many copies, she simply doesn't order them. We've tried, but we just can't get anywhere with her. About the only use most of that collection ever gets is from faculty members who take books home for their kids. I just won't go begging to her anymore. We try to work around her as best we can, I guess."

Morvillo decided that further conversation with Bosely would be futile. Because he was not familiar with children's literature he regularly consulted with Kuhn. Unless she concurred, he ordered no more than one copy and many requests he simply ignored. This reduced the amount being ordered by about half.

After a while, Orpha Bosely began to realize what Morvillo was doing. In no mood to see her life's work compromised, she literally went on the warpath. What surprised everyone was the way she chose to defend the children's collection. At a tea several weeks later, she cornered President Wall and tearfully related how this young man who knew nothing of Aurora and its history was bent on destroying the Ethel Caldwell Children's Room, and all she had worked so hard for over the years. McEnroe himself witnessed the final dramatic moments of her impassioned plea.

The following Monday, he called Morvillo into his office.

"Joe, you weren't at the president's reception yesterday, were you?"

"No. I was out of town."

"But I suppose you heard about it?"

"I sure did. That woman must be out of her mind!"

"She may be out of her mind, Joe, but this is a serious problem. Don't forget that you may see her as someone who's just screwing up something you think is very important, but she has built one of the best children's literature collections in the country. It has a national reputation—and that's about all Aurora is famous for. And don't think the president doesn't know it, too.

"You and I may know that too much is being spent on kiddy lit, but the president doesn't know it. Miss Bosely has been around here a long time, and the president is likely to listen to her. I simply can't afford to run the risk of getting our budget cut over something like this."

"I guess I know what you mean," Morvillo said, "but I'm very serious about this business of building a decent collection here. I don't mean this as a threat, but I'm not about to waste my time here as an order clerk. I don't object to that, but it's only part of my job as I see it."

"Joe, relax. You're doing a good job and I don't want you to leave Aurora, but I can't risk getting the book budget cut either. You wouldn't want that. It would be the end of any effort to improve things. One thing I'm not going to consider is going back to an allocated budget simply to control her. I fought that battle quite a few years ago and it wasn't an easy one. I think the best and, realistically, the only way out is to convince the president that you're doing the right thing. So, get me a good strong justification as soon as you possibly can—how about a week? If it's good enough, I'll go talk with the president. But like I said, she's been around a long time. The president knew her father and he'll listen to her. So if I'm going to try to explain all of this to him, I think you'll have to prove how much we should spend for that stuff, how big the collection should be, and that sort of thing. That's about it, I guess."

"Okay. It won't be easy, but I'm not willing to stand by and let the money be wasted. I'll think about it and get something to you."

Morvillo left McEnroe's office without knowing exactly what to do, but determined to fight for balanced spending so that he could continue to work at building a solid basic collection in the humanities and social sciences.

●　●　●　●　●

The library at Aurora State College is typical of many others in the country in that an outstanding collection has been built as the result of the single-minded dedication of one individual. The conflict between Morvillo and Bosely illustrates the dilemma facing such libraries. Should Aurora continue to maintain this outstanding collection of children's literature even at the expense of the rest of the collection, or should it abandon this one area of excellence in favor of a more balanced collection?

If you agree with Morvillo, how would you go about preparing a memo to McEnroe? Outline the major points you would cover and the sources of information you would use to support your arguments.

On the other hand, if you disagree, what arguments would you offer in support of Bosely?

What alternatives are open to McEnroe and Morvillo if they cannot obtain the support of President Wall to limit the growth of the children's literature collection?

2.
"You've Got the Books, and I've Got the Media"

$\bullet\ \ \bullet\ \ \bullet\ \ \bullet\ \ \bullet\ \ \bullet\ \ \bullet\ \ \bullet\ \ \bullet\ \ \bullet\ \ \bullet\ \ \bullet\ \ \bullet\ \ \bullet\ \ \bullet\ \ \bullet\ \ \bullet\ \ \bullet$

Iva Korte had been Chief of Public Services at Murdock University Library for eight years. When Kenneth Ferrell, the director for many years, retired, she was appointed director. The library was organized into three divisions: technical services, public services, and the audiovisual center. Along with her new responsibilities came a number of administrative problems, one of which was a badly-needed reorganization of technical services. Equally serious was the matter of the audiovisual center. For years, the director of the center, Robert Stitts, had expressed resentment at being administratively responsible to the director of libraries, largely because he felt he had not received his fair share of the budget. Of a total library staff of 85, excluding student assistants, to serve a student body of over 16,000, eight were in the audiovisual center. Of a total budget for books and other materials of $402,923, audiovisual materials received $16,206. Stitts argued that this was inadequate. The center was responsible for films, filmstrips, tape and disc recordings, videotapes, and slides. The media library contained 886 8mm and 16mm films, 5,984 filmstrips, 136 tape recordings, 8,090 disc recordings, 43 videotapes, and 1,008 slides. On the other hand, the library's collection included 352,451 books, 48,215 volumes of bound periodicals, 56,633 bound government documents, 257,376 microform units, and 25,217 maps, along with a variety of other material such as pamphlets and pictures.

The arguments never varied. Stitts always had on hand long lists of film requests from various departments, including 30 from psychology alone. He was fond of calling the present level of support a "band-aid approach." In his latest five-year goal statement, he called for an initial augmentation of $125,000 along with an annual allocation of $25,000 for films alone. In response Korte outlined, as had Ferrell before her, equally serious deficiencies in library resources, and argued that allocations for nonprint materials were

5

more than generous. She pointed out that in recent years the center's media budget had increased at a greater rate than the library's book budget. The library collection was weak in a number of areas, but especially in its periodical holdings. The library's five-year goals specified the need to increase periodical subscriptions from 3,341 to about 4,000.

Stitts did not limit his campaign to increasing his budget. He took advantage of every opportunity to advance the cause of a separate learning resource center. He argued that a number of related services including the audiovisual center, the university's FM radio station, the Theater Service Department, responsible for projection and sound systems for noninstructional programs, and perhaps even the computer center could be brought together to offer better service to the entire university. He also argued that the present organizational structure prevented the audiovisual center from providing adequate production facilities and equipment for instructional television, as well as an instructional development program.

When Ferrell announced his retirement, Stitts began to intensify his efforts to separate the audiovisual center from the library. Korte's appointment only strengthened his determination. Stitts said that as long as the university administration insisted on "preserving this senseless, artificial organization, at least they could have replaced Ferrell with someone who knew something about our problems."

The matter was further complicated the following fall by the retirement of the fine arts librarian, who was replaced by Cheryl Bauer. Bauer was particularly interested in art history, and had taken 15 graduate units in that field during the three years she worked at Williams University immediately after receiving her M.L.S.

Bauer arrived on the first of September, and soon after met with the members of the art history faculty to discuss their programs and needs. The chairman of that department was so impressed with her knowledge that she offered her the opportunity to teach a two-unit course next fall in bibliography and research methods in art history. Following this meeting, Bauer worked hard to evaluate and develop the collection. She took advantage of the fact that the book budget was not allocated by subject to order a great many titles. By early spring, she had done most of the basic work on the book collection and established a standing order program for exhibit catalogs. From there, she turned her attention to prints and slides, but she soon learned that slides were the responsibility of the audiovisual center. Before talking with Stitts, she spoke with Jay Iverson, Head of the Reference Department, and explained first that she felt it made no sense to keep slides in the audiovisual center, for even though it was in the same building it had a separate entrance. "Slides should be near all the other material on art, here on the second floor," she explained. Then she asked Iverson for advice on how to proceed. He warned her that she would probably run into trouble with Stitts.

His warning proved to be an understatement. Bauer outlined her activities and asked how much money was available for slides.

"None, my friend," Stitts replied, "absolutely none. What is more, there won't be a penny spent on slides until my budget for films reaches $25,000."

Bauer explained that she was trying to build a balanced collection of book and nonbook materials to support the art history program. Stitts told her that if a faculty member wanted slides for his lectures he could order them from the audiovisual center's production department.

"But," Bauer pointed out, "the faculty over there do have a collection. I'm not talking about that, I'm talking about students who need them for their work."

"You're only talking about a handful of students," said Stitts, reaching for his list of films that had been requested but not ordered. "These are a lot more important in serving the instructional needs of this campus. Last year the audiovisual center showed nearly 6,000 films. If you figure the average class size is 20, we're reaching a lot of students with our film library. You couldn't come near that with a slide collection. There are probably not more than 20 art history majors."

"In the first place, I'm not asking for anything like what your film budget is. In the second place, what about the record collection?"

"It's not the same kind of thing," Stitts replied. "We had well over 20,000 uses of records and tapes last year."

"Okay, and I'll bet there aren't any more students in musicology than in art history."

"That's right, but music is different. Student listening isn't just for class assignments. But if someone wants to look at pictures, they get a book, not a bunch of slides.

"No, slides just don't get the same use, but even if they did, I won't spend a dime on slides until my film budget is $25,000 and budgets for other materials are brought up to a satisfactory level. That's all there is to it."

"I just can't believe this," Bauer said. "Not only doesn't it make sense to me that you have a large film and record collection, but almost no slides, but it is equally senseless that the few slides we do have are kept separate from the rest of the materials on art."

"It's simple," Stitts answered. "You've got the books, and I've got the media. And I say slides can't be justified until we are developing our other resources more fully."

Somewhat stunned, Bauer went directly to Iverson's office to ask him if he would try to convince the director to do something about this situation. She summed up by saying that she couldn't do her job properly unless she could build a collection that included all the materials needed to support the art history program. Iverson expressed some pessimism, but promised to do whatever he could.

When Iverson spoke with Korte several days later, she explained, "I wouldn't want you to tell Cheryl, or anybody for that matter, but I think Bob Stitts is nothing but an empire builder. He has never been happy with the audiovisual center under the library and he never will be. My only consolation is that he has only five years more to go until retirement. I'm in an awkward position and I can't take a chance on giving him anymore arguments for splitting off from the library. Ferrell should never have let him have a separate entrance and complete control of the records, slides, and other things, but that's the way it is. It's awfully hard to change."

"I know. But I've got a real problem, too. Cheryl is one of the best librarians we've got and I don't want to risk losing her."

"Yes. I realize her loss would be serious, but I've got to wait a little while. I think we can keep Vice President Wentworth from making any change if we just don't give Stitts anything to hang us on. That means we can't do much right at this moment, but I do want to make some basic changes ultimately."

•   •   •   •   •

Do you agree with Korte that the problem is simply caused by an ambitious audiovisual center director, and it will be solved once he retires?

Do you feel there is any justification for his complaints?

Do you believe the budget for library and audiovisual material (Appendix A) is fairly divided? If not, what changes would you make?

What do you feel are the advantages and disadvantages of allocating money by form of material? Would you favor retaining or abandoning the present system of dividing the budget by form of material? How would you allocate funds? Or would you even attempt to allocate?

Assuming the possible consequence of supporting Bauer is the separation of the audiovisual center from the library, and that to take no action might mean the loss of Bauer, what would you do? What is the benefit of keeping these two units together?

APPENDIX A
MURDOCK UNIVERSITY LIBRARY BOOK BUDGET

Type of material	Allocation
Books	$266,769.00
Current periodicals	90,292.00
Periodical backfiles	4,920.00
Newspapers	1,776.00
Microform	18,169.00
Maps	2,367.00
Ephemeral material	2,424.00
Films	10,440.00
Filmstrips and loops	2,165.00
Discs/tapes/cassettes	3,601.00
TOTAL	$402,923.00

3.
"It's Not as Simple as You Think"
. . . .

It seemed as though Carolyn Shackelford had always been interested in science. Her interests were broad and not limited to a single discipline. Choosing a major in college was not an easy task, but she finally selected biology. No sooner had she made this decision than she was confronted with the problem of what to do after graduation. Graduate work would only require more narrow specialization. During her junior year she spent a great deal of time thinking about her future and talking with many people. Some suggested teaching while others mentioned possibilities in journalism or scientific publishing. However, one of her professors suggested that she consider a library career and added that a number of universities offered broad master's programs in the sciences. He pointed out that this kind of program was usually intended for science teachers, but that it might serve her particular needs. This possibility interested her enough to talk with a couple of librarians at the university library. What they said interested her even more. During the summer months she continued to think about the whole matter and finally concluded that she did want to go to library school and later to take a master's degree in natural sciences. With a good grade point average, she had no trouble being accepted.

As graduation from library school approached, she set about finding a position. She wrote letters to a number of libraries and interviewed for any position that seemed at all related to her interests. Two offers came at about the same time. One was for the position of science bibliographer at Dent University, and the other for science librarian at a smaller college. After a great deal of thought, she finally decided to accept the offer from Dent. In reaching this decision, she carefully weighed the advantages and disadvantages of each. She concluded that while the other position was probably better, Dent was located in a large metropolitan area only seventeen miles from Stoney Creek

University, which offered a multidisciplinary master's program that was exactly what she wanted. It required 32 units of work in the life, earth, and physical sciences. As soon as she accepted the offer from Dent, she applied and was admitted to the program at Stoney Creek.

Relieved of the pressure of finding a job, Shackelford was free to devote all of her energies to completing her library school degree. At the same time, she was also making plans for the coming year. She had hoped to visit Europe that summer because she knew it would be at least a few years before she would again be able to take a long vacation. However, Robert Turner, Assistant Director for Collection Development and her future department head at Dent, insisted that she begin work there on the first of July. While this disturbed her initially, she was soon grateful because it gave her some time to study the collection before the faculty returned from vacation. The day after she reported, Turner set aside two hours to talk with her. In his mid-forties, Turner was a thin, intense chain-smoker. He had spent almost all of his career at Dent, first as a reference librarian, later as head of the reference department, and for the last seven years in his present position.

He began by explaining that the role of the librarian in collection building was not to replace the faculty's traditional involvement, but rather to supplement it. Shackelford asked him what he meant. He replied that he felt the faculty knew what they needed, and that "too many librarians nowadays are trying to take over book selection from the faculty. Often librarians just don't know enough to make good decisions."

"Okay," Shackelford responded, "what if some faculty member says, 'Order this,' and it's just wrong?"

"Carolyn, after you've been at this awhile, I think you'll come to realize that if you talk long enough with a faculty member, you'll find there is a pretty good reason for what he wants."

"I'll agree with you most of the time, but I'm sure also there are a few problem people. What do you do about them?"

"I think you're looking for trouble before you find it. I haven't found it necessary to reject any faculty request, and I don't expect you will either. Let's not cross that bridge until we come to it. If you see something that bothers you, we'll talk it over."

At this point, Turner changed the subject and reviewed each of the departments for which she would be responsible. In his years at Dent, he had come to know many of the faculty. His observations were perceptive. However, as she left this first meeting, Shackelford was somewhat disturbed by his passive approach to collection development.

That afternoon she began to familiarize herself with the collection. Before the summer was over, she had already identified a number of gaps. During this period, she met Richard Wherritt, assistant professor of geology. He had just completed his first year at Dent, and was teaching summer session. Wherritt and Shackelford talked on several occasions about library needs. He explained that the geology collection was very poor, owing to neglect over the years, because no one in the department was active in research. To confirm this, Shackelford first checked *BCL* (*Books for College Libraries*), and found that the library indeed held only 77 percent of the geology titles listed. In a later conversation, Wherritt said that he felt probably the best thing the library could acquire would be the various state geological society guidebooks and state geological surveys. Shackelford agreed, and spent much of the following year working with the geology collection along these lines. In fact, she took a course in invertebrate paleontology as part of her program at Stoney Creek.

At the end of her first year, she reflected on her work and felt considerable satisfaction over what she had accomplished. Her apprehension about Turner's philosophy of collection building was largely unrealized. Even though the main reason she had not encountered difficulty was perhaps because most faculty members were not interested in research, she was, nevertheless, relieved. In addition, she was grateful for the help Turner gave her in working with faculty members. She often found it useful to talk with him before meeting with someone she had not gotten to know. His observations made it possible for her to handle a number of difficult situations successfully. He was also especially helpful in drawing her attention to many library-oriented, younger faculty members.

She also came to understand Turner himself better during the year. In talking with other librarians she learned that, when the previous director had left Dent three years ago to accept the directorship of a large university library, Turner and the present director, who was then assistant director of technical services, both applied for the position. Turner was quite bitter about not being made director. However, he decided not to leave until his children were out of school. But from that point on, he was very sensitive to criticism and sought, above all else, to prevent librarians and teaching faculty from going to the new director with anything that might be taken as criticism. This seemed to explain his attitude, at least in part.

Her success in building the geology collection was especially gratifying. While the number of current books did not increase substantially over the previous year, she more than doubled the number of retrospective titles ordered. Standing orders were placed for the publications of thirteen state geological surveys. For next year, she had plans to search through dealers' catalogs for volumes that were no longer in print. She also worked hard on all other areas of the sciences. She was particularly happy about increasing the number of symposia and societal publications added to the collection. These often difficult-to-identify publications took a great deal of time to acquire, but were very much appreciated by a number of faculty members.

At about this time, she learned that the chairman of the geology department was stepping down. Apparently none of the present members of the department was an acceptable replacement because an off-campus search was made. The man who was selected, Gustav Opheim, had a national reputation in the field of metamorphic petrology. Shackelford made a note on her calendar to see him the following fall, after the semester was underway and things calmed down a little. Eventually an appointment was made. Shackelford opened the conversation by reviewing what had been done in the past year to strengthen library holdings in geology. Opheim, a stiff, formal man, made a noncommital response, which Shackelford felt implied that he did not regard her efforts favorably. As the conversation progressed, it became clear to her that Opheim saw her role primarily in traditional "fetch and carry" terms. He believed that the whole problem with the geology collection was that there simply had been no concern with acquiring research material, especially journals.

He went on to say that he did not feel he could count on the rest of his faculty right now to help in building the collection, but that he would work at it as time permitted. However, he had been fortunate enough to receive a catalog several days back, which listed some good runs of basic journals in geology. He handed it to Shackelford, pointing to a group of entries (see below).

Science Catalogue N. 125	U.S. $
3764. Neues Jahrbuch Fuer Geologie und Palaeontologie Abhandlungen. Vols. 92–139, 1950–1973	6,000.00
3765. Nues Jahrbuch Fuer Geologie und Palaeontolgie. Monatshefte. Years 1950–1973	1,600.00
3766. Neues Jahrbuch Fuer Mineralogie. Abhandlungen. Vols. 81–115, 1950–1973	2,800.00
3767. ———, Monatshefte. Years 1950–1973.	2,700.00

He instructed her to order all of these immediately, before they were sold. Shackelford replied that she did not know much about geology because she had majored in biology, but that to her, this material looked too specialized. Opheim patiently explained that the *Neues Jahrbach* was a basic journal, much like the *Bulletin of the American Geological Society*, and that many of the world's leading geologists, Winkler, for example, published in it. He concluded by saying that if Dent was to have any pretensions to scholarship whatsoever, it must acquire this basic journal.

Because she was not in a position to argue, Shackelford raised no more objections. But she did make an appointment with Edward Collins, her geology instructor at Stoney Creek. She explained the problem and expressed reservations about the purchase, which would cost $13,100.

"I agree with you completely," Collins said. "If you had a Ph.D. program, you'd have to have it. But that department only offers the master's and the faculty there isn't very strong either. I hear that's why they brought in Opheim. And, even a research-oriented faculty won't use it often. I'd use it about once a year, maybe. That's about average. Another thing is that there must be half a dozen runs available in libraries within a hundred-mile radius and anyone can use one of those. You know, Carolyn, you might just solve this problem by subscribing to one of the abstracting services that covers the geoscience journals."

"Okay," Shackelford answered, "but now let me ask you something else. Last year I worked with one of the other geologists at Dent, and he said the best thing for us would be to get the guidebooks published by the various state geological societies and the state geological surveys. That made a lot of sense to me, but when I talked to Professor Opheim about it, although he didn't come right out and say so, I felt he didn't think much of it. What do you think?"

"I think you're on the right track. That's what students really need. They can go and see things in the states when they can't go to Europe or North Africa. It's a much better way to spend your money."

With that information, she went to Turner and explained the problem.

Turner responded, "I understand your feelings. In fact, these journals probably shouldn't have such high priority, but I remember making a point of explaining when you first came here that it isn't wise to say no as long as the money lasts. And we do have the money to make this purchase."

"I feel pretty strongly about this," she answered. "It's not just a few volumes; it's $13,100 now and more later if we fill in the whole set. I find that there are seven complete runs in this area. What you're really telling me is that it's okay to waste $13,100. That's more than I make in a year, and it really makes me begin to wonder just what my job is."

"It's important, Carolyn, that you understand one thing clearly: it's not as simple as you think. The money isn't going to be wasted. True, we could perhaps buy more important things right now. But this will be used. Also, I've explained to you before that your job isn't to decide what to get, but to round out the collection and to fill in what the faculty miss."

"I'm sorry, Mr. Turner, but I don't see how you can say the money isn't being wasted. I talked with my geology instructor over at Stoney Creek. He's sharp, and he said that a research-oriented geologist probably would use this on the average of once a year. Because we have only two research-oriented people in geology now, and because there are plenty of sets nearby, it's pretty clear to me that this is just a waste of money. I really believe our responsibility involves more than running errands for the faculty and tidying up after them."

"I'm sorry, Carolyn, but that's the way it is. There is no point in arguing further. The matter is closed."

• • • • •

Carolyn Shackelford realized that if she went to the director to protest Turner's decision, she might very well have to leave Dent. Turner was a hard man to understand, but her intuition told her that he would react strongly. In fact, she felt he might even be prone to petty reprisals. On the other hand, she knew little about the director. He seemed pleasant enough, but she had not gotten to know him, and therefore could not judge how he would respond. She wanted to stay at Dent long enough to finish her master's program. Dent had been generous in giving her released time to take courses. Yet she felt very strongly about the issue.

What should Shackelford do? How would you evaluate the arguments offered by Opheim and Turner in favor of this purchase, and those of Shackelford and Collins against it? What other evidence might be offered in support of either position?

4.
"I'll See What I Can Do"

· · · · · · · · · · · · · · · · · · ·

"Betty Rosen! I'm Mary Green, Assistant Director for Technical Services. It's probably unfair of me to bother you right now, since this is only your second day. I'm sure you're more interested in getting your feet on the ground and learning something about the reference collection before school starts next week than you are in my problem, but I've been holding up some things waiting for you to arrive on campus, and I really need your help. You're the first real science reference librarian we've had for several years. Your immediate predecessor really wasn't qualified for this position. He didn't have a science degree, and he really wasn't too interested in book selection."

"You're right," Rosen answered. "I do have an awful lot of things I want to do before school starts, but I'll certainly do whatever I can for you."

"Thanks. We've been having a terrible time with the science periodicals. They're a mess. You know how science is—it's a never-ending problem. I'd appreciate it if you'd go through the science periodicals subject by subject, and come up with some recommendations for new titles."

"That's the sort of thing I'm interested in, but I don't know very much right now. I'll probably make a lot of mistakes, but I'll do what I can."

"I'm sure with your background you'll make a lot fewer mistakes than any of us, even with our experience," Green observed. "Start with biology. That's our biggest headache right now. They're especially insistent. I've got a list of new titles they want in my office together with a list of what we're getting now. We can't get anything near what they want, so I'd like to know what you think we really need."

"I'll need more than just that list," Rosen said. "The lines between disciplines aren't very watertight, so I'll need lists at least for psychology, chemistry, and physics."

"No problem. We have them for every subject. I'll give them to you if you'll drop by my office. I should add that the list of current periodicals in biology isn't strictly limited to biology. We've got a nursing program, and some of their journals are also on that list."

"Another question," Rosen added, "how many new subscriptions are you talking about?"

"Well, I generally start by projecting a percentage of the total holdings onto the number of new titles I think we can afford to add. This year we're talking about a hundred new titles. We have some 3,721 current subscriptions, of which about 275 are in biology. That would give you somewhere between seven and eight titles. Okay?"

"Not really. I'd question that kind of approach to science periodicals. Since new titles are coming out in the sciences at a much faster rate than in other fields, they really should get a larger percentage of the new subscriptions."

"Perhaps, but let's just start out this way, and if you figure you really need more, go ahead and argue a case. Also, see if you can eliminate any subscriptions to specialized research journals that we originally got for faculty members who have either left or changed their research interests.

"The list of recommended new titles from biology includes about thirty items. You don't necessarily have to be limited by that list, but if you think we ought to have something else, it ought to be pretty basic and pretty important."

"I'll see what I can do."

The following day Rosen began to accumulate information about the biology program. First, she obtained lists of biology, physics, chemistry, and psychology titles currently received (Appendixes A–D), as well as the list of titles requested by the biology department (Appendix E). Then she went through the university bulletin and found that the biology department offered a standard undergraduate curriculum, as well as a master of science program allowing for specialization in botany, microbiology, or zoology.

To establish the relative importance of the biology program as compared to other programs, she checked through reports in the director's office and found that, out of a total of 134,535 credit hours generated by the university in the fall semester, 4,625 were in biology—3,855 for freshman and sophomore courses, 649 for upper division courses, and 122 for graduate courses. She compared these figures with chemistry, which generated 579 lower division credit hours, 801 upper division credit hours, and 151 graduate credit hours, and physics, which reported 1,481 lower division units, 432 upper division units, and 115 graduate units. There were 161 biology majors, and a total of twenty-nine undergraduate and three master's degrees had been awarded in the last year.

Next, she met with the department chairman and several other members of the department to learn more about the biology program, and especially about the research interests of the members of the department. From the departmental annual report, she found that the nine faculty members had published fifteen papers in the past year, exclusive of notes, in major professional journals and that two had received outside grants. Because she was not able to contact every member of the department, she did not obtain uniform information about their research interests. However, she made notes and listed the following.

Alves: Assistant professor. Ribosomes, changes produced by drug resistance. Evaluation of photoreaction of transforming DNA enzymes from Jansenula species. Three articles.

Becker: Assistant professor. Effects of cobalt 60 on snake venom. Labeling snake venom with radioisotopes. No publications (one article last year).

Bremond: Professor and chairman. Fungi. Two articles.

Doerr: Associate professor. Breeding habits of fish. Water pollution. One article in a regional journal.

Erikson: Assistant professor. Neuroendocrinology. Loss of a circadian adrenal corticosterone rhythm following suprachiamatic lesion in the rat. Two articles.

Johnson: Instructor. Immunology. No publications (one last year).

Molstad: Professor. Physiology and embryology of mosquitoes. Insect physiology. Hatching stimuli and pollution. No publications.

Rickard: Professor. Neurotransmitters of the gut of the cockroach. Three articles.

Scantlin: Associate professor. Genetics. Cellular biochemistry. Radiochemistry. One article.

Swanson: Assistant professor. Reproductive physiology. No publications.

Sweeney: Associate professor. Antibody structure, method of operation. Two articles.

Tyson: Instructor. Microbiology. No publications.

Wheelahan: Assistant professor. Parasitology—hosts. Shiztosomes. One article.

Young: Assistant professor. Fly ash (industrial wastes)—growing plants in it. Native grass (cover) studies. No publications.

• • • • •

Examine the list of periodicals being received. If you were Betty Rosen, what new subscriptions would you recommend? Which existing subscriptions, if any, would you recommend be dropped? What specific justifications would you provide for each recommendation?

APPENDIX A

BIOLOGICAL SCIENCES PERIODICALS CURRENTLY RECEIVED

ADA Forecast
Acta Physiologica Scandanavica
Acta Physiologica Scandanavica Supplements
Advances in Colloid and Interface Sci
Agricultural History
Am Biology Teacher
Am Fern Jrl
Am Fisheries Society Transactions
Am Forests
Am Jrl of Anatomy
Am Jrl of Botany
Am Jrl of Clinical Nutrition
Am Jrl of Epidemology
Am Jrl of Mental Deficiency
Am Jrl of Nursing
Am Jrl of Ophthalmology
Am Jrl of Orthopsychiatry
Am Jrl of Physical Medicine
Am Jrl of Physiology
Am Medical Association Jrl
Am Microscopical Society Transactions
Am Midland Naturalist
Am Zoologist
Analytical Biochemistry
Anatomical Record
Anatomy Anthropology Embryology Histology
Animal Welfare Institute Information Report
Annals of Botany
Annals of Human Genetics
Antonie van Leeuwenhoek, Jrl of Microbiology and Serology
Applied Biochemistry and Microbiology
Applied Microbiology
Aquatic Biology Abstracts
Archiv fuer Hydrobiologie
Archiv fuer Microbiologie
Archives Neerlandaises de Zoologie
Archives of Physical Medicine and Rehabilitation
Audubon Magazine
AUK
Australian Entomological Society Jrl
BSCS Newsletter
Bacteriological Reviews
Bedside Nurse

Behaviour, An International Jrl of Comparative Ethnology
Biken Jrl
Biological Abstracts
Biological and Agricultural Index
Biological Bul
Biological Psychiatry
Biological Reviews
Biologist
Biometrika
Bioresearch Index
Bioscience
Biotechnology and Bioengineering
Botanical Gazette
Botanical Review
British Mycological Society Transactions
Bul of Entomological Research
Bul of Environmental Contamination
Bul of Marine Sci
Bul of the History of Medicine
Canadian Entomologist
Canadian Jrl of Botany
Canadian Jrl of Genetics and Cytology
Canadian Jrl of Microbiology
Canadian Jrl of Physiology and Pharmacology
Canadian Jrl of Zoology
Canadian Nurse
Cancer News
Cancer Research
Cellule; Recueil de Cytologie et d'Histologie
Chromosoma
Clinical Medicine
Coleopterists' Bul
Comparative Miochemistry and Physiology
Copeia
Crustaceana
Current Contents, Life Sciences Edition
Cytobios
Deep Sea Research and Oceanographic Abstracts
Developmental Biology and Teratology
Ecological Monographs
Ecology
Economic Botany

Endocrinology
Entomological News
Entomological Revue
Entomological Society of America Annals
Entomological Society of America Bul
Entomological Society of Canada Bul
Entomological Society of Canada Memoirs
Entomological Society of Washington Proceedings
Entomologist
Entomologist's Monthly Magazine
Evolution
Experimental Brain Research
Experimental Cell Research
Experimental Neurology
Federation of Am Societies for Experimental Biology Proceedings
Fiziologicheskii Zhurnal
Forest Sci
France. Centre National de la Recherche Scientifique. Bulletin Signaletique Microbiologie Virologie Immunologie Biologie et Physiologie Animales Biologie et Physiologie Vegetales Science Agricoles
Genetica
Genetical Research
Genetics
Geoderma
Giornale di Batteriologia Virologia ed Immunologia
Giornale di Microbiologia
Grana Palynologica
Health Sciences TV Bul
Heredity
Herpetologica
Herpetological Review
Hilgardia
Home Garden and Flower Grower
Hoppe-Seyler's Zeit fuer Physiologische Chemie
Human Biology
Human Development
Human Genetics
Human Heredity
Humangenetik
Hydrobiologica
ICLA Bul
Immunochemistry
Immunology

Index Medicus
International Jrl of Radiation Biol
International Jrl of Systematic Bacteriology
International Zoo News
Jrl of Animal Ecology
Jrl of Applied Physiology
Jrl of Bacteriology
Jrl of Biological Education
Jrl of Cell Biology
Jrl of Cell Sci
Jrl of Cellular Physiology
Jrl of Comparative Neurology
Jrl of Ecology
Jrl of Economic Entomology
Jrl of Electron Microscopy
Jrl of Embryology and Experimental Morphology
Jrl of Entomology
Jrl of Experimental Biology
Jrl of Experimental Medicine
Jrl of Experimental Zoology
Jrl of Fish Biology
Jrl of General Microbiology
Jrl of General Physiology
Jrl of General Virology
Jrl of Genetics
Jrl of Helminthology
Jrl of Heredity
Jrl of Immunology
Jrl of Infectious Diseases
Jrl of Insect Physiology
Jrl of Lipid Research
Jrl of Mammalogy
Jrl of Marine Research
Jrl of Medical Genetics
Jrl of Membrane Biology
Jrl of Molecular Biology
Jrl of Molecular Spectroscopy
Jrl of Morphology
Jrl of Neurophysiology
Jrl of Occupational Medicine
Jrl of Parasitology
Jrl of Protozoology
Jrl of Soil and Water Conservation
Jrl of Soil Sci
Jrl of the History of Biology
Jrl of Theoretical Biology
Jrl of Ultrastructure Research
Jrl of Virology
Jrl of Vitaminology
Jrl of Zoology

Kansas Entomological Society Jrl
Lancet
Leukemia Abstracts
Life Sciences
Madrono
Mathematical Biosciences
Medical Library Association Bul
Menninger Clinic Bul
Metabolism, Clinical and Experimental
Michigan Entolmologist
Microbiologia Española
Microbiology
Microbios
Micronesia
Milbank Memorial Fund Quarterly
Molecular Pharmacology
Morris Arboretum Bul
Mutation Research
Mycologia
Mycopathologia et Mycologia Applicata
National Tuberculosis Association Bul
National Wildlife
Natural History
Nature
Naturwissenschaften
Nervenarzt
Netherlands Jrl of Zoology
New Phytologist
New York Entomological Society Jrl
New Zealand Jrl of Agricultural Re-
search
New Zealand Jrl of Botany
Nursing Forum
Nursing Outlook
Nursing Research
Oecologia
Ohio Jrl of Sci
Pan-Pacific Entomologist
Parasitology
Paris Institut Pasteur Annales
Paris Institut Pasteur Bul
Pfluegers Archiv
Photochemistry and Photobiology
Physiologia Plantarum
Physiological Reviews
Physiological Zoology
Physiology and Behavior
Phytochemistry
Phytomorphology

Phytopathology
Plant and Cell Physiology
Plant Physiology
Pollen et Spores
Primates
Princeton Univ. Industrial Relations Se-
lected References
Psyche
Quarterly Review of Biology
Research Jrl of the Reticuloendothelial
Society
R.N.
Radiation Botany
Radiation Research
Rehabilitation and Physical Medicine
Revista de Biologia Tropical
Revista Latinoamericana de Micro-
biologia
Royal Entomological Soc London
Transactions
Royal Soc of London Proceedings Series
B. Biological Sci
Sabouraudia
Senckenbergiana Biologica
Society for Experimental Biology and
Medicine Proceedings
South African Museum Cape Town An-
nals
Southern California Academy of Sci Bul
Soviet Genetics
Special Education
Stain Technology
Star
Theoretical and Applied Genetics
Tissue and Cell
Torrey Botanical Club Bul
Virology
World Health
World Hospitals
Zeitschrift fuer Naturforschung
Zeitschrift fuer Vergleichende Physi-
ologie
Zeitschrift fuer Wissenschaftliche Zoolo-
gie
Zoologica
Zoological Jrl of the Linnean Society
Zoological Record
Zoological Society of London Transac-
tions

APPENDIX B

CHEMISTRY PERIODICALS CURRENTLY RECEIVED

Academy of Sci USSR Bul
Accounts of Chemical Research
Acta Chemica Scandinavica
Acta Crystallographica Part A and B
Advances in Colloid and Interface Sci
Analog
Analytica Chimica Acta
Analytical Abstracts
Analytical Chemistry
Analytical Letters
Angewandte Chemie
Annalen der Chemie, Justus Liebigs
Annales de Chimie
Applied Spectroscopy
Atomic Absorption Newsletter
Berichte der Bunsengesellschaft fuer Physikalische Chemie
Biochemistry
Bulletin de la Societe Chimique de France
Bulletin of the Chemical Society of Japan
Bulletin on Environmental Contamination and Toxicology
Bureau of Standards Jrl of Research Physics and Chemistry
Canadian Jrl of Biochemistry
Canadian Jrl of Chemical Engineering
Canadian Jrl of Chemistry
Canadian Jrl of Physics
Canadian Jrl of Physiology & Pharmacology
Chemica Scripta
Chemical Abstracts
Chemical Communications
Chemical Engineering
Chemical Instrumentation
Chemical Review
Chemical Berichte
Chemistry
Chemistry in Britain
Collection of Czechoslovak Chemical Communications
Coordination Chemistry Reviews
Critical Reviews in Analytical Chemistry
Discussions of Faraday Society
Electrochemical Society Jrl
Electronic Design
Environmental Sci and Technology

European Jrl of Biochemistry
Experientia
Helvetica Chimica Acta
Hoppe-Seyler's Zeit fuer Physiologische Chemie
Indian Chemical Jrl
I & EC Fundamentals
I & EC Process Design and Development
Inorganica Chimica Acta
Intra-Sci Chemistry Reports
Jrl of Agriculture and Food Chemistry
Jrl of Am Chemical Society
Jrl of the Am Oil Chemists Society
Jrl & Abstracts of Applied Chemistry and Biotechnology
Jrl of Analytical Chemistry of USSR
Jrl of Association of Official Analytical Chemists
Jrl of Biological Chemistry
Jrl of Catalysis
Jrl of Chemical Documentation
Jrl of Chemical Education
Jrl of Chemical Engineering Data
Jrl of Chemical Physics
Jrl of Chemical Society
    Dalton Transactions
    Faraday Transactions part I
    Faraday Transactions part II
    Perkin Transaction part I
    Perkin Transaction part II
Jrl de Chimie Physique et de Physicochimie Biologique
Jrl of Chromatographic Sci
Jrl of Chromatography
Jrl of Crystal Growth
Jrl of Electroanalytical Chemistry
Jrl of General Chemistry of USSR
Jrl of Organic Chemistry of USSR
Jrl fuer Praktische Chemie
Jrl of Mass Spectrometry and Ion Physics
Jrl of Medicinal Chemistry
Jrl of Organic Chemistry
Jrl of Organometallic Chemistry
Jrl of Physical Chemistry
Jrl of Polymer Sci—Part A-1
    Polymer Chemistry, Part A-2
    Polymer Physics, Part B
    Polymer Letters, Part C

Jrl of Protein Research, International
Jrl of Quantum Chemistry, International
Jrl of Quarterly Reports on Sulfur
  Chemistry, Part B
Jrl of Solid State Chemistry
Kinetics and Catalysis
Macromolecules
Makromolekulare Chemie
Microchemical Jrl
Mikrochimica Acta
Molecular Pharmacology
Monatshefte fuer Chemie
Organic Mass Spectrometry
Product Research and Development
Pure and Applied Chemistry
Radiochimica Acta
Quarterly Reviews
Record of Chemical Progress
Recueil des Travaux Chimiques des
  Pays-Bas
Reviews of Pure and Applied Chemistry

Revue de Chemie Minerale
Russian Chemical Reviews
Russian Jrl of Inorganic Chemistry
Russian Jrl of Physical Chemistry
Separation Science
Spectrochimica Acta Part A and B
Steroids
Synthesis
Synthesis in Inorganic Chemistry
Talanta
Tetrahedron
Tetrahedron Letters
Theoretica Chimica Acta
Theoretical and Experimental Chemistry
Thermochimica Acta
Zeitschrift fuer Analytische Chemie
Zeitschrift fuer Anorganische und Allge-
  meinie Chemie
Zeitschrift fuer Physikalische Chemie
Zeitschrift fuer Physikalische Chemie
  (Neue Folge)

APPENDIX C

PHYSICS PERIODICALS CURRENTLY RECEIVED

APL Technical Digest
Acoustical Society of Am Jrl
Advances in Physics
Am Geophysical Union Transactions
Am Jrl of Physics
Am Physical Society Bul
Annalen Der Physik
Applied Optics
Applied Physics Letters
Australian Jrl of Physics
Biochemical and Biophysical Research
  Communication
Biochimica et Biophysica Acta
Biochimica et Biophysica Acta Previews
Biophysical Jrl
British Jrl for the Philosophy of Sci
Bul Geodesique
Bul of the Atomic Scientists
Canadian Jrl of Physics
Chemical Physics Letters
Combustion, Explosion, and Shock
  Waves
Comments on Nuclear and Particle
  Physics
Comments on Solid State Physics
Communications on Pure and Applied
  Mathematics

Contemporary Physics
Cosmic Research
Faraday Society Transactions
  Physique I
  Physique II
  Physique Nucleaire
  Structure de la Matiere
  Biophysique Biochimie
  Combustibles Energie
Geophysical Jrl
Geophysics
Health Physics
Helvetica Physica Acta
IEEE Transactions on Audio and Elec-
  troacoustics
Indian Jrl of Physics
Infrared Physics
Institut Henri Poincare Annales Sect A
International Atomic Energy Agency
  Atomindex
International Atomic Energy Agency
  Bul
International Atomic Energy Agency
  List of Bib
International Jrl of Mass Spectrometry
  and Ion Physics
International Jrl of Solids and Structures

International Jrl of Theoretical Physics
JETP Letters
Japanese Jrl of Applied Physics
Jrl of Applied Physics
Jrl of Atmospheric and Terrestrial Physics
Jrl of Chemical Physics
Jrl of Mathematical Physics
Jrl of Physics and Chemistry of Solids
Jrl of Physics, A. General Physics
Jrl of Physics, B. Atomic and Molecular Physics
Jrl of Physics, C. Solid State Physics
Jrl of Physics, D. Applied Physics
Jrl of Polymer Sci Part A-2 Polymer Physics
Jrl of the Mechanics and Physics of Solids
Jrl of Vacuum Sci and Technology
List of References on Nuclear Energy
Molecular Physics
Moscow University Physics Bulletin
Nuclear Data
Nuclear Data Section B
Nuclear News
Nuclear Physics
Nuclear Sci and Engineering
Nuovo Cimento Supplemento
Optical Society of Am
Optical Spectra
Optics and Spectroscopy
Paris Universite Institut H.P. Annals Sect A
Physica
Physica Status Solidi
Physical Review Ser 1, 2, 3, Index
Physical Review Letters
Physical Society London
Physical Society London Reports on Progress in Physics
Physical Society of Japan Jrl

Physics and Chemistry of Glasses
Physics Education
Physics Express
Physics of Fluids
Physics of Metals and Metalography
Physics Today
Physik der Kondensierten Materie
Polymer
Progress of Theoretical Physics
Quarterly Checklist of Geophysics
Quarterly Checklist of Physics
Quarterly Reviews of Physics
Review of Scientific Instruments
Reviews of Geophysics and Space Physics
Reviews of Modern Physics
Rheologica Acta
Rheology Bul
Royal Society of London Proceedings Series A Math and Physical
Sci Abstracts Section A Physics Abstracts
Solar Energy
Solid State Abstracts
Soviet Jrl of Nuclear Physics
Soviet Physics, Crystallography
Soviet Physics, JETP
Soviet Physics Jrl
Soviet Physics Semiconductors
Soviet Physics, Solid State
Soviet Physics, Technical Physics
Soviet Physics, Uspekhi
Studies in Applied Mathematics
Tectonophysics
    Section A Physics & Chemistry
    Section B Mathematics & Mathematical Physics
Zeitschrift fuer Angewandte Physik
Zeitschrift fuer Astrophysik
Zeitschrift fuer Naturforschung
Zeitschrift fuer Physik

APPENDIX D

PSYCHOLOGY PERIODICALS CURRENTLY RECEIVED

APA Monitor
Acta Psychologica
Adolescence
Am Academy of Child Psychiatry
Am Behavioral Scientist
Am Behavioral Therapy

Am Imago
Am Jrl of Mental Deficiency
Am Jrl of Orthopsychiatry
Am Jrl of Psychiatry
Am Jrl of Psychoanalysis
Am Jrl of Psychology

Am Psychoanalytic Association Jrl
Am Psychologist
Animal Behavior
Archives of General Psychiatry
Behavior Notes
Behavioral Sci
Behavior Research and Therapy
British Jrl of Educational Psychology
British Jrl of Medical Psychology
British Jrl of Social and Clinical Psychology
British Jrl of Social Psychiatry
Canadian Jrl of Psychology
Character Potential
Child Development
Child Development Abstracts and Bibliography
Cognitive Psychology
Community Mental Health Jrl
Comprehensive Psychiatry
Conditional Reflex
Contemporary Psychology
Counseling Psychologist
Darshana International
Developmental Psychology
Educational and Psychological Measurement
Gifted Child Quarterly
Group Psychotherapy and Psychodrama
Hospital and Community Psychiatry
Human Factors
Human Relations
Humanitas
Indian Jrl of Psychology
Individual Psychologist
International Jrl of Group Psychotherapy
International Jrl of Psychoanalysis
International Jrl of Social Psychiatry
Jrl of Abnormal Psychology
Jrl of Analytical Psychology
Jrl of Applied Behavior Analysis
Jrl of Applied Behavioral Sci
Jrl of Applied Psychology
Jrl of Behavior Therapy and Experimental Psychiatry
Jrl of Clinical Psychology
Jrl of Comparative and Physiological Psychology
Jrl of Counseling Psychology
Jrl of Creative Psychology
Jrl of Educational Measurement
Jrl of Educational Psychology

Jrl of Experimental Child Psychology
Jrl of Experimental Education
Jrl of Experimental Psychology
Jrl of Experimental Research in Personality
Jrl of Experimental Social Psychology
Jrl of General Psychology
Jrl of Genetic Psychology
Jrl of Humanistic Psychology
Jrl of Individual Psychology
Jrl of Mathematical Psychology
Jrl of Parapsychology
Jrl of Personality
Jrl of Personality and Social Psychology
Jrl of Personality Assessment
Jrl of Psychiatric Research
Jrl of Psychology
Jrl of Psychosomatic Research
Jrl of Rehabilitation
Jrl of Social Psychology
Jrl of the Experimental Analysis of Behavior
Jrl of the History of Behavioral Sciences
Jrl of Verbal Learning and Verbal Behavior
Literature and Psychology
Menninger Clinic Bulletin
Merrill-Palmer Quarterly of Behavior and Development
Mind
Organizational Behavior and Human Performance
Parents Magazine and Better Family Living
Pastoral Psychology
Perception and Psychophysics
Perceptual and Motor Skills
Personnel Psychology
Professional Psychology
Progressive
Psychiatric Quarterly
Psychiatry
Psychoanalytic Quarterly
Psychological Abstracts
Psychological Bulletin
Psychological Record
Psychological Reports
Psychological Review
Psychologie Francaise
Psychologische Forschung
Psychology
Psychology in the Schools
Psychology Today

Psychometrika
Psychonomic Science
Psychopharmacology Abstracts
Psychophysiology
Psychosomatic Medicine

Sociometry
Soviet Neurology and Psychiatry
Soviet Psychology
Sythese
Theoria

APPENDIX E

PERIODICAL SUBSCRIPTION REQUESTS FROM BIOLOGY

Acta Pathologica et Microbiologica Scandinavica
Acta Zoologica (International Jrl of Zoology)
Arkansas Academy of Sci Transactions
Atmospheric Environment
Australian Jrl of Biological Sci
Biologia Plantarum
Biologisches Zentralblatt
Brain Research
California Fish and Game
Cellular Immunology
Comparative and General Pharmocology
Developmental Biology
Forestry Abstracts
Great Basin Naturalist
Growth
Herbage Abstracts
Insect Biochemistry

International Bul of Bacteriological Nomenclature & Taxonomy, now called International Jrl of Systematic Bacteriology
International Jrl of Biochemistry
Jrl of Experimental Botany
Jrl of General & Applied Microbiology
Jrl of Hygiene
Jrl of Molecular Evolution
Kentucky Academy of Sci Transactions
Marine Biological Assn of the United Kingdom Jrl
Neuroendocrinology
Nucleic Acids Abstracts
Planta
Progressive Fish Culturist
Public Health Laboratory
Soil Sci
Worm Runner's Digest
Zeitschrift fuer Psychologie

5.
"There's Just
No Way to Do This"

· · · · · · · · · · · · · · · · ·

Pratt State College was a liberal arts institution with approximately 2,100 FTE students, offering master's programs in several fields of the humanities and social sciences. Its library was well supported, with 294,693 volumes and a book budget, not including periodical subscriptions, of $146,167. Most of this money was used for new publications; what was left was spent for retrospective material. The staff of the acquisitions department included William Farlow, Head of the Department, John Huang, Assistant Acquisitions Librarian, 3.5 clerks, and 90 student assistant hours. Since the department was also responsible for periodicals and serials, Farlow and his staff had barely been able to keep up with the work. In fact, most out-of-print requests were set aside in a separate file, arranged by subject, that by now contained some 7,000 cards.

Some of the cards in the o.p. file dated back many years. Faculty requests accounted for about 70 percent of the total. Most were probably suitable for the collection, but some were considerably more important than others. Perhaps as many as a third of the titles were too specialized for the programs at Pratt. The remaining 30 percent of the cards were generated by librarians. The bulk of these were selected to fill gaps in the collection that reference librarians had identified while working with students over the past decade. However, about a quarter of these had been generated as a result of checking bibliographies. One reference librarian had checked parts of the *Lamont Catalog* many years ago, and another had checked several basic bibliographies in geography and anthropology. The name of the bibliography was typed at the bottom of each of these cards.

Occasionally, antiquarian booksellers checked through the o.p. file and supplied titles from stock. Occasionally, too, want-lists were sent out for urgently needed titles, and every once in a while Farlow would check an especially good catalog against the file.

That morning, Farlow had an appointment with the head librarian, Geraldine Bell, to talk over the budget for the coming year. Farlow, usually a quiet man, smiled broadly as he returned from that meeting, and shouted across the room, "Get some coffee, John, and come into my office!"

As Huang settled into a chair, Farlow lit a cigarette and said, "Well, it looks like we're finally in business. Guess what?"

"There's only one thing that could get you this excited," Huang observed, "and that's a bigger budget for next year—a lot bigger budget!"

"Right! Fifty thousand dollars more in the book budget. It looks like we can finally get to work on our out-of-print file."

"Okay," Huang cautioned, "but before you go any further, are we going to get enough staff? We certainly can't do it with what we've got."

"Well, that's a problem all right. We'll get another clerk, but no more."

"That's just not enough. There's no way we can purchase that many titles from the o.p. file with one clerk. I don't know exactly how much time we spend now per book. It varies from month to month, depending on what percent of the titles we check are actually ordered, what percent we get, and how much is foreign. But I'd guess we average about 50 minutes per title. We don't really have to be any more accurate to know that we just can't do it. Figure it out for yourself."

"Well," Farlow paused for a moment to review the figures in his mind, "perhaps it wouldn't take a full 50 minutes. We've already done the bibliographic checking on the o.p. stuff."

"Bill, I know you're excited about this extra money, but there's just no way. I don't have any figures, but you know o.p. books take a lot more time. My guess is twice as much. That's because for in-print books we probably get between 85 to 90 percent of what we order from the jobbers. With the o.p. titles, we'll be lucky to get 25 percent. Let's face it; that's why those cards have been sitting in that file so long."

"Yeah, you're right," Farlow conceded. "I suppose we can always buy some big sets, some journal backfiles, or microfilm collections at the end of the year. The reference people always have something or other they want. But we've already bought so much of that out of year-end funds the administration has come up with. That's just not what we really need.

"It looks like we ought to spend some time thinking about how we can get the most with what we have. There are quite a few ways to get out-of-print books. We could go over catalogs, we could go to bookshops, we could send want-lists, we could order copyflo copies, or we could even advertise."

"Copyflo is the easiest," Huang explained. "We have a catalog of what's available, and they say they'll try to get any book we want. Want-lists involve more work, and we wouldn't get back a very high percentage. Checking catalogs is time-consuming and so is going to bookshops, but prices are lower. Advertising involves a lot of work to keep records of quotes."

"You're right, but we've got to think of the costs. Copyflo is expensive, and some booksellers really charge an arm and a leg when they start searching."

"Right. You pay either way; it's basically a trade-off. If the bookseller searches for us, he has to charge for his work; it takes a lot of time. But if we don't have enough staff, that may be our only alternative."

"You know, there's another thing we might consider," Farlow added. "If we type up want-lists and send them out, you say we'll be lucky to get 25 percent in a year. Now what would happen if we sent the lists to booksellers with a letter saying 'Send what you have in stock within one month'? Then we could send them on to another dealer each month. What do you think we'd get?"

"I haven't had any experience with that, so I'd just be guessing. But I'd say around 5 percent from each dealer until about a third of the list had been filled. Then it would taper off."

"Not too good," Farlow observed. "You know, there's just no way to do this. It would take more staff, which we can't get, and I don't know where I'd put anyone anyway. But we've simply got to come up with some kind of plan or we're going to wind up spending the better part of $50,000 on things we really don't need all that much."

• • • • •

Collection building in many academic libraries is often influenced as much or more by acquisitions procedures than it is by selection policies and procedures. Farlow and Huang view this problem as one of reducing the backlog of o.p. requests that have accumulated over the years. Is this the real problem? The administration is anxious to build a strong collection to support graduate and undergraduate programs. While funds are limited, every effort is made to support the library. Usually, substantial amounts of year-end money are transferred each June to the library. However, because staffing has always been short, and all funds must be encumbered before the end of the fiscal year, this money has been used for backfiles, expensive sets, and microfilm material. Librarians, faculty, and administration all recognize the need to acquire older monographic material.

What do you think is the best way for Farlow and Huang to develop retrospective holdings within the limits of available staff and money during the coming fiscal year? Should they consider alternate ways of getting material such as purchasing book collections en bloc, reprints, or ultramicrofiche collections? Should they consult with others before they go ahead, even though the college librarian has not indicated that they should? If so, with whom?

6.
"Just a Bunch of Old Fuddy-Duddies?"

· · · · · · · · · · · · · · ·

Hammond University was an institution where prestige, real or fancied, was taken very seriously, and the library was one place where traditional faculty perquisites were seldom challenged. In part, this explained why Rogers Library was above all else a traditional library, but there were many other reasons. Fiscal limitations had made it almost impossible for the library to develop much beyond its traditional role. The current total library budget of just over $2,500,000 represented only 3.4 percent of Hammond's educational budget. Bad as this was, the percentage of funds allocated to the library had increased over the past two years and the rate of acquisitions had nearly doubled over the last ten years to roughly 62,000 volumes a year.

To characterize Rogers Library as traditional reflected on almost every aspect of its resources and services. Most notable was the fact that its collection was limited almost exclusively to books—1,463,172 of them. In terms of number of volumes per FTE student, this was only half as many as held by a similar private university in the northern part of the state. As for nonbook holdings, until two years ago there was virtually nothing. At that time, the library held only 13,190 reels of microfilm, 52,631 maps, 10,785 records in the Music Library, and 43,572 slides in the Fine Arts Library.

Yet, the institution was changing and everyone knew it. Two years ago a new president had been appointed. He stated publicly that the university needed a better library. Soon after his arrival he made an appointment with Paul McClaren, Director of Libraries, and at that meeting showed that he understood libraries much better than most university presidents. He explained that it would take some time before the library could expect to be funded adequately. First, he would have to increase income from grants and gifts, so fund raising would be his number-one priority. The two agreed that if the li-

brary was ever to be adequate, more material would have to be acquired in
microform, because there simply was not enough money to purchase original
editions or reprints.

Following this conversation, McClaren announced that, if available, material should be ordered in microform. He accurately predicted the chorus of
faculty protest that followed, but with strong backing from President
Crandall, the director was pleased to be able to do what he had not felt he
could do before.

In the two years that followed, McClaren made every effort to apprise the
president of library needs. This seemed to account for the substantial increases in year-end allocations of money. In the past, this money had been
used principally to purchase back files of periodicals and newspapers. As soon
as he was notified by the business office that $29,000 had been allocated for li-
brary acquisitions, McClaren informed Herbert Darr, Assistant Director for
Public Services, of the amount and told him that since it was too late in the
year to consult the Library Committee he could allocate the money as he saw
fit.

The amount took Darr completely by surprise, and as he reflected on how
best to use it, he concluded that to spend these funds on individual titles would
create havoc in the acquisitions department. Acquisitions always seemed to
complain, but he knew they did have staffing problems. The only solution
seemed to be to purchase a collection or some expensive sets.

Decisions of this sort were not easy to make because the library had no acquisitions policy. About eight months earlier, Darr had talked with the bibliographers, all of whom reported directly to him, about such a policy, but
there was little enthusiasm for it. They objected on the grounds that it would
be too much work and that there would be little benefit because they already
knew what was needed. The group felt that an acquisitions policy would neither help them to understand needs better nor convince faculty members to
moderate their requests. Darr recognized that there was some truth in this,
because he knew only too well that most faculty members felt that librarians
had no business concerning themselves with book selection. On the other
hand, he felt that an acquisitions policy would support the director in showing
the president the need to allocate more money for collection building.

Lacking better information, he decided that about half of the special allocation, or $14,500, should be spent to continue developing holdings on Africa.
Africa was one of the ten fields in history in which the doctorate was offered,
and an interdisciplinary African studies program (Appendix A) was also offered.

After he made his decision, he spoke with Judy Sorenson, history bibliographer. She agreed that Africa was an area of critical need, but she expressed
concern about her ability to choose wisely, because at this time of the year almost the entire faculty had already left the campus for the summer. Yet, the
money had to be encumbered by the end of August. She knew a little about

African history, but was by no means a specialist. In spite of this obvious handicap, she agreed to review what was available and report back as soon as possible.

In checking the collection she found that most of the important current books had been acquired as published since the mid-sixties. Periodical back files were not a serious problem either, because most titles began during this period and the others had already been acquired for the most part. Holdings of newspaper back files and government documents on microform, while still far from adequate, had improved. Clearly, the most serious weakness at this point was in the area of older monographs. After contacting several specialist booksellers, she located two collections that were available. The first, for which she had a prospectus from the dealer (Appendix B), had been acquired from a retired university professor in Spain. The second, a collection of 296 volumes, almost all of which were published between 1920 and 1950, mostly in German, French or Italian, concerned Fascist Italy's claim to Ethopia and Nazi Germany's African colonial policies. The price for this collection was $1,295.00. In addition, her files contained a letter (Appendix C) describing a new microfiche collection.

As she weighed the advantages of the two book collections against the microfiche collection and considered the library's new emphasis on microform material, she became increasingly disturbed, because the microform material she had already acquired was being used little, if at all. She decided to talk the matter over with Darr. After describing the collections that were available she went on to say, "This really bothers me. We bought a lot of microfilm last year, but if it's not being used what good is it? I get an awful lot of complaints from the faculty. Are they really just a bunch of old fuddy-duddies? I'm not sure. Of course, I know some of the complaints are exaggerated. Douglas in medieval history insists that he had to get a new pair of glasses.

"What bothers me about the *African Heritage Library* is that it isn't like periodicals, newspapers, technical reports, or that sort of thing. With that kind of material, people just read short excerpts. These are whole books— they're different from most kinds of things in microform collections. I know the cost per book is low, but any cost is too high if it won't be used.

"I realize the economies of microform have a strong appeal to the president and the director, but I don't think everything is suitable to that format. This kind of material ought to be looked at differently."

"Of course, they prefer books," Darr answered, "and I know it's true many students and faculty never use microform material, but the same can be said of libraries generally. The people you and I have talked to have used these materials and continue to use them even though they are upset, and we couldn't get a fraction of what they need any other way. I suspect that most of the material in the *African Heritage Library* is either so expensive or so hard to come by that we never could expect to get it otherwise. If we're going to build a decent library, how else can we do it?"

"I know that," Sorenson answered, "but I'm far from convinced that we should buy books on microform, and I do want to make sure we spend our money in the best possible way, especially for the African studies program, because it hasn't been supported properly."

• • • • •

Assuming that both the collections and the *African Heritage Library* are as described, what would you recommend to Darr if you were Judy Sorenson? How would you justify your choice?

APPENDIX A

HAMMOND UNIVERSITY GRADUATE SCHOOL BULLETIN:
AFRICAN STUDIES

Interdepartmental African Studies Program Committee: John Becker (Political Science) Director, African Studies Program; R. A. Okpara (Geography) Associate Director; Harold Ambers (Law School), Joyce Babcock (Linguistics), Edwin Barclay (Anthropology), Phillip Cook (Sociology), Donald Deuel (Economics), Jeffrey Diemer (Medical School), Luther Helmer (Journalism), Michael Labunski (Industrial Engineering), Samuel Lee (Management), Thomas Ohlson (Music), Owen Startzman (History), Carla West (Art).

The African Studies Program provides a center for the coordination of teaching and research among scholars in a number of disciplines who are interested in Africa. The program is concerned with the systematic study of African people, culture, and institutions both historically and in the present. It covers a wide range of fields and provides for integrated study of Africa across a broad spectrum of disciplines. Comprehensive course offerings include economics, geography, history, law, linguistics, music, political science, and sociology. The program awards an African Studies Certificate to those meeting the specific requirements in languages and upon completion of 36 graduate credits, including 20 chosen from the African Studies core curriculum. However, graduate degrees are always taken in a particular discipline. Many of the students who have completed the program have gone into university teaching and research. The program has also led to careers in government, commerce, journalism, and missions.

African Studies:
   268 Africa: An Introductory Survey
   538 Interdisciplinary Seminar in African Studies

Anthropology:
   220 Peoples in Cultures of Africa
   351 African Philosophy
   520 Seminar: African Ethnology
   553 Seminar: Traditional African Political Institutions

Art:
   363 African Art

541 Nigerian Sculpture
582 Seminar: African Art

Economics:

375 Problems of Africa
429 Economics of Agriculture in Tropical Africa
629 Seminar: Economic Problems of Tropical African Agriculture

History:

361 History of Africa to 1880
362 History of Africa since 1880
430 National Movements in the Near East and North Africa
475 History of West Africa
476 History of East Africa
477 History of North Africa
478 History of Equatorial Africa
661 Seminar: History of Africa
665 Research Seminar: History of Africa

Law:

580-581 Seminar: African Law

Linguistics:

141-142 Elementary Swahili
143-144 Elementary Xhosa
145-146 Elementary Southern Sotho
147-148 Elementary Hausa
161-162 Elementary Arabic
241-243 Intermediate Swahili
243-244 Intermediate Xhosa
245-246 Intermediate Southern Sotho
247-248 Intermediate Hausa
261-262 Intermediate Arabic
341-342 Advanced Swahili
347-348 Advanced Hausa
361-362 Advanced Arabic
405 Introduction to African Oral and Written Literatures
414 Traditional Literature of West Africa
415 Modern Hausa Literature in Translation
437 Swahili Literature
440-441 Oral Traditions of Southern African Literatures
443-444 Central African Literatures
445 Camerounian Oral and Written Literatures
453 Modern African Literature in English
454 Modern African Literature in French
455-456 Southern Bantu Literature
502-503 African Linguistics Structures
521 Typology of African Languages
530 Linguistic Characteristics of an African Language Area
601 Seminar: Modern African Literature

603 Seminar: African Linguistics
620 Seminar: Structure of Southern Bantu Languages
621 Seminar: Comparison and Classification of African Languages
630 Seminar: Hausa Literature
640 Seminar: Central African Literature
650 Seminar: African Thought in Oral Tradition
655 Seminar: African Mythology

Music:
401 African Music

Political Science:
344 African Political Systems
462 African International Relations
561 Seminar: African Politics

Sociology:
327 Comparative Social Structure in Africa
525 Urbanization in Africa

APPENDIX B

Knapp & Wagner, Booksellers

Spanish Africa

A collection of 739 volumes, most of which are unbound. All were published between 1870 and 1960.

Most of the books in the collection are rare. The following is a small selection of some of the fundamental items in the collection:

Baroja, J. C., *Estudios Sahrianos*, 1955.

Cabrera, A., *Los Mamíferos de Marruecos*, 1932.

Campoamor, J. M., *La Actitud de España ante la Cuestión de Marruecos, 1900–1904*, 1951.

Catálogo de Materias (Obras relativas al Islam y Africa) de la Biblioteca General del Protectorado, 1952.

Hernandez-Pacheco, *El Sahara Español, 1949.*

Las Cagigas, J. de, *Tratados y Convenios Referentes a Marruecos*, 1952.

Velez Villanueva, J., *Recopilación Legislativa Vigente en la Zona de Influencia de España en Marruecos*, 1917.

$12,000.00

APPENDIX C

Educational Microimages, Inc.

Dear Librarian:

The *African Heritage Library* offers your library an opportunity to acquire a definitive collection of 10,000 volumes, selected by twenty leading scholars in the field. While it will include titles published up to 1960, the major emphasis will be on books published between 1900 and 1940. Coverage will be continent-wide and include every aspect of the African experience, social, cultural, and political.

The *Library* will provide an invaluable resource for African studies courses. It will find heavy use in departments of history, anthropology, art, political science, and linguistics.

Duplication will be minimal. Many volumes are held by only a few very large American university libraries, and some titles are rare books existing in only one or two copies.

The *Library* has been carefully selected and the entire process has been coordinated by an editorial advisory board made up of scholars and librarians. Selection is based on the following criteria:

1. The historical significance of the title—its intrinsic excellence.
2. How well it reflects the African experience—a variety of works are included to insure diversity and avoid bias.
3. Educational value—the potential contribution of the work to an understanding of the African experience.

The price is $14,000, and this includes a complete set of Library of Congress catalog cards together with a printed book catalog. The cost to acquire original editions of these works is estimated at nearly $250,000. Over and above this the figure would be the costs of ordering, cataloging, and processing.

The collection will be available this fall on 3-by-5-inch microfiche.

Let me know if you would like more complete information on the *African Heritage Library*. I will be glad to send you our new 16-page booklet that describes the *Library* in greater detail.

Sincerely,

Lloyd G. Zuendel
President

7.
"I Just Don't Know What They Want"
· ·

Russell Dobbins had always been a bookish man. He read widely and had a remarkable ability to recall the authors and titles of books. Thus it seemed only natural that he took a job in a bookstore after graduating from college. While he enjoyed many aspects of his work, he was never entirely comfortable in the business world. After two years, he decided to return to school to work on an M.L.S.

Two months before graduating, he accepted an offer from Northern Plains University for the position of assistant acquisitions librarian. At that time, the library of this state-supported institution, established sixty years ago, numbered 258,336 volumes and the book budget was $98,000. The acquisitions department was headed by Peggy Nolan, whose staff included two full-time clerks and sixty student assistant hours per week. Since Dobbins' position was a new one, their first task was to divide responsibilities between them. Nolan concentrated on serials and the budget, while Dobbins took care of bibliographic checking and ordering.

From Dobbins' point of view, this arrangement was ideal because it gave him an opportunity to work with books and book dealers. He especially enjoyed looking at new books as they came in. The Director of Libraries, Frederick Alterman, was pleased too. He felt his choice had been a good one because, while Nolan was good at handling the business end of the department, she had little feeling for books. Alterman began to urge Dobbins to become active in selecting books. In years past, Alterman used to work at this in order to fill in gaps left by faculty selections. However, as the institution grew, he had less and less time and, for the last five years, he had been able to do almost nothing at all. Dobbins needed little encouragement. His knowledge of books enabled him to go right to work filling gaps here and there. Whenever he came across something the library needed, he filled out a card and processed it through.

Dobbins felt he was indeed fortunate. Northern Plains seemed to offer him an almost ideal situation. He talked frequently with other acquisitions librarians, especially at meetings of the Mountain-Plains Library Association. Most of them had almost no opportunity to get involved in book selection because of rigid allocation of funds to departments. Dobbins believed that Alterman was responsible for the fact that this condition did not exist at Northern Plains. He protected the library and the librarians from the faculty by keeping them at arm's length. They did not challenge library policies. On several occasions, Dobbins had overheard Alterman setting senior professors straight about library matters. The story of one strong-willed professor who went over Alterman's head to the president because Alterman would not order several runs of periodical back files for him was well known on campus. After that, all of his requests wound up in a special deferred file.

However, not all of the librarians shared Dobbins' admiration of Alterman. He was an old-fashioned administrator and quite a few found him a hard man to work for. Peggy Nolan was one of those. In Dobbins' eighth year at Northern Plains, she received an offer from another institution. While she was not anxious to move, she was far from satisfied with conditions at Northern Plains. Alterman's strong personality and managerial style were especially frustrating. She felt he gave her far less responsibility than she needed, and that he would not allow her to introduce long-overdue changes. Repeatedly she suggested ways to make her department more efficient, only to find him unwilling to let her go ahead. His usual response was that a certain amount of inefficiency was necessary in case funds were ever cut back.

Three things troubled her in particular—accessioning books, bibliographic checking, and accounting. She could not get Alterman to give up accessioning books, even though he would admit that there was no need to continue the process. Both the acquisitions and cataloging departments did their own checking. In spite of extensive duplication of effort, he could not be persuaded to change existing procedures. Finally, he saw no need to keep accurate accounting records, even though the business office had a reputation for frequent mistakes. For instance, a single posting error the previous April, which Nolan did not discover until after the close of the fiscal year—too late to recover the money—resulted in the loss of $2,338 in book funds. Failure to make any progress left her discouraged and, after considerable thought, she accepted the new job.

Shortly before Nolan left, Alterman called Dobbins to his office. In his usual avuncular manner, he began, "Russ, sit down. I haven't had much time to talk with you this semester because I'm so heavily committed this year on that academic governance committee.

"Peggy's about to leave, and I think it's a good time for us to talk things over. Actually, this may be best for us in the long run. I've always thought she got herself too wrapped up in all that scientific management business—trying to have everything just so, but she never knew anything about what she was working with—books.

"Now you've done a great job building the collection, and I think you'd do a fine job as head of the department."

"Well, I have enjoyed working with the books," Dobbins replied, "and I have ordered a lot of things we need. I like that, but I don't think I'm ready for the responsibility of running the whole department. I know what you mean about Peggy, but the way she and I had things divided up worked pretty well. She did a good job of running things, and I had time to work on the collection. I like it that way and I don't think I'd be happy spending my time looking after all those people in the department. I just don't think that's very professional."

"Exactly! That's just what I mean. You've worked with Peggy a long time, Russ—too long perhaps. All that management business—she never saw the forest for the trees. I don't think it's all necessary, nor do I see any reason why you couldn't have plenty of time to do just what you've been doing all along. I'll get you an assistant who wants to work with the serials so you won't have to worry about that."

The two talked on for another twenty minutes, at which time Dobbins asked for some time to think things over. They met again a week later, and he finally agreed to accept the position.

As time went by, Dobbins came to feel he had made the right decision. Naturally there were problems. Most serious was staffing. While the book budget increased, his staff did not grow at the same rate. Trying to keep up proved harder and harder. At length, he appealed to Alterman for relief. After some thought, the director decided to abandon accessioning. However, this alone was not enough and Dobbins again appealed to Alterman. This time the director asked him if it would not be better to issue want-lists for o.p. books. As long as he had been at Northern Plains, one of the clerks checked dealers' catalogs against the desiderata file. Dobbins admitted that this would save time, but objected on the grounds that o.p. book dealers who search charge too much. While Dobbins abandoned the old procedure of regularly going through catalogs, he could not bring himself to issue want-lists. This procedural change made it possible for him to spend the budget by concentrating on in-print titles, but the o.p. file began to grow.

It was no surprise that faculty complaints began to increase. At first, Dobbins was able to satisfy most of them. Rather than argue with them, he would promise to do everything possible to expedite their o.p. requests. Sometimes he took catalogs home to check in the evening or over the weekend. However, more often than not, as soon as he began to work on one faculty member's problem, another would come in with a similar complaint. He could no longer get it all done. Far from appreciating what he tried to do, most faculty members began to feel Dobbins was not being honest with them. Several went to Alterman, but received little comfort. He took obvious pleasure in telling them that he was understaffed and overworked.

Things went from bad to worse the following year when the book budget was increased from $151,000 to $174,000. Alterman knew he had to make some change in order to enable Dobbins to spend the money. He remembered that Peggy Nolan was always fussing about duplicated effort in bibliographic checking. He called in Dobbins and the head of cataloging to discuss the problem, only to find that they were opposed to any change. Dobbins viewed Alterman's suggestion that acquisitions do full bibliographic checking as an added burden for his staff, one they could not accomodate. The head of cataloging expressed doubts that acquisitions could ever do the kind of checking that her staff needed. After thinking it over, Alterman abandoned this approach, but he recalled having read that approval plans save staff time. Dobbins' initial reaction was not favorable. He doubted that the vendor would really know anything about the needs of Northern Plains University or that the firm would send all the needed titles. But he finally concluded there was no other way out, and agreed to go ahead.

Dobbins exercised great care in the selections. In the first full year of the program, he spent approximately $90,000 on approval books. During this period he received little comment from any quarter about the project. Only one faculty member expressed strong opposition, and Dobbins referred him to Alterman. Thus it seemed strange to him to learn from one of the reference librarians that some faculty members were critical of the program. He was upset because they knew little about it and had not come in to talk with him. The fact was that several reference librarians were also disturbed about the program, but this was not reported to Dobbins. They felt that he had returned several important reference tools they needed.

Two years later, Alterman announced plans to retire at the end of the academic year. In order to select a successor as soon as possible, a number of candidates were screened by Alterman, the Library Committee and the academic vice president. The list was narrowed to three who were brought to the campus for interviews. William Frost, the successful candidate, had spent three years as librarian of Cascade College in the Pacific Northwest. At the time he was interviewed, Professor Dennis Wescoat, Chairman of the Library Committee, asked him the same question he put to each candidate. "Mr. Frost, what is your opinion of these so-called on-approval plans?"

"I can't honestly answer you because I've never worked with one and I have no experience with this kind of program. At Cascade the faculty was responsible for letting us know what they wanted. The only complaint I ever got was that there wasn't enough money."

Three months later, on the first of July, Frost assumed his new duties. During the summer months he met a number of faculty members, some of whom were critical of the approval program. His conversation with John Larson, Associate Professor of Music Literature and a member of the Library Committee, was in many ways typical.

"Welcome to Northern Plains. Are you getting settled?"

"After a fashion, I guess. Our furniture arrived only ten days ago and we're not completely unpacked yet. But we should be settled down before too long."

"Well, I do hope everything goes smoothly. I guess you weren't here long enough last spring to get a good look at things. But tell me, how does the library look to you now?"

"Quite honestly, I still haven't been here long enough to answer that question. I've been busy just meeting people and reading reports. But from what I can see, things look like they're in pretty good shape."

"Of course," Larson answered. "I know it's too early, but there is one thing that bothers quite a few of us a lot, and that's the approval books business. Many of us just don't think we need all that stuff they send. Frankly, I think we're wasting a lot of money."

"There's no doubt that many of the faculty need more than just an approval program. Many of you also need older material, and I think we ought to be able to devote a fair percentage of the budget to that sort of thing. But I'd like to know what we are getting on the approval program that doesn't fit into our needs. You know that we can send anything back we don't like. How often do you get over to look at the shipments?"

"Well, I haven't had the time lately," Larson admitted. "I'm just swamped trying to get a manuscript off to the publisher and revising my nineteenth century course. I'm already four months late on my book. But I don't have to look at all those books to know that a lot of people don't like this program, and that we just aren't getting the things we need. When this program was first set up, I tried to convince them that it would eat into our already meager funds and prevent us from getting the really important books. Alterman was pretty pig-headed and never would listen to anyone. Well, now a lot of the committee members want to take a hard look at this program. I, for one, think it's high time we gave it up. Why, do you know that fellow back there— Dobbins, that's his name—has thousands of cards that never will be ordered? That's what I'm concerned about."

As the conversation drew to a close, Frost promised to look into the matter. It was obvious that Larson did not know much about the approval program, but that he did feel strongly about it. Other faculty members did too. One common complaint was that their requests were ignored. Another source of irritation was the fact that Dobbins routinely returned cards for titles they had noticed in their professional journals with the explanation that they would probably come in on approval.

Frost determined to evaluate the whole situation carefully. First, he reviewed each approval shipment for a period of several weeks. He was especially impressed with the quality of the selections. From what he knew of

Northern Plains, the books Dobbins had chosen appeared to mirror accurately the instructional programs on campus. There was no question that Dobbins knew books and spent a lot of time reviewing them.

Second, he asked Dobbins to review the operation of the department with him. Dobbins explained how order cards were received and processed. First, they were sorted. Cards for current imprints were checked against the vendor's list of publishers. Any that appeared on that list were returned to the requester. Next, cards for titles that seemed inappropriate were set aside. Sometimes they were sent back, but if the requester was likely to complain, they are usually held. This saved a lot of unnecessary argument, Dobbins explained. Foreign titles, societal publications, and symposia were also set aside because it took longer to process them. These were held until the department was caught up on its other work. The remaining cards were checked in the public catalog and order file to eliminate duplicates and then they were priced in *Books in Print*. Out-of-print titles were placed in a separate file, which contained over 8,000 cards and was growing rapidly. Again, if the department was caught up on other things, the staff checked dealer catalogs against the file. Orders for in-print titles were typed and mailed to the vendors. When they arrived, they were checked to make sure the vendor supplied what was ordered. The books were then sent to cataloging for bibliographic checking.

Frost found this review helpful and commented, "Russ, now that you've told me what you're doing I can see—and I think anyone who took the time could see—that you're doing a great job of selecting books on the approval program. Yet a lot of faculty members I've met are pretty upset about it. In fact, a good number want to scrap the whole thing. How would you explain this?"

"I really can't, Mr. Frost. In fact, I just don't know what they want. I guess some of them are upset about what I'm doing, but I don't know why. Maybe it's because I don't have enough people to do the job. We're spending $184,000 this year on books and $83,000 on periodicals and serials. To do this we only have—let's see—seven full-time people, a half-time clerk and about two-and-a-half student positions. That just isn't enough to do things the right way.

"I've talked to a lot of faculty, but they never seem to understand. Mr. Alterman used to talk with them. He may not have satisfied them, but at least they didn't keep coming back to bother me all the time, and I could get some work done. Now the only time I can really get anything done is if I come in on weekends. I certainly hope you aren't thinking of cancelling the plan, Mr. Frost. I honestly don't see how I could keep up if that happened."

Frost left the conversation with a better understanding of what went on in acquisitions, but with a number of questions about Dobbins. How efficient was he? Frost had no way to answer that question because he had no background in acquisitions. On the other hand, how much of the problem was a result of difficulties Dobbins had in communicating with others? Or was that Alterman's fault? Frost wanted to continue to build a good collection, and he was sure Dobbins knew his business. Yet it looked as though something would have to be done.

Two weeks later Elizabeth Wasaff, Head of the Reference Department, came into his office to ask if her reference librarians could look at the approval books. She explained that while she was sure that Dobbins did a good job, occasionally he sent back reference tools they needed. Frost asked her why she did not ask Dobbins himself. She explained that she had brought it up over a year ago. He voiced no objection, and in the beginning he called after the shipments were unpacked. But gradually he stopped letting her know when to come. Moreover, the books were in a corner where they were hard to reach. Frost agreed to schedule a meeting with the three of them to work out a way for the reference librarians to review the books.

At the first meeting of the Library Committee in September, the approval plan was brought up for discussion. While one member supported it, all the others expressed varying degrees of opposition. Frost's defense of the plan appeared to have no impact on the members. A resolution calling for cancellation of the program was introduced, and would easily have passed had Frost not asked for a semester to look into the matter more deeply. The committee agreed to postpone formal action for a semester.

Frost felt it was important that the library continue to acquire the new books it needed. He had succeeded in delaying the committee long enough to come up with a solution, but he saw no simple answer. As he reviewed the problem, he tried to sort out its components.

First, and most obvious, was the fact that much of the criticism was not based on substantive objection to the program. Rather, it focused on other aspects. He asked himself whether he could expect to pacify the faculty within such a short span. Probably not. Should he then, like Alterman before him, ignore them simply because he felt they were wrong? He wondered whether those he had spoken with accurately reflected faculty opinion in general. What other sources of support were there? He was sure the administration would not care one way or the other. Second, and less clear to Frost because of his lack of technical services experience, was the question of what could be done to satisfy the needs of the faculty for o.p. books. Clearly Dobbins was understaffed, yet Frost suspected that acquisitions was not a model of efficiency. And even if he could solve this problem now, was it too late?

Third, and even more vague, was Frost's feeling that Dobbins was trying to do too much. He asked himself what the head of acquisitions should be doing. In a library like Northern Plains, could one person handle both the administration of the department and collection development?

Frost wondered whether there was any way he could abandon the approval program and still achieve the same results. Unfortunately, Alterman had not hired reference librarians on the basis of their subject knowledge. Two had majored in history and the other three were former school teachers. They possessed no particular subject competence and showed no interest in collection building.

•   •   •   •   •

What should Frost do?

8.
"We've Got a Good Thing Going"
. . . .

The librarians at Olton State University were proud of the collection they had built. For many years they worked hard and gained the respect of most of the faculty for their efforts. Public Services was organized into four divisions, humanities, social sciences, science, and education, and each of the librarians was assigned responsibility for a specific part of the collection. LC proof slips served as the basic tool for selecting current imprints. These were sorted by subject in the acquisitions department and sent to the various divisional librarians. Other selection tools included *Publishers Weekly, Choice,* publishers' catalogs and blurbs, as well as journal reviews. By meeting often with faculty members and getting to know the advanced graduate students, the librarians kept aware of current research activity in their areas of responsibility. Some even made regular trips to a local bookstore to look at the latest titles and pick out those that faculty members or graduate students might want right away.

So well did this system work that the Director, Oscar Rounds, had not had a complaint about the acquisition of books and periodicals for many years. In fact, he had received a number of letters complimenting the staff on their effectiveness in getting specific books. In these letters, faculty members often wrote that new publications were ordered before they had even heard of them. Because of this, over three quarters of the book selection at OSU was done by librarians. The success of the acquisitions program was one reason the divisional librarians had an esprit de corps that enabled Rounds to recruit and retain good librarians, many of whom held graduate degrees in their areas of responsibility.

While their routines varied somewhat, each of the librarians maintained a file of titles they had ordered to avoid duplication. When faculty members sent purchase recommendations, they checked their own files without going to acquisitions and returned cards for titles already ordered. Notification slips were sent to them from the catalog department after the books had been cataloged and the subject specialists pulled the slips from their own files.

Most faculty members recognized that the librarians were doing an outstanding job and were happy to let them continue. The administration was equally impressed. This had brought the library substantial increases in its book budget, which gradually began to create a problem because the librarians found it increasingly difficult to spend the available funds. There just was not enough time. Rounds knew that he could not expect any additional specialists beyond the ten now on the staff. For these reasons, he was interested in talking with Robert Lynch, who was in charge of the approval program for a large book jobber, and Louis Janowitz, manager of the nearest branch office. Rounds invited the two to come to OSU to make a presentation. They spent nearly two hours describing and outlining the major advantages of the program to Rounds, the head of the acquisitions department, and the heads of the four divisions. Lynch and Janowitz explained procedures and discussed experiences of a number of other institutions.

The following week, Rounds met with the same group again briefly to discuss the proposal. He argued that it would save time and work and free the subject specialists to devote more time to other activities such as retrospective collection building, library instruction, and long-range planning for future library needs. None of the others shared his enthusiasm. The general reaction was summed up in the words of Richard Miller, head of the humanities division: "While I'm willing to go along with you on this, I feel that we're taking a chance on it. We've got a good thing going, and I don't believe the approval program will be as good. They aren't going to get all the titles we need. I hate to see us take a chance on damaging our relationships with the faculty, which I believe are so good simply because of the work we've been doing over the years. The real answer is more staff."

"I'd like to see that, too," Rounds replied, "but we don't have a leg to stand on. With 33 librarians, 50 clerks, over 90,000 student assistant hours, and a million and a quarter books, we're ahead of the pack by every measure—percent of the institutional budget, expenditures per FTE student, volumes per student, right down the line."

No further objections were raised. The group acquiesced to the director's proposal and consented to adopt the program on a trial basis for six months.

Janowitz was delighted and came that same week to talk with each specialist. From these conversations he constructed an outline that specified collecting levels for each field, and added a variety of other modifiers such as form of material, level of specialization, geographical area, and language to refine the selection process even further.

Soon books began to arrive, and almost immediately the fears of the subject specialists seemed to be confirmed. Coverage was spotty. Many of the books received had already been ordered by the subject specialists long before the approval program had begun. Others were not suitable for the collection. As many as half of the titles sent were being returned. What bothered them even more was the fact that many important books were apparently not being sent. Because of this, most of them continued to review *Publishers Weekly* and other sources just as they had done for years. Thus, the librarians found themselves doing the same work they had done before, and the approval plan became nothing more than a frustration.

It was not long before others also began to object to the program. Formerly, close to 80 percent of the orders for current imprints were made from proof slips and no verification by the catalog department was necessary. Books arrived from the acquisitions department with a copy of the proof slip. With the change to the approval program, it was decided there would be no need to route the proof slips to the subject specialists, but rather to set up a proof slip file for the catalog department. However, this meant that the approval books had to be searched through the proof slip file. Moreover, the library had always rush cataloged books needed by faculty members. These changes seemed to make it necessary to do more temporary cataloging, which had to be redone later. It was not surprising that the head of the catalog department became one of the most outspoken opponents of the program.

Other librarians complained about having to examine the books themselves. Many, especially in the sciences, felt that the proof slips gave them all the information they needed and that it was a waste of time to read prefaces and tables of contents, or to skim through the books.

Before long, the head of acquisitions joined the opposition because his work load had also increased. The divisional librarians were continually asking his staff to find out whether a particular book had been received on approval or to check with the vendor about the status of a title. Returning large numbers of unwanted books was an additional burden.

The experience of Ellen Hill, Life Sciences Librarian, illustrated what happened to most of the subject specialists. One afternoon soon after the program was inaugurated she received a call from a close faculty associate who asked whether a new university press publication on the shrubs and woody vines of the Midwest had been ordered. In the past, she could easily have checked her order file and provided information immediately on the status of the book. Now she had no record. She felt uneasy at being unable to give an answer right away. All she could do was promise to call back later. The acquisitions department reported that it had not received the book. She checked other tools and found an LC proof slip as well as a listing in a recent issue of *Publishers Weekly*. The acquisitions department sent a form letter about the book to the vendor, who replied "not available yet." She called the faculty member back and reported what had happened. He expressed surprise because he had seen a copy of the book on display at a conference he had attended the week before, and said he needed it for his research.

Angrily she immediately called Janowitz personally. He told her that the book certainly would be shipped as soon as it arrived. When Hill asked why he had not received it when it had already been published, he explained his problems with publishers and how unreliable some of them, especially the university presses, were. She called the faculty member once more and explained that he had probably seen an advance copy, even though she was not satisfied that this was really the case.

From that point on, she began to check *PW* regularly and to look at the proof slips again to see what was really being sent. Within a short time she identified several other important titles that had not arrived. Soon she was spending as much time selecting current books as before.

Within four months after the approval program began, most of the librarians were pleading with Rounds to abandon it. It irritated him every time the matter came up because he felt they were not giving the program a fair chance. Their reaction surprised and confused him. He wondered what to do, and reluctantly he began to draft a letter cancelling the program.

• • • • •

Approval programs have worked successfully at many academic libraries, yet not all librarians agree that they are desirable. What are the arguments for and against approval programs? What factors govern the success or failure of such a program? Can they be predicted in advance? What do you think accounts for the apparent failure of the program at OSU? Was Rounds correct in believing that an approval program could succeed? If so, was he correct in going ahead with the program in the way he did it?

Should he send the letter cancelling the program or should he seek to correct the defects in the program?

9.
"But What About the Students, Professor Reid?"

. . . .

Ann Harnack had not seen John Meyer for nearly five years. Both began their professional careers as reference librarians at the same university. Meyer remained and had become associate director at that library, while Harnack went on to head the reference department of a New England university and then to become librarian at Elmburg College. When they ran into each other between meetings at the ALA conference that year, both were delighted that their schedules allowed them some time to talk. They exchanged information about mutual friends, reminisced about their early years, and then moved on to the present.

In talking about Elmburg, Harnack was quick to praise her president because he had been generous with the library in many respects. Salaries were above average and she had been able to attract a competent staff. In fact, financial support for the library as a whole was good—6.5 percent of the college budget. Yet all was not well. The president was too busy with other problems to take an active interest in the library. Because of this, a group of senior professors dominated the library through the Library Committee. Even though this group clung to its perquisites and opposed many changes Harnack sought to introduce, she had made some progress toward reducing the committee's influence on library matters over the years. Yet she felt this was hardly more than a drop in the bucket.

One area in which the committee took a special interest was the budget. For many years, funds for library material had been severely limited, and arguments over even a few dollars in the departmental allocations were not uncommon. Each spring usually brought bitter controversy that occasionally erupted into personal animosity as the committee prepared the budget for the coming year.

A number of years ago, Harnack had read an article in *Library Quarterly* on budgeting by formula. The article convinced her that this was the best way to avoid these divisive struggles. It was not difficult to get the committee to agree with her. She and a member of the economics department were directed to develop such a formula for Elmburg, based on such factors as the credit hour production of each department, the rate of publication by subject, and the average cost of books by subject. In addition, each department was assigned a weighted library dependency factor, based on the committee's judgment of how heavily each one used the library. While it was easy to get agreement on a formula in principle, there was considerable debate over the specifics. Nevertheless, it was adopted and it became known as the Mostellar formula. At the time it was approved some faculty members expressed dissatisfaction, but most either supported it or were neutral. In the years that followed, a couple of powerful committee members were able to modify the formula to their own advantage, although this was not general knowledge.

During the same period, Harnack succeeded in reducing the allocated portion of the total book budget from 57 percent to 47 percent. Most of this gain was offset by the cost of new periodical and serial subscriptions, but there was some additional money to purchase reference books and general titles for the collection.

In spite of the progress she had made, Harnack was far from satisfied. The responsibility for book selection remained almost exclusively in the hands of the faculty. Only a few books could be ordered each year by the library. These procedures created many gaps in the collection because most faculty members failed to take an active part in choosing titles. Others picked only titles they felt were useful to them.

Students often came to the reference desk for help in locating books they needed for their papers and other assignments. All too often they could not find what they needed because the library was weak in that particular area. About a year ago, Harnack had checked several issues of *Choice* and found that over 40 percent of the books she thought the library should have had not been ordered.

It seemed to her that this situation was caused by the fact that funds were allocated to departments; break that and the problem would be solved. But how?

At this point Meyer broke in: "Have you ever considered an approval program, Ann?"

"No, it never occurred to me. I just don't think we're at that level, and I don't see how we could afford it."

"Don't be too sure. I can think of some libraries that aren't spending much more than you are and they've gone into it. It's not just the allocation problem you ought to think about. There are other considerations. With an approval program you'd not only get a balanced selection, but you'd get the books on the shelves a lot faster and probably save staff time too."

The conversation then drifted to another topic, but after they parted, Harnack did think about Meyer's suggestion. The next day she dropped by the booth of one of the vendors offering an approval program. There she met Ed Marcucci, manager of the approval program. Since it was almost noon, he suggested that they have lunch together to discuss the matter fully.

After they had gotten settled, Marcucci opened the conversation by asking Harnack to tell him something about Elmburg College. She explained that Elmburg, established in 1822 as a denominational college, later abandoned its sectarian affiliation and was now a liberal arts college that offered a number of master's degrees. The collection numbered 163,000 volumes and the budget for library books and periodicals was $186,000.

Marcucci responded by reviewing the experiences of several other small and medium-sized colleges he had worked with, and then he spent a few minutes analyzing publishing trends. Next, he explained that $70,000 was about the minimum required for an approval program. Anything below that would not work because his staff could not be sufficiently selective. He warned that normally libraries should not spend much more than 30 percent of their total book budget on an approval program. A slightly higher percentage of the budget could be used for this purpose if existing holdings were well selected and relatively few retrospective materials were needed.

After the meeting Harnack reflected on what Marcucci had said. While it was true that the collection had a number of gaps, eventually most important titles did get ordered. The more she thought about it, the more it seemed that much of the problem was caused by the fact that it took so long for the faculty to get around to ordering the important books. An approval program seemed an ideal solution. No longer would the library have to wait for basic titles; they would come in right away.

After she returned to Elmburg, Harnack talked first with her two reference librarians, George Rowland and June Richards. They were closest to the students and understood their problems best. Each reported a number of recent instances in which students became frustrated trying to prepare papers and reports. While both agreed the plan would solve a number of problems, Rowland wondered if it would not be just as effective and cost less to order the titles reviewed in *Choice*. However, he thought either way would represent a major step forward. Richards was especially bitter toward the faculty. With an M.A. in English, she kept up with her field, and was keenly aware of areas of weakness in the collection. To correct these, she took time, often on weekends, to read reviews in the *Times Literary Supplement, Publications of the Modern Language Association*, and other sources. She typed order cards, frequently copying excerpts from the reviews, and sent them to members of the English department hoping they would sign and return them. Less than a third ever came back approved. At times it seemed hardly worth the effort, but she continued in spite of the poor return because even that amount was better than nothing.

Next, Harnack spoke with the acquisitions librarian, Frances Waters. To Harnack's surprise, Waters proved even more enthusiastic. Pressed for staff, she viewed an approval program as a way to eliminate the constant stream of requests for books already on order or cataloged. She explained that if the faculty understood that books from certain publishers would be received automatically as soon as they were published, precious staff time would not be wasted on unproductive work. The volume of duplicate order cards was one of her main complaints. They came not only from different departments and different faculty members in the same department as they read reviews in their professional journals, but sometimes even from the same faculty member. To make matters worse, many cards were hand written, and her clerks could barely decipher some of them. Others left off important data or used the wrong entry. Many were so bad that she had to check them herself. The present system, she concluded, was a major cause of low morale.

Harnack was encouraged by her staff's response, but she knew the next hurdle would be much harder. Before doing anything further, she called Professor Joseph Malouf of the history department to arrange a luncheon meeting at the faculty center. Malouf was a strong supporter of the library. Harnack had been pleased when he was elected to the Library Committee last spring because he, unlike the majority of the members, consistently backed her efforts to improve the library. More than once, he argued against proposals that would either interfere with the internal administration of the library or commit the library to an unwise policy. As a result, she often consulted him in advance about matters to be brought before the committee. In the case of the approval program, she realized this would be a hard victory. Because it would deprive the faculty of direct control over the budget, she wanted to find a way to present her proposal that would perhaps appeal to the committee and the faculty generally.

Harnack outlined the plan to Malouf, who asked a number of questions. When she finished, he expressed reservations about the quality of the material that would be received. With so little money, he felt that it would be better to wait until reviews appeared in the scholarly journals and then to make selections from them. He had been doing this for many years and it seemed perfectly satisfactory. Harnack explained that while he was conscientious, most faculty members were not. Malouf conceded this point, agreed to back her, and added that the program could easily be abandoned if it did not work. However, he warned her that he doubted whether the other members of the committee would accept the program.

After the conversation, Harnack gave the matter considerable thought. First, she attempted to determine how the members of the committee would vote. She concluded that two would oppose, and two, including Malouf, would support it, while three were uncertain. Second, she decided to talk with the three in question individually in hopes of winning their support. Before making appointments, she spent a week reviewing the literature on the sub-

ject and carefully organizing her arguments. Then she arranged a meeting
with Professor Charles Reid, a musicologist who had been on campus for
over twenty years. She carefully outlined the major advantages of the program:

1. Automatic receipt of material needed by the library. The dealer would
develop a profile of Elmburg's needs. Books that matched this profile would
be shipped. The library would hold them for review and any that were not
suitable could be returned.

2. Important books would be made available more rapidly. The dealer
would send the books as soon after publication as possible. Faculty and students would not have to wait for books they needed.

3. Costs would be reduced. Staff time would be saved processing orders. At
present, some titles had already gone out-of-print by the time a faculty member got around to ordering them, and the cost for o.p. books is usually much
more than the original price.

After she concluded her remarks, Reid responded, "I'm sorry Miss Harnack, I simply cannot support your proposal. This scheme would do nothing
more than fill the library up with whatever happened to be published without
regard to its merit. It would prevent us from purchasing the things we truly
need."

"Many schools have found just the opposite to be true," Harnack answered. "As I mentioned, the first step is to carefully construct a profile of
our needs. The dealer sends only what fits into it. Then we put the books on
review shelves and make them available to all the faculty for a week. You and
your colleagues can come and look them over. We'll send back anything you
don't like."

"That might work as far as I'm concerned, but there is no one else in my
department who cares enough to take the time. I suspect things are about the
same in most other departments. Now you understand that one professor
simply can't be familiar with all areas of his discipline. If the others don't care
enough to do it the right way, I can't see why they need books at all. But
that's not my only objection. My field depends on historical works, reprints,
and foreign publications. It takes a couple of years to establish whether a
book is any good in the first place. I just can't understand why we have to
rush out and buy every book that's published."

"But what about the students, Professor Reid? You're talking about research material, but ours is not a research library. It's mainly for students. I
wish it were otherwise, but it's not because we just don't have enough money.
The president has been as generous with the library as he possibly could be,
but right now we're not even meeting student needs. They come to our reference librarians asking for new books for their papers that we don't have.
Quite honestly, I think it's much more important that they get a new book to
do a term paper than for the library to acquire some specialized study in
French or German. Very few students can work with any foreign language.
But it's not just getting books as soon after publication as possible. There are

a lot of things that either never get ordered or that nobody orders for five or ten years. There are many gaps in the collection."

"Miss Harnack, I'm confused. You surely understand that when it comes to what students need, it is I and my colleagues on the faculty who know that and therefore what ought to be in the library. To be honest, I don't see why you seem so disturbed."

"Actually, Professor Reid, you'd be surprised how broad student interests are. Many times they aren't reflected in the curriculum or in the interests of one of their professors."

"What surprises me, Miss Harnack, is that *you* keep telling me what students need. To be perfectly honest, neither you nor your librarians know, and least of all does some bookseller who probably never set foot on this campus. Frankly, I am mystified that you would even suggest abandoning a perfectly good system that has served us well for years in favor of one that would fill the library with a lot of trash."

Harnack could easily have pressed further with arguments based on saving money, but Reid was no longer listening. The level of his voice had been rising and she realized that she would only antagonize him more. She shifted the conversation to another topic as quickly as possible and ended the discussion a few minutes later.

For the rest of the day and well into the evening she was preoccupied with this encounter. Reid was adamant. This both angered and frustrated Harnack, because he rejected her plan without a fair hearing. His response left her more firmly convinced that the approval plan was a good idea and that it should not be thwarted by individual faculty members who knew so little about libraries.

•   •   •   •   •

What should Harnack do now? Has she proceeded in the best way up to this point?

Although she studied approval programs carefully, has she thought out all considerations? For example, can Elmburg College really support an approval program? Are there perhaps other ways she could accomplish her goal? Could this be done more gradually? Are there other possible sources of backing for the approval program? If so, how should she exploit these?

Should she present her proposal to the Library Committee? If the committee rejects the proposal, should she go ahead and implement it? If the idea of an approval program is dropped because of faculty opposition, are there ways the existing system of book selection might be improved?

10.
"Surely There Must Be Some Mistake!"

· · · · · · · · · · · · · · · · · ·

Professor Eugene Fields of the mathematics department had a reputation as the campus watchdog. As he prowled about the campus of Dennison College, he always seemed to notice whatever was wrong—sometimes wasted money, an infraction of the rules, or poor maintenance. He was well known to every campus administrator, including Edward Rankin, the college librarian. Indeed, one of his most celebrated crusades had involved the library several years earlier. Standing in the lobby looking at an exhibit of fine printing that Rankin had assembled, Fields noticed a student leaving the unguarded exit with several books that had not been charged out. He demanded that Rankin institute an exit control. Rankin explained that he could not because he did not have the staff, and he spent two hours showing Fields the entire operation. Convinced that Rankin could not possibly provide the 64 hours of student assistant time needed to guard the exit to Schaffer Library, Fields shifted his campaign to the president and finally secured funding for a door check.

Now Fields was again in Rankin's office, and as he sat down the librarian wondered to himself, "What now?" He dreaded the thought of another crusade, but then no one on campus looked forward to a visit from Professor Fields. As Rankin looked up he noticed that Fields was carrying an armload of books. Before sitting down, he carefully laid them out on the librarian's desk. It was then that Rankin noticed that each one was stamped "Withdrawn." Fields opened the conversation by explaining that he had been taking a shortcut to his office, because he had arrived late that day and the parking lot he usually used was full. This route took him past the loading dock of the library. In passing, he spied a trashcan full of books and stopped to examine them. All bore the "Withdrawn" stamp. While a great number were old textbooks, some were not. Fields continued, "I gathered up as many as I could carry to show you. Perhaps you aren't even aware of what your staff is doing, but I can't believe that with all the money problems we're having you would turn around and throw out perfectly good books. Surely there must be some mistake!"

Rankin thought to himself, "Why don't they keep the lids on those cans and only put them out at five o'clock? I've warned them about this before." Then he patiently began to explain that during the summer months he, together with the reference and acquisitions librarians, customarily went over the collection and weeded out volumes that were no longer needed. This was standard practice at many colleges, and especially necessary at Dennison because the building was designed to accommodate only 155,000 volumes, and provided seating for 400 students, just under a third of the student body. Now, with 125,000 volumes already on the shelves and approximately 6,000 volumes a year being added, the building would be full in five years. It was only six years old, and an addition was out of the question for at least seven or eight more years. Rankin knew that some seating could be taken out, since the reading areas were never more than half filled. Yet, he had not seriously considered this alternative because the Schaffer family had been generous in providing funds for the library. They were proud of the building and he felt that to make changes in the interior layout might run the risk of upsetting them. The college hoped to get a substantial gift from them for the future addition as well.

Rankin went on, "Many volumes, especially those that are essentially texts, are no longer useful. Newer and more accurate information is all that is needed in a number of disciplines. In other cases, some books are very specialized. Quite a few were ordered by faculty members who have left or for other reasons are no longer used. I remember that somebody did a study some years back of branch libraries at a large university and found that 25 to 70 percent of the collection satisfied 99 percent of the needs. That suggests that we don't really have to retain the books that aren't being used."

"Now I'm even more disturbed," Fields broke in. "First, I find out that we're ordering a lot of textbooks, and I thought we didn't. Then you tell me that a faculty member can order anything he wants, and when he leaves or doesn't use it anymore, you just throw it away."

"Well, you can't make any hard and fast rules on textbooks. We try to order as few as we can, but in some disciplines, there isn't much else. So, we just accept the fact that in five or ten years it's time to throw them out. Your other point is a little more complicated. I review all order cards and often talk with individual faculty members about their orders. Sometimes I say 'no,' but things get complicated in a situation like this: Professor X is teaching a seminar and he has a particular area of specialization within that field. More often than not, he wants to concentrate on that area. It's given once every other year. If he stays here five or six years, that means he may teach that seminar two or three times. Then he takes a job someplace else. Then what? Another man comes in. He'll teach the same seminar but his interests are likely to be different, and the chances of those books ever being used again is pretty remote."

Breaking in again, Fields bellowed, "We can't have that! We can't afford to support this kind of purchasing! If you can't control it, I'll propose that the Library Committee review all purchases. Maybe they can make some hard decisions around here. And even if a book is a little old or esoteric, we shouldn't throw it away. I can think of hundreds of times I've driven thirty miles across town to use the library at Nelson University or down to the public library to find a book we didn't have, or even worse, waited three weeks for something on interlibrary loan. I wonder how many of the books you've thrown out would have been just what somebody needed at some time. We've got plenty of storage space under the bleachers in the stadium, and we could put them there if you don't have enough space here. And another thing, how do you decide a book should be thrown out?"

"We keep up with new books, and when something new comes out that supersedes another work, we generally discard the earlier edition. Duplicates are also a problem. We often have to buy multiple copies of a particular book to put on reserve. Later on they're not used, and we throw them out. But for most things, the emphasis is primarily on how often the title is used. In some fields, they get all excited about a particular topic, and then in a few years they lose interest and switch to something else. Education is a good example. Not too many years ago, everybody was all concerned with the gifted child, and now they're off into other things. We gradually throw books like that out, because they're not used any more. In literature, authors are popular and then people lose interest in them. They could become popular again, but it may take fifty or sixty years. I figure if a book hasn't been used for four or five years, it's a prime candidate for the trash barrel. We look them over, and sometimes we find it useful to check with the department. Some faculty members can be very helpful."

After Rankin concluded, the two of them went over each of the books Fields had salvaged (Appendix A). All of them fit the criteria Rankin had outlined, except for an art book that had been replaced because many of the illustrations had been cut out. Fields argued that if students cut up books they should live with the results.

Although Rankin felt he had very effectively explained and defended his policies, Fields was unconvinced. As he stood up to leave, he announced that he would take the matter to the president and the dean, as well as to the Library Committee, to propose not only that no esoteric books be ordered, but also that Rankin stop throwing out books that might be useful to someone else in the future.

● ● ● ● ●

Weeding is one solution to the problem of too many books. What are the alternatives? What are the advantages and disadvantages of each?

What is the best solution for Schaffer Library?

If you believe weeding is advisable, are Rankin's policies reasonable? Did he go about implementing them in the right way? How could he have protected himself in this situation against the kind of criticism expressed by Professor Fields?

APPENDIX A

Alberti, Rafael. *A Year of Picasso Paintings: 1969.* New York: H. Abrams, Inc., c. 1971.

Doubman, J. Russell, and Whitaker, John R. *The Organization and Operation of Department Stores.* New York: John Wiley & Sons, Inc., 1927.

Fiske, Horace Spencer. *Provincial Types in American Fiction.* Chautauqua, N.Y.: The Chautauqua Press, 1907.

Jackson, J. D. *The Physics of Elementary Particles.* Princeton, N.J.: Princeton University Press, 1958.

Kingsnorth, G. W. *Africa South of the Sahara.* London: Cambridge University Press, 1962.

Muir, John M. *Geology of the Tampico Region, Mexico.* Tulsa, Okla.: American Association of Petroleum Geologists, 1936.

Schieder, Theodor, & Ernst Deuerlein, eds. *Reischsgrundung 1870/71: Tatsachen, Kontroversen, Interpretationen.* Stuttgart: Seewald Verlag Stuttgart, c. 1970.

Shoenberg, D. *Superconductivity.* Cambridge: Cambridge University Press, 1960.

Watson, John B. *The Ways of Behaviorism.* New York & London: Harper & Brothers Publishers, 1928.

Wilson, Angus. *A Bit Off the Map.* New York: The Viking Press, 1957.

Wilson, Angus. *The Wild Garden.* Berkeley & Los Angeles: University of California Press, 1963.

Woods, Frederick Adams. *Mental and Moral Heredity in Royalty.* New York: Henry Holt & Co., 1906.

11.
"You've Wasted
a Lot of Our Money!"

. . . .

Mitchell Library, like many other libraries, sent extra copies of multipart order forms to faculty members to notify them that books they had ordered had been received. Hugh Hudson, Associate Professor of English, found an envelope with some of these slips in his box one morning on his way to class. He put them in his briefcase, and after class he looked them over in his office. One upset him so much that he got up and went immediately to the office of David Sofer, Assistant Librarian. As he burst in, he thrust the slip at Sofer and said, "I'd like to know what's going here. I sent an order card for this book and now I find out that you paid $17.50 for a reprint edition. Just a few days ago I saw a good copy of the original edition in Kerlin's Bookshop for only $9.00. You've wasted a lot of our money! Our departmental allocation this year is only $2,100, and we can't afford to waste a penny of it."

Sofer answered by explaining that it takes a great deal of time to order out-of-print books and that faculty members often need things in a hurry, so he always tries to get the books as quickly as possible, and that out-of-print books are often in poor condition. For these reasons, library policy was to buy reprints whenever they were available.

Hudson responded, "I would suggest that you spend a little less time shuffling papers and get out and visit bookshops once in a while. We have a number of excellent ones, in case you don't know. I would really think that a librarian would want to do something like that and save some money at the same time."

"There's nothing I'd like to do better, but there just isn't enough time. I can barely keep up with the orders as they come in."

Even more irritated, Hudson shot back, "It's foolish for me to bother sending orders over to you except for simple in-print titles. In the future I'll buy the out-of-print books we need at bookshops and have them sent to you. Even with an occasional duplicate, we'll be hundreds of dollars ahead by the end of the year."

. . . . .

How would you answer Hudson?

12.
"It's Time
to Put an End to This!"
. . . .

The final responsibility of the outgoing chairman of the Senate Library Committee was to call the first meeting of the year in the fall and oversee the election of a new chairman. Normally this was a routine task, but this was not a normal year at Spalding University. Student enrollment had fallen short of the projected 18,500 FTE, and the administration was faced with having to make severe budget cuts. The library's allocation for books, periodicals, and nonbook material was $840,518, which was $82,928 below the previous year. While the possibility of cuts had been common knowledge the past spring, the committee had not discussed it at that time. Now, however, feelings were strong among the members, and the chairman found it impossible to prevent discussion of this matter. The general view was that the committee, speaking for the faculty, must voice strong opposition to the cuts. The voice of Professor Roger Kerwin, the committee's humanities representative, rose above the others as he called for better budgetary support, but added, "First, however, the library must put its own affairs in order!"

Obviously taken by surprise, Director of Libraries Ralph Dillon responded that the library was run as efficiently as possible.

"I'm not talking about efficiency," Kerwin answered. "What bothers me is that there seem to be no restrictions on the number of copies a faculty member can order. I've always worried about this, but now it's a critical issue. Each duplicate copy means that another book someone needs for research can't be purchased. It's time to put an end to this!"

"Certain titles must be duplicated," Dillon explained. "We try to watch this as carefully as we can. Actually most of the duplication isn't done by the teaching faculty at all, but by librarians. The teaching faculty want duplicate copies for reserve. If the class is large enough and the use is likely to be intensive, we'll buy extra copies.

"However, use is the main factor. There is a basic core of heavily used material and we have to acquire extra copies to satisfy demand. It's a fact that many libraries of our size—we're at about a million and a half volumes now—have separate undergraduate libraries, some with a hundred thousand or more volumes, all of which are duplicates. These are titles used mainly to support undergraduate instruction.

"Another category of duplication involves the branch libraries. With nine branches, not counting law and medicine which are under the deans of those colleges, there's bound to be a lot of duplication. There's so much overlap between a number of them, especially engineering, chemistry-physics, and to a degree geology; agriculture and biological sciences; and architecture and fine arts. Mathematics and education don't have as much overlap with other branches, but all of them duplicate to a degree the holdings of the main library. It's not uncommon to buy several copies of a book. The branch librarians review new books and order some extra copies, and the teaching faculty order even more."

As Dillon was speaking, a troubled look came over Kerwin's face, and he showed signs of becoming increasingly agitated. No longer able to contain himself, he exclaimed, "Good God! If our faculty and graduate students can't even walk a few blocks to get a book or fill out a card to reserve a book that's checked out, this university is in pretty sorry shape."

Equally disturbed at his inability to control the discussion, the outgoing chairman broke in, "Forgive me, gentlemen, but first things first, and we must attend to the matter of electing this year's chairman."

Before he could continue, Kerwin added, "Just let me say one more thing, then. I'm going to introduce a formal motion at the next meeting to restrict faculty and library staff from purchasing duplicate copies."

The Senate Library Committee at Spalding University was originally constituted as a policy committee. This meant, according to the constitution of the Senate, that it did have authority to make formal policy for the university. On the other hand, Dillon had made it clear to the administration that he would not accept this role for the committee. While the president and academic vice president told him that they understood the problem, they pointed out that changing the constitution was in the hands of the Senate and, ultimately, the general faculty. When he asked for backing in case a dispute arose, they told him that each case would be judged on its own merit. So, while he always referred to the committee as advisory, and some members agreed, the matter had been left unclear and Dillon did his best to avoid open conflict. Further, he was unsure of how most of the members would react to the matter of purchasing duplicates. Three were new that year, and the issue Kerwin raised was different from those the committee had discussed in the past.

• • • • •

Based on the information presented in this case, what are the pros and cons of Kerwin's argument and Dillon's defense?

How would you as director of libraries respond to Kerwin's motion when the matter is discussed by the committee?

13.
"It's Going to Take a Lot of Books to Get Accredited"
. . . .

Highland College was eight years old. Four years ago it had moved to its present location near a small town and dropped its formal denominational affiliation in an attempt to attract more students. With an enrollment of 750, the college offered bachelor's degrees in the liberal arts, education, and business.

In the words of the Carnegie Commission, Highland was one of the "invisible colleges." With a total budget of less than a million dollars, the college was severely strapped for funds. The fact that the institution had allocated only 3.3 percent of its budget to the library for the current year explained why the collection numbered only 15,685 volumes.

Recognizing that one way to improve the fiscal picture would be to increase enrollment to approximately 1,000, President Kruse announced at the first faculty meeting of the academic year that he would direct attention in the coming year toward improving the institution with a view to seeking accreditation in three or four years.

Inez Herriot was elated. During the three years she had been librarian, she had tried unsuccessfully to increase acquisitions. At her next meeting with the academic dean, Verlin Hendrix, she expressed her feelings and added, "I'm sure President Kruse realized when he announced his plans to seek accreditation that one important factor will be the library. It's going to take a lot of books to get accredited. We're adding less than 1,500 volumes a year now, and almost half are gifts. I'm afraid we'll need a lot more money to build up our library."

"I think we ought to talk with the president about this," Hendrix said. "In fact, let's go over right now. He may be free for a moment."

They did find that the president was able to see them. He ushered Herriot and Hendrix into his office, and the academic dean outlined the problem. President Kruse replied, "This is an excellent time to talk this over. We certainly do have a problem, and I have been giving it some thought. I can't offer much hope for increasing the budget. The money just isn't there, so we've got to try some other way. It looks like we can do two things. First, let's see if we can get some money from foundations, and then let's really go out after gifts. I'll send a special letter to every alumnus and to the families of all our students." Turning to Herriot he added, "You could write your own colleagues at some of the larger state-supported institutions and try to get duplicate books from them. I've heard of other colleges like ours getting a lot of excellent material this way."

"I think it is only fair to tell you," Herriot explained, "that I do send out letters each year to a number of institutions and we do get some things that way. But I will make an extra effort."

In the following months, the president sent his appeal to the alumni. In fact he went even further by appealing to civic and fraternal groups and businesses. Results for the first year were encouraging. One foundation granted the college $2,750 to purchase history books, and a total of $587 in cash was received. There were also two excellent gifts. One came from the parents of a student whose grandfather had been a professor of ancient history. In his will, his books and a small collection of papyrii were divided among his three children. The family donated what it had received, seventeen volumes and two papyrii dating from about 180 B.C. Another collection came from the mother of an alumna who was recently widowed and planned to move to a retirement community in Arizona. She donated her husband's collection of eighty-one volumes on the Lewis and Clark expedition.

In addition, over 2,000 miscellaneous books came in from a variety of sources. Lacking the staff to process them immediately, the librarian set them aside on shelves and in boxes in the receiving area. During the summer, Herriot finally got around to looking at some of these volumes. While some were suitable, most were not.

In the past, she had screened gift books carefully. But now she wondered whether she should be a little less selective, so she went to President Kruse. The president expressed admiration for the care she had exercised in the past in choosing books, but went on to say, "If we are going to survive as an institution, and I believe that Highland College is worth saving, we must be able to attract more students. Accreditation is our only hope. For now, then, put whatever you get on the shelves. When we get accredited maybe we can do a little better by you."

"You mean, " Herriot asked, "you want me to catalog everything we've received?"

"Certainly, I can't see why not."

Somewhat taken aback, Herriot retreated without further protest. She worked at the gifts as time permitted, but progress was slow and it took a long time to get them organized. She found eighty-seven dental and medical books, most of which had been donated by a recently retired dentist, and were ten-to-fifteen-year-old textbooks that he had kept in his office. There were 381 paperbacks ranging in quality from the best to the worst. Quite a few had been used for classes and were marked up, while others were old, with paper that was already beginning to deteriorate. There were seventy-six religious and self-help books. There were duplicates and in several cases three copies of a title. There were ninety children's books, most of which were badly worn. Except for some of the better quality paperbacks and children's books, she boxed all the rest and set them aside. Then she filled a range of shelves with the remainder, and instructed a student assistant to list the books, check them against the card catalog, mark those in the library with a check and the others with a circle, and return the list (Appendix A) to her office.

• • • • •

Would you go ahead and catalog all of the books as President Kruse directed, or would you attempt to convince him once more that some of the material should not be added to the collection? If so, what should not be added and how would you attempt to convince him?

Are there other things Herriot could do to stimulate giving?

APPENDIX A

O Adams, Kramer. *The Redwoods*. Popular Library, n.d.

✓ Andrist, Ralph. *Steamboats on the Mississippi*. American Heritage Publishing, 1962.

O Armstrong, Edward. *Syntax of the French Verb*. Henry Holt & Co., 1909.

O Ashmore, Harry, & Baggs, William. *Mission to Hanoi*. Putnam, 1968.

O Baker, Elizabeth. *Printers and Technology*. Columbia University, 1957.

O Bader, Ray. *American Chronicle*. Charles Scribner's Sons, 1945.

O Baedeker, Karl. *Belgium and Holland*. Karl Baedeker, 1905.

O Baldwin, Lillian. *Music to Remember*. Silver Burdett Co., 1951.

✓ Bambrough, Renford. *The Philosophy of Aristotle*. New American Library, 1963.

O Bancroft, Caroline. *Six Racy Madams of Colorado*. Bancroft Booklets, 1965.

✓ Barrie, J.M. *Margaret Ogilvy*. Charles Scribner's Sons, 1896.

O Baum, L. Frank. *The Road to Oz*. Reilly & Lee, 1909.

O Blodgett, Harold, ed. *The Story Survey*. Lippincott, 1953.

✓ Blum, J., & Catton, Bruce. *The National Experience*. Harcourt, Brace, & World, 1963.

O Boyd, Ernest. *Guy De Maupassant*. Little, Brown, & Co., 1928.

O Bradford, Barbara, ed. *Children's Stories of Jesus*. Lion Press, 1966.

✓ Bromberg, Walter. *The Mind of Man*. Harper & Bros., 1954.

O Bryan, William. *The Old World and Its Ways*. Thómpson Publishing, 1907.

O Buffum, Douglas. *Stories from Merimee*. Henry Holt, 1920.

O Burnell, Elaine. *Asian Dilemma: U.S., Japan, and China.* Center for the Study of Democratic Institutions, 1969.

O Burrell, Angus, & Cerf, Bennett, eds. *The Bedside Book of Famous American Stories*. Random, 1936.

✓ Cecil, David. *Melbourne*. Bobbs-Merrill Co., 1939.

O Chrisman, Arthur Bowie. *Shen of the Sea*. Dutton, 1925.

O Chrystie, Frances. *Riddle Me This*. Walk, 1940.

O Claire, Mabel. *The World's Modern Cook Book*. World Publishing, 1941.

O Cleland, Thomas, ed. *Evangelical Hymns*. T. T. Skillman, 1828.

O Cooley, John. *A Primer of Formal Logic*. Macmillan, 1949.

O Cote, Levey, & O'Connor. *Ecouter et Parler*. Holt, Rinehart, & Winston, 1962.

O Cozzens, James Gould. *By Love Possessed*. Harcourt, Brace & Co., 1957.

O Crowe, John. *You Can Master Life*. Prentice-Hall, 1954.

✓ Crunden, Robert. *A Hero in Spite of Himself.* Alfred A. Knopf, 1969.

✓ Cundiff, Hannah, & Dykema, Peter. *School Music Handbook*. C. C. Birchard, 1950.

O Dacey, Norman. *How to Avoid Probate!* Crown Publishers, 1965.

O Dale, John & Magdalene. *Cours Moyen de Francais*. D. D. Heath & Co., 1956.

O Dale, John & Magdalene. *Cours Elementaire de Francais*. D. D. Heath & Co., 1964.

O D'Alonzo, C. Anthony. *The Drinking Problem—And Its Control*. Gulf Publishing, 1959.

O Dane, Clemence. *The Flower Girls*. W. W. Norton & Co., 1955.

✓ Daniels, Josephus. *Tar Heel Editor*. Chapel Hill, 1939.

O Davis, Adelle. *Let's Eat Right to Keep Fit*. Harcourt, Brace, 1964.

✓ Defoe, Daniel. *Robinson Crusoe*. Jacobs, n.d.

O De Whurst, Coppock, Yates, & Assoc. *Europe's Needs and Resources*. Twentieth Century Fund, 1961.

O Durrell, Lawrence. *Mountolive*. Dutton, 1959.

O Ekert-Rotholz, Alice. *The Time of the Dragons*. Viking Press, 1958.

O Elisseeff, Serge, & Reischaur, Edwin. *Selected Japanese Texts*. Harvard-Yenching Institute, 1944.

✓ Farber, Seymour, & Wilson, Roger, eds. *Control of the Mind*. McGraw-Hill, 1961.

O Fast, Howard. *The Unvanquished*. World Publishing, 1956.

O Flye, James. *Letters of James Agee to Father Flye*. Braziller, 1962.

O Fowles, John. *The French Lieutenant's Woman*. New American Library, 1969.

O Fox, Genevieve. *Mountain Girl*. Junior Literary Guild, 1932.

O Gillespie, Cecil. *Accounting Systems*, 2nd ed. Prentice-Hall, 1962.

O Goetschius, Percy, ed. *Symphony Number Five by Antonin Dvorak*. Oliver Ditson, 1958.

O Graf, Max. *From Beethoven to Shostakovich*. Philosophical Library, 1947.

✓ Graves, Maitland. *The Art of Color and Design.* McGraw-Hill, 1941.

O Guest, Edgar A. *When Day is Done.* Reilly & Lee Co., 1921.

O Gray, Elizabeth. *The Cheerful Heart.* Viking, 1959.

O Harris, J., & Leveque, Andre. *Basic Conversational French*, 3rd ed. Holt, 1963.

O Headley, J. T. *Stanley and Livingstone in Africa.* Spencer Press, 1937.

✓ Hendrick, Burton. *The Life and Letters of Walter H. Page.* Doubleday, 1923.

O Henry, Marguerite. *Album of Horses.* Rand McNally, 1951.

✓ Hicks, John. *The American Nation.* Houghton Mifflin, 1946.

O Hodgins, Eric. *Enough Time?* Doubleday & Co., 1959.

✓ Kazan, Elia. *The Arrangement.* Stein & Day, 1967.

O Keefer, Frank. *A Text Book of Military Hygiene and Sanitation.* Saunders Co., 1914.

✓ Lampart, Felicia. *Cultural Slag.* Houghton Mifflin, 1961.

O Lehninger, Albert. *The Mitochondrion.* W. A. Benjamin, 1964.

O Leif, Alfred. *Brandeis.* Stackpole, 1936.

O Lewis, Ethel. *Decorating the Home.* Macmillan, 1950.

O Litwack, Gerald, & Kritchevsky, David, eds. *Actions of Hormones on Molecular Processes.* Wiley, 1964.

O Lowe, Robert. *Visages de France.* Odyssey Press, 1964.

✓ McKinney, Howard & Anderson, W. R. *Discovering Music.* American Book Co., 1943.

O Malamud, Bernard. *The Fixer.* Farrar, Straus & Giroux, 1966.

O Mathieson, Elizabeth. *The Complete Book of Crochet.* World Publishing, 1946.

O Maugham, W. Somerset. *Cakes and Ale.* Doubleday, 1930.

O Merton, Robert K. *Social Theory and Social Structure.* Free Press, 1957.

O Millis, Walter. *The Martial Spirit.* Literary Guild of America, 1931.

O Mulhauser, R., D. Desberg, & Saisselin, R. *Le Francais d'aujord'hui.* Ginn, 1962.

O O'Hara, John. *Ten North Frederick.* Random House, 1955.

O Peattie, Roderick. *How to Read Military Maps.* Stewart Publishers, 1942.

O Pitman, Robert. *Alcohol and the State.* National Temperance Society, 1878.

✓ Prince, Morton. *The Disassociation of Personality.* Meridian Books, 1957.

✓ Radt, F. *Elsevier's Encyclopedia of Organic Chemistry.* Springer-Verlag, 1959.

O Raphael, R. A., Taylor, E. C., & Wynberg, H., eds. *Advances in Organic Chemistry*, Vol. 2. Interscience Publishers, 1960.

O Raswan, Carl. *Drinkers of the Wind.* Creative Age Press, 1944.

O *Reader's Digest Condensed Books*, 10 vols. 1954–1969.

O Remmers, H. H., & Gage, N. L. *Educational Measurement and Evaluation.* Harper, 1955.

O Roth, Philip. *Portnoy's Complaint.* Random House, 1969.

O Ryan, Mildred. *Your Clothes and Personality.* Appleton-Century, 1937.

O Sandall, Robert. *The History of the Salvation Army, 1865–1878.* Nelson & Sons, 1947.

O Savage, Minot. *Our Unitarian Gospel*. George Ellis, 1900.

O Schulz, Charles. *For the Love of Peanuts!* Fawcett, 1952.

O Shellabarger, Samuel. *Lord Vanity*. Little & Brown, 1953.

O Sonet, E., & Shortlife, Glen. *Review of Standard French*. Harcourt & Brace, 1954.

O Spurgeon, Charles. *My Sermon Notes*. Funk & Wagnalls, 1888.

✓ Steinbeck, John. *Travels with Charley*. Viking, 1962.

O Styron, William. *Set This House on Fire*. Random House, 1960.

O Sugimoto, Etsu Inagaki. *A Daughter of the Samurai*. Doubleday, Doran & Co., 1930.

O Temple, Daniel Jr. *Life and Letters of Rev. Daniel Temple*. Congregational Board of Publication, Boston, 1855.

O Tumulty, Joseph. *Woodrow Wilson as I Know Him*. Doubleday, 1921.

O Updike, John. *The Same Door*. Fawcett, 1954.

O Van der Weyde, William, ed. *The Life and Works of Thomas Paine*, 10 vols. Thomas Paine National Historical Association, 1925.

O Vaughan, Bill. *Bird Thou Never Wert*. Simon & Schuster, 1962.

O Vincent, Marvin. *The Age of Hildebrand*. Scribner, 1900.

O Wambaugh, Joseph. *The Blue Knight*. Little, Brown & Co., 1972.

O Warner, Susan. *The Wide, Wide World*, 2 vols. Edward Publishing, n.d.

O Waters, Frank. *People of the Valley*. Sage Books, 1941.

O Wellman, Dane I. *The Chain*. Doubleday & Co., 1949.

O Wheeler, John Harvey. *Democracy in a Revolutionary Era*. Center for the Study of Democratic Institutions, 1970.

✓ White, William Allen. *Woodrow Wilson*. Houghton Mifflin, 1924.

O Whittier, John. *The Poetical Works of John Greenleaf Whittier*. Houghton Mifflin, 1848.

O Williston, Seth. *Five Discourses on the Sabbath*. E. & F. Hosford, 1813.

O Wilson, Eugene. *Wings of the Dawn*. Connecticut Printers, 1955.

✓ Winkler, Franz. *Man: Bridge Between Two Worlds*. Harper & Bros., 1960.

O· Yerkes, Robert. *Chimpanzees, A Lab Colony*. Yale University Press, 1943.

O Young, James Harvey. *The Toadstool Millionaires*. Princeton University Press, 1961.

14.
The Half Millionth
Volume—One Too Many?

• •

Historically, Mesa University was an undistinguished institution. In fact, the term "university" reflected little more than the ambition of its founders. All but a few of its students came from the surrounding community. The others came mostly because they were unable to gain admittance to better colleges and universities. The policy was to accept almost any applicant with a high school diploma, and the faculty was under strong pressure not to fail anyone. The faculty was no better. The number holding the doctorate was so low that when Mesa was recently reaccredited, the report called attention to this problem.

Mesa was a branch of the state university, whose main campus was located at the other end of the state about 250 miles away. In addition, there was a second branch, which emphasized science and technology. Mesa offered the doctorate in education, psychology, anthropology, history, and English, master's degrees in the social sciences and the humanities as well as in mathematics, and bachelor's degrees in almost all fields including the sciences. The quality of its graduate programs was uniformly weak. For the most part, Mesa trained teachers.

The situation at Mesa was principally the result of administrative and fiscal difficulties. For years, the institution floundered under a president who ruled with an iron hand through his vice president. The president sought to avoid any publicity, fearing that it might call attention to the institution's condition. In a politically conservative state which was far from wealthy, adverse publicity could easily result in budgetary slashes.

Five years ago the vice president retired. This marked the first step in a long process of reversing the pattern of mediocrity that had for so many years characterized Mesa University. Although he had been eligible to retire earlier, the president persuaded him to remain until reaching mandatory retirement age. Less than a year after losing his strong right-hand man, the president himself retired. To replace him, the trustees selected Charles Bowers, who had served for several years as academic vice president at a large midwestern university. Mesa interested Bowers because in it he saw an opportunity to develop a strong liberal arts program, strengthen graduate programs, and improve the quality of the students and faculty. He knew that the state was not a rich one and that he could not expect enough money for these changes from that source alone. What impressed Bowers was that the community was proud of this institution in spite of its poor quality. Early in its history, Mesa had been a municipal university. Close ties developed between the community and university that continued after it was taken over by the state. Bowers felt he could attract more fiscal support from the community to supplement state funding.

In the three years since he was appointed, Bowers had already met with a certain amount of success. To fill the vice presidency, he selected Howard Dart, a noted renaissance scholar. He recruited a number of promising young faculty members and added new courses in the social sciences and humanities, and enrollment grew to 10,000 FTE, while at the same time entrance requirements were raised slightly.

During this period, Mesa's long-time library director also reached retirement age. Bowers took a personal interest in this appointment. Over the years, he had developed a genuine interest in books and had come to know several antiquarian booksellers. He felt that an active special collections program would assist him in achieving two of his important goals—improved community relations and a better faculty.

A search committee was formed to screen and evaluate candidates. Several were invited to come to Mesa to meet with the selection committee, the faculty library committee, librarians, deans, and a number of academic administrators. Among the applicants was James Gray, who had been head of public services for six years at a similar, but larger, state university about 600 miles away. Gray was immediately attracted to Mesa after meeting Bowers, who talked of his plans to solicit gifts of books and money to develop special collections.

From others, Gray learned that the collection as a whole was weak. While the volume count exceeded 400,000, a substantial number of these were obsolete textbooks, especially in education. This was partly the result of a policy, abandoned about twelve years ago, requiring the library to purchase unsold copies of textbooks from the bookstore. Also, there were many gaps in the collection, and the need to improve the quality of holdings in the humanities was widely recognized.

When the selection committee submitted its recommendations, Gray's name was among the top candidates. Dart recommended Gray to the president without reservation. No other applicant shared the president's interest in special collections while at the same time appearing to be a competent administrator, which was Dart's major concern.

Eighteen months after arriving at Mesa, Gray reflected on his accomplishments. He felt fortunate indeed, especially in light of the close relationship that had developed between the library and the administration. The president's strong, active interest suggested that the library might look forward to a period of growth that would make up for years of neglect. Although the book budget was still far from adequate it had increased to $281,826. In only one respect had his plans been thwarted. Bowers' efforts to attract gifts and funds from outside sources to build special collections proved unsuccessful. The major cause was crop losses for two years in a row, which cut farm income and dampened most segments of the local economy.

Nevertheless, Gray did everything possible to develop outside support. He established a friends of the library group and, while their account contained only $351, he was certain that in better times they would prove effective in stimulating gifts and interest in the library. In spite of limited success, Bowers was delighted. He went out of his way to tell Gray how pleased he was with the progress he had been making and to express confidence that with time outside funds and donations would be forthcoming.

In the meantime, Bowers showed an active interest in the collection by occasionally sending over catalogs from antiquarian booksellers in which he checked items for purchase. These were generally well-chosen landmarks in the history of printing. While Gray realized the money could be better spent on badly needed periodical back files or out-of-print monographs, he raised no objection. This seemed a small price to pay for the close relationship that he enjoyed with his administration.

In fact, Gray hardly gave the matter a thought. His hands were full with a variety of projects including preliminary planning for an addition to the library building and the reorganization of public services. The number of service points had to be reduced because the staff was spread too thin to give good service. In addition, he spent many hours talking with faculty members about library problems. Many were pressing for a "better library," which meant more books, because of their own interest and because they wanted their students to use the library more. Concern with the collection was particularly strong at this time of the year as many instructors were beginning to plan courses for the next semester. Within a month, Gray talked to about a dozen. The fact that many of them said almost exactly the same thing underscored the pressing need to improve the collection.

A conversation he had with Anthony Wold was typical in many respects. Wold, who had recently received his doctorate in art history, was among the promising appointees made since Bowers' arrival. The administration looked to Wold to strengthen the art department at MU. Soon after arriving on campus, he made it a point to meet Gray. Wold was interested in the library and expressed a desire to use it more heavily in his teaching. Gray was encouraged by the enthusiasm Wold and some of the other young faculty members showed. In spite of the problems, their interest in the library made him feel confident that progress would be made.

One morning, Gray saw Wold in the outer office and went out to talk to him. After they exchanged greetings and went back to Gray's office, Wold explained, "I've only got a couple of minutes before class, but I wanted to talk about next fall for a moment. I'm giving a seminar called 'Techniques of Art History,' designed for senior art history majors. I want them to learn research methods by preparing a research paper. The problem is that I don't know how I'm going to do it. The library is so bad, Jim. I know you can't change things overnight, but I simply don't stand a chance of doing a halfway decent job unless it's improved.

"Periodical back files are probably the number one problem, but there are also lots of basic studies and some sets we need. I don't suppose we have half of what we need. Just let me give you one example—our subscription to *Burlington Magazine* doesn't start until 1949. The back file has been reprinted, but it's terribly expensive—something over $2,000.00 I think.

"I could name lots more titles that are just as important and just about as expensive. You can see what the situation is. That's why I came over. I'd like to find out what you can do."

"I wish I could be more encouraging, Tony, but you know as well as I do how little money we have. We're barely able to keep up with the new things, let alone all the older stuff you need. I can probably scrape up an extra thousand, but that's about it."

"Jim, I know what you're up against, but I can't even teach properly, let alone do any decent research here. Betty and I have just gotten settled and we hate to think of another move, but things just don't look very encouraging."

"I wish I could do more," Gray answered, "but quite a few people have come in with the same problems and I've got to think of them too."

"I know you do. I'll drop around later; maybe you can get some extra money somewhere."

"I'll try, but I'm not too optimistic."

The implication of Wold's remarks jolted Gray as none of the previous conversations had. He was particularly disturbed by Wold's obvious pessimism about improving the library. Unless something could be done, he feared Mesa might lose the young faculty members he hoped would use the library in their teaching and transform it into an important educational resource on campus. What is more, the loss of these good new faculty members would represent a setback for the president. That night and over the next few days Gray worried a great deal about the whole problem. He was keenly aware, too, that in addition to the dozen who called on him, there were probably many others who did not even bother because they felt it would be a waste of time.

The following Tuesday the problem was thrown into even sharper focus.

The afternoon mail brought a catalog from an antiquarian book dealer, on which the president had written the following note: "Jim: If my memory is correct you're getting close to the half-million mark. Wouldn't item 5 make an excellent half-millionth volume? The newspaper would give it good coverage, and we need a good story to bring in some gifts and new Friends."

The entry in the catalog read as follows:

> 5. AUGUSTINUS. St., *De Civitate Dei.* 274 leaves, Roman letter, 50 lines to the page, with 2 fine illuminated initials and marginal flourish on the first leaf of text. Folio, vellum, Venice: Johann and Wendelin de Spria, 1470. $1500.
>
> First Venice edition of *The City of God.* A very fine example of early Venetian printing, and the fourth book printed at Venice. "This work is indispensable to the collector of early typography. . . ." Dibdin.
> *Bib. Spenceriana.* Johann and Wendelin de Spria were the first printers at Venice. Johann completed only three books before this. He died during the printing of the work, and it was completed by his brother, Wendelin. This is the earlier issue having blank spaces for the capitals at the beginning of each book, and having the illuminated initials, in place of the woodcut border on the first page of text. This is a very fine and tall copy (393 by 274mm.). Stillwell A1092. Hain 2048. *BMC* V, 153. *Gesampt. Kat.* 2877. Updike I, 72 (plate 26).

This was far more expensive than anything Bowers had previously ordered. Gray began to wonder what the total cost of the president's orders amounted to. He found that with *The City of God*, the total for the year would come to $3,115. While he recognized and supported the president's goals, he suddenly realized that expenditures of this sort damaged those very goals in other ways. He knew it would be difficult to get this point across to the president. Repeatedly he had tried to explain to Dart and Bowers that the collection simply was not adequate to support existing instructional programs, and he never passed up an opportunity to transmit comments he had received from faculty members. True, Dart and Bowers were sympathetic, but they did not seem to grasp the seriousness of the problem. Bowers' preoccupation with special collections seemed to make him oblivious to other library problems. Gray recognized that somehow he must approach this problem from another direction, yet he was at a loss as to how to proceed.

• • • • •

Does Gray fully understand the problem himself? Has he contributed to it in any way? If so, how? What alternatives are open to him? What are the possible results of each of these? What course of action would you take?

15.
"Why Duplicate?"
· · · · · · · · · · · · · ·

Scene: The office of Herbert Miller, Academic Vice President at Barnham University, a private institution located in a metropolitan area of 800,000 people. Barnham enrolls nearly 5,000 full-time students and about 4,000 part-time students. It offers master's programs in business, education, and engineering, as well as the arts and sciences. The library has 327,601 volumes and 2,979 current periodical subscriptions. Miller is reviewing the library budget request for the coming year with Edwin Logan, Director of Libraries. During their conversation, Miller keeps glancing distractedly at papers and memos on his desk that he must attend to.

"Okay," Miller said, "so much for the supplies and services. Now let's move on to the book and periodical accounts, especially the periodicals. Every year you keep repeating in your justification that subscription costs are going up 13 percent, or something like that. We just don't have 13 percent more each year to maintain current subscriptions, and we certainly can't afford the 125 new titles you feel are 'essential'."

"I'd like to explain the problem in a little more detail. We now have 2,979 periodical subscriptions. That just isn't enough to support our program."

Without giving Logan a chance to finish, Miller broke in. "Ed, I don't for a moment question what you say, but you've got to face some of the realities of this situation. You and I have been going over this each year for three years now, and each time you come back with the same thing. You need to recognize that I can't give you a higher percentage of the university budget without damaging other programs, and I'm not about to do that unless you've some better arguments than you've come up with so far. The budget increases you're asking for this year would eat into other things. I've just got to cut your requests down, and since we're short on time and this will have to be our final budget conference this year, I simply have to be arbitrary. I'm going to propose no increase in the budget for periodicals. I don't see any reason why you shouldn't, in fact, cut down on the number of periodicals. We have a number of good libraries in this city. The research people can use them. The public library has about three quarters of a million volumes and a good strong literature collection. OU's got a lot better library than ours, and one of the best science libraries in the country. There's no reason our people can't go over there. It's only eight miles. The art museum has a couple of rooms full of books. And even though it's about twenty miles away, the teachers' college has been in business for a good many years, and they've got a first-rate library for anything relating to education. I just can't see any point in our subscribing to expensive periodicals that are available practically down the street! Why duplicate? It just seems silly to me."

● ● ● ● ●

Assuming that Logan has not anticipated this turn of events, how might he respond to Miller's decision and what arguments might he offer to salvage all or part of the proposed budget for periodicals? Which arguments might be most effective with a man in Miller's position?

16

"They Are Biased, Immoderate, and Will Probably Mislead Our Students"

Mercer Community College was situated on a postage-stamp sized modernistic campus, dominated by a strikingly conventional and ugly ten-story classroom and office building that looked something like a prison administration building. It blended with the harsh lights and dead-end streets of its urban setting. The entire campus looked like something that had been financed from unused municipal bonds that the city fathers felt should go to contractor–allies as rewards for services rendered.

MCC had recently appointed a new academic dean, Alfred Whitman, who was determined to make the institution rise above its setting and the blue-collar students who made up its primary clientele. Whitman, to whom the director of the Educational Media Center reported, was a man who believed in standards. When his conversation was not about recruiting a "better-qualified faculty," it was likely to deal with "academic standards," "demanding more from students," or "restoring proper balance" to MCC, all of which meant deemphasizing vocational and technical programs.

The Educational Media Center, located in the main classroom building, reflected the strong emphasis on vocational training at MCC. Many of its 61,588 books, as well as its nonbook resources, had been selected to support programs in commercial art, business, engineering technologies, health sciences, and law enforcement.

Five days before the start of the fall semester, Jane Hickman, a reference librarian, walked into the office of John Tillman, Acting Head of the EMC. Indignation radiated from every pore of her body. Her gray eyes were flashing and her back was ramrod straight. As she entered the office, she exclaimed, "Now he's really done it! This is completely inexcusable and unjustified!" She waved a stack of about thirty cards in her hand.

"Sit down, Jane," Tillman replied, as he prepared to listen to a long tirade.

"Whitman has gone too far and he's not going to get away with this, if I have to organize all the women on this campus! These cards reflect a careful selection of books about women, and he's returned every one of them with this note." The note, which she shoved at Tillman, read, "The books represented on these order cards do not meet the standards of high scholarship we expect here at Mercer. They are biased, immoderate, and will probably mislead our students. They are returned to you and will not be submitted for purchase."

Because the EMC was currently without a permanent director, Whitman insisted on personally approving all book, film, and periodical orders before they were sent to the college bookstore for puchase.

Hickman, who had been a reference librarian for five years at Mercer, was devoted to the cause of women's rights and the women's movement. "The women's movement is a healthy thing," she continued, as she looked down at her rejected order cards. "It's refreshing and quite wonderful to see women affirm their loyalties to each other and their mutual interests."

Now, more soft spoken, but still highly articulate, Hickman indicated that she was prepared to defend her choices even to the extent of enlisting her husband, an attorney, to take legal action. "Young men and women here need the points of view expressed in these books. I've read many of them myself. Too often newspapers portray us as a group of kooks. Our students deserve better information than that.

"During my lifetime, I have met women of capability, depth, and courage, and it seems to me they were being held out of the mainstream of American life or were allowing themselves to be held out. For the most part, this school is oblivious to the issues that are boiling about it. So many forces exist here that tell the students to learn the tools of a job or profession and get on with being a good suburbanite. They are programmed to accept society as it is. They are conditioned to think of themselves as unintellectual, incapable, and somehow inferior."

"But anyway, off the soap-box and back to the real issue. Whitman simply isn't in touch with the real world. To call these books 'biased' or 'immoderate' or whatever he called them displays complete ignorance of the feminist movement. Beyond the rhetoric—and you have to go beyond the rhetoric—these books reflect an effort to create an image women can identify with in a more humane world."

As she spoke, Hickman began shuffling through the cards. The first one she tossed on his desk was for *Combat in the Erogenous Zone*. "I'll bet that one really got him. But it's a beautiful book. It shows with such honesty just how real psychic damage from the oppression of women is. It's a very touching book."

Next she tossed out cards for *Sexual Politics* and *The Female Eunuch*, commenting, "Scholarly? No, but basic to an understanding of the resurgency of feminism. But where he really doesn't have a leg to stand on is that crap about 'scholarship'." Pulling out cards for Flexner's *Century of Struggle*, Scott's *The Southern Lady*, Wolff's *Love between Women*, and Bardwick's *Psychology of Women*, she concluded, "These are good solid studies. They're as scholarly as just about anything that's being written today. This is a good selection, John, and you've got to get the dean to reverse his stand."

Grimly, Tillman took the rest of the cards and thumbed through them. They were similar to the examples she had showed him. He noted that they represented a number of points of view. True, most of them were not scholarly dissertations or learned sociological tracts, but they did spell out the social ferment that was going on in American society.

"It's important that we defend our right to order books like this," Tillman replied, "and we must establish our freedom from administrative censorship. I'll talk with Whitman this afternoon."

• • • • •

Does a community college educational materials center need these kind of books, when they are probably also available at public libraries near the students' homes? Does the dean's argument that these books are not sufficiently scholarly have validity?

Can external administrative review of library purchases be justified at any time? If so, under what conditions?

Are there any legal ground for challenging the dean? How would you present your case to the dean?

17.
"Like Atomic Energy, Teacher Power Can Be Used for Many Purposes"

• •

The Learning Resource Center's collection at Commonwealth College presently contains 31,500 books and 1,070 films, as well as tapes, discs, film-strips, and other materials. A year ago, the Library-Audiovisual Committee of the faculty undertook jointly with the staff of the Learning Resource Center a study of the administration of the materials budget, which is currently $45,000 per year. In the past, all purchase requests had been routed through the director of the LRC, and no records were kept of spending by discipline. On the recommendation of the committee, however, it was decided, beginning with the current year, to allocate a definite percentage of the materials budget to each department. The acquisitions librarian was responsible for all order-ing, keeping accounts, and reporting expenditures and balances monthly to each department. The new system was intended to enable each department to make long-range plans for developing resources in its field. Departmental al-locations were approved by the committee. For the first year, they accepted the recommendations of the director with only minor changes. In addition to funds allocated to departments and for subscriptions and standing orders, $3,800 was reserved for the LRC staff to purchase reference, reserve, and rec-reational books.

The chairman of the Library-Audiovisual Committee that year was How-ard Bidwell. Admired by his faculty colleagues, Bidwell was intelligent, hard-working, and devoted to the college. He was an excellent chairman, and Jane Seeger, the Learning Resource Center Director, was very pleased to have such an effective faculty member in this important post.

Bidwell had one characteristic, however, that had caused some comment among the faculty, although it did not seem to affect the respect in which he was held. He was bitterly opposed to teacher unions and to political action on campus. This made him an exception. Seventy percent of the faculty belonged to the American Federation of Teachers, and even more were committed to political activity that would further the cause of education, teachers' rights, or salary benefits. All six members of the professional staff of the LRC were AFT members.

Early one morning, Seeger received a phone call from Bidwell and after she put down the phone, her apprehension over the conversation grew. He was disturbed that the LRC had recently purchased seventeen volumes on collective bargaining for teachers, and asked for a meeting in her office at 3:00 P.M.

Promptly at 3:00, Bidwell entered Seeger's office. He came right to the point. "Jane, this doesn't have anything to do with my personal feelings, but I just don't understand why the precious book funds of the college should be spent for books on collective bargaining when there are so many things we need much more urgently to teach our courses. We allocated $3,800 for your staff to purchase reference and reserve books and to fill in gaps. Certainly we need too many things to be spending part of the library allocation in the field of labor relations."

Because Seeger recognized that this could be an important confrontation, she spoke slowly as she answered and tried to choose her words carefully. "You're right, Howard, we do have many more needs than the budget will ever enable us to fill. But the reason for the special allocation was partly to let us buy books needed to fill in information gaps—things not covered by any department. That's what we were doing when we bought these books. We felt collective bargaining was a timely topic, the books were recommended in *Choice*, and they do fill a gap in our information resources."

Without pursuing the matter further, Howard Bidwell stood up and, getting ready to leave, announced, "I am calling a meeting of the Library-Audiovisual Committee next week to discuss this matter, Jane, and I trust you will be prepared to answer the questions of the members at that time."

"Howard, before you go, let me explain further. Unionization and collective bargaining are serious issues in higher education today, regardless of what any of us feels personally. It's even more important at Commonwealth, because I'm certain we're going to have a vote on collective bargaining within a year. These books don't hold to any single point of view. They're intended to inform. The potential impact of this movement on our campus is immense.

"I can't quote word for word, but one writer compared teacher power with atomic energy. His point was that like atomic energy, teacher power can be used for many purposes. Like it or not it's here; the question is what do we do with it. It can have an important effect on issues such as educational opportunity, tax reform, and environmental improvement. In addition, collective bargaining among teachers will revolutionize educational finance, educational philosophy, and the ways our schools and colleges go about educating young people. Free speech on campuses, due process in regard to disciplinary actions, participatory management of schools can result. A new world is opening up and our faculty and students should have more information about it!"

Bidwell was obviously unconvinced. "I'll let you know in a day or two exactly when the committee will meet, and I intend to discuss this purchase with as many members of the faculty and administration as I can before that time."

Unable to change his mind, Seeger began to think about how best to handle this situation. She knew each of the books. They were all good and could be defended on the basis of reviews, at least in *Choice*. What was in question, then, was whether books on broader issues had a legitimate place in the LRC. She shifted her thoughts to how the committee might react. While four of the seven members belonged to AFT, she was not at all sure they would support her. Bidwell was a persuasive man and his arguments might well win them over. As was the case at many institutions, the authority of the committee was vague. In the last analysis, administrative support would be critical if she could not convince the committee to support her. Yet she was not at all certain she would receive the backing of the dean of instruction, to whom she reported, and who would probably handle the matter. He had said little about unionization although she suspected he opposed collective bargaining. On the other hand, he might not want to antagonize the faculty members who belonged to the AFT, and he might back off if the union made an issue of this matter. In any event, his actions would not be based on the merits of the case. Then too, an appeal to the union might seriously damage the LRC program. Seeger concluded that the LRC was in danger of being catapulted into a school-wide donnybrook over this issue.

• • • • •

In the absence of a policy statement defining the scope of the collections at Commonwealth College, what argument might Seeger use to defend the acquisitions of these books.

Are there any steps you would recommend she take in advance of the next meeting of the Library-Audiovisual Committee?

Since Seeger holds that the LRC was acting within the policies established by the Library-Audiovisual Committee in making these purchases, what value is there in further discussion? Can the committee contribute to a resolution of the problem? If so, how?

18.
A Great Issues
Collection in Thirty Days
· · · · · · · · · · · · · · · · · ·

Phillip Jamestown left a note on the desk of John DeVere, Technical Services Librarian, and moved on to his office behind the circulation desk. At 7:45 in the morning, he had three hours to gather his papers and notes together before flying to Chicago for a community college library preconference planning session at American Library Association headquarters. A recent library school graduate and the newest member of the Instructional Materials Center's professional staff, DeVere was not due at his desk until 8:15.

Jamestown glanced carefully through as much of the building as he could see from his glass-fronted office. It was an old habit that stemmed from the time many years ago when he was the only librarian at Hathaway Community College and when the library, during the evening hours, had been manned mostly by a clerk and student assistants. He thought briefly of the beginning of Hathaway ten years ago and of the drafting room in a converted elementary school building where the library had first been housed. Now the school had grown to around 2,800 full-time and 5,200 part-time students and the media center had its own building, with a collection of 51,119 books as well as tapes, films, slides, video cassettes, and a graphic studio. Jamestown sighed briefly as he thought of the work that had brought the center from the drafting room to this.

He turned once again to the task of packing his briefcase and stifled an early morning yawn. John DeVere walked in shortly after this exhibition of bodily rebellion.

"Good morning!" DeVere greeted the head of the Instructional Materials Center with all the cheerfulness of youth.

Jamestown smiled, "Good morning, John. Perhaps you've heard that I'm leaving today for Chicago. This puts us in a bind, and I wouldn't go except that I promised to do it and I really can't back out now. But I would like to talk to you about the problem. Last week the board granted $35,000 to the college to be spent before the end of the fiscal year to strengthen the learning climate at Hathaway Community College."

DeVere brightened as he asked, "Does that mean we get it for the Instructional Materials Center?"

"Not exactly," Jamestown answered. "The president conferred with the academic vice president a few days ago and decided that the money might be assigned either to the IMC or to the Related Trades Division to purchase numerical control machines, whatever they are. But after discussing it a little more, the two of them decided to give it to whomever can write the best proposal, and that applies campus-wide. I've been working on this for two days, but I'm only half finished with it. What I've done so far describes a special great issues collection of books, tapes, slides, movies, and video cassettes, but I haven't gotten to the part describing how we'd spend the money in one month, the tools and resources we'd use to select the materials, and how this collection would be housed and organized for use.

"I'd like you to complete the proposal for me while I'm gone so that it will be ready for next Tuesday's deadline. That gives you four days, and we'll have a day to revise and retype your draft."

"What's your basic idea behind this collection?" DeVere asked.

"Well," Jamestown paused as he collected his thoughts, "it goes something like this: even though our students are basically blue-collar, they should be exposed to contemporary issues and ideas in a problem-centered way totally unlike the building-block approach practiced in this college.

"We're a comprehensive community college surrounded by a highly industrial community, and it comes as no surprise that our curriculum is heavily weighted toward vocational education. There are courses in history, art, literature, and music, but these are presented in a systematic fashion and in a highly formalized classroom situation that's not always appropriate for our students.

"We live in a highly technological society in which the individual has more and more time to discover himself and to understand the world around him. I contend that this college sees its mission as limited to producing workers for our technological society and that it hasn't done enough to help people live a richer and fuller life at a time in history when they have been given the leisure to explore themselves and their changing world. We haven't produced people who look at, listen to, read, and use works of art or literature with personal interest, understanding, and love, nor those who approach society as a whole with educated comprehension.

"Well, anyway, the function of this collection would be to do something about this; to enable our students to feel and to know beauty in a relaxed and natural manner and to understand the social phenomena around them. I believe that our student body, coming as it does from the industrial worker class, can particularly benefit from this opportunity for exposure to a synthesis of the arts and ideas in this kind of issues collection. We could pick perhaps ten issues after consulting with the faculty and students and build a collection of materials. Here is the draft of my proposal. The last section of my draft just begins to touch on what I'm asking you to do, so you may want to leave that part out or incorporate it into what you're going to be doing."

DeVere took the document (Appendix A), and looked at the opening paragraphs. From the expression on his face, Jamestown could tell that he was fascinated with the problem. "I agree with you 100 percent," he said when he had finished reading, "and I'm anxious to get to work on completing it."

• • • • •

If you were DeVere, how would you complete Jamestown's proposal?

What kinds of issues would be appropriate, how would you propose establishing consultative procedures with the faculty and students, and what selection tools should DeVere consult? How should the collection be organized and serviced?

Are there any problems Jamestown has neglected in his draft? Would you want to change any part of Jamestown's draft? If so, what and how?

APPENDIX A
DRAFT PROPOSAL: GREAT ISSUES COLLECTION

Charges of irrelevancy of general education to a particular major, and of a community college education to what students and the public perceive as the real world, stem largely from the failure of higher education to make palpable the relationship of the parts to the whole. There are remedies: college curriculum proposals have suggested freshman seminars, for example, and transdisciplinary approaches to the study of themes or issues to demonstrate how the disciplines relate to each other and to current social concerns. Certain programs already provide a measure of practical experience—student teaching is the principal one—enabling students to see the relationship between the intellectual content of their courses and their chosen careers. Some colleges have encouraged their students to seek these relationships less formally in the social laboratory by taking leaves of absence from their studies.

Regardless of how the community college chooses to meet the problem of demonstrating relevancy, the harbingers of change are already here in observable phenomena. Of necessity, the Instructional Materials Center will be developing new modes of response to these phenomena, for it has become increasingly clear to librarians that the needs of the academic community are changing, and that library services must be modified to satisfy these needs. New modes of response must be developed to satisfy:

1. A growing disenchantment with the lecture–textbook method of instruction. More and more, instructors are coming to rely on assortments of paperbacks

and outside readings as information sources. There are several reasons for this conversion—the limitations of traditional texts, the increasing quantity of information within the disciplines, and a tendency to concentrate on method rather than information within the classroom are a few—and the result has been to extend the IMC's function from one of support to that of a pivotal agency of instruction. The instructor has time to do little more than introduce a student to a subject, and it rests with the student to seek out applicable information. The IMC is a principal source of information for students, and has found it necessary time and again to extend the parameters of the collection to include more and more specialized materials. The collection will grow, and problems of housing it, servicing it, and teaching students how to use it will grow along with it.

2. More independent study. Honors programs and independent studies programs have their effect, but it is mainly within the framework of traditional courses that students are being encouraged to pursue their own ideas and do research projects. Students are being asked to identify problems, investigate them, and reach conclusions about them, where before instructors were more inclined to ask students to work with standard, set problems. Often, this approach stimulates a degree of enthusiasm in undergraduate scholarship that was heretofore lacking, and students are more likely to engage in more thorough investigations. The point where the student begins his investigation is a crucial one, and the library is seeking to permit students to perform their preliminary work in a setting that will not confront them with a complex, highly organized corpus of information. Ways are being sought to encourage students to use IMC resources without overwhelming them with something so awesome that they are frightened away.

3. More interdisciplinary activity. Degree programs, courses, and books and other materials that directly demonstrate the relationships between disciplines attack the problem head on. In many ways, the IMC is ideally suited to provide a mode of demonstrating interdisciplinary relationships. Materials relating to one discipline are arranged in juxtaposition to materials relating to other disciplines, and students using the IMC will, for example, be able to bring information sources in philosophy and religion to bear on questions in literature. Many students, however, do not learn how to use the IMC well. The classification system that was developed to bring order to chaos carries with it its own tyranny, and ways must be found to overcome it. Courses in IMC use may be the answer. Such courses will provide a medium through which students can broaden their knowledge of IMC resources, and enable them to bring information from more diverse sources to bear on problems they are working with.

In summary, the IMC believes that the community college should continue to seek ways to demonstrate to the students—and to the public—the relevance of a college education, and the relevance of the intellectual to the "real" world. The phenomena noted above, and others not listed in this brief paper, show that the college recognizes the need to demonstrate relevance and that it is making efforts to do so. The IMC supports these efforts, and is attempting to develop modes of response to the new needs brought about by changes to the curriculum and in teaching methods.

As a means of solving some of the problems outlined above, the IMC proposes to establish a special collection focusing on *current issues*. The aim of such a collection of books, graphics, films, and tapes is to permit students quick and easy access to information on topics of high interest to them. Timeliness would be a key feature of the collection, and a relatively high turnover rate of subjects covered is likely. In some ways, the collection parallels the idea of a topic-centered general education program.

A new program has recently been instituted whereby the bookstore is supplying materials, chiefly paperbacks, from student bestseller lists, and student response to this new approach has been most gratifying. The current issues collection will, in all probability, be an expansion of this program.

The planning model is as yet insufficiently developed to provide much detail about the collection, and the IMC is far from developing an operational model. Briefly, some of the questions that have to be dealt with and some tentative answers are:

1. *Will the collection be cataloged?*
   Probably not in the same way that the main collection is cataloged. A goal is to make the materials available within as short a time as possible, and time-consuming processing will be cut short where feasible. If the collection remains small, perhaps no cataloging, effectively speaking, will be required.

2. *What will the collection contain?*
   Ideally, the collection will contain basic interdisciplinary material on topics of concern to students, probably with heavy duplication. Controversial topics will be represented from opposing points of view. It is the hope of the IMC that students reading in the current issues collection will be led to investigate the topic in the main collection. As suggested above, all types of learning resources will be included.

3. *What will the turnover rate be?*
   Interest and popularity will be the chief criteria. As long as materials are circulating, they will stay in the collection. When a particular item stops circulating frequently, it will be removed.

4. *Will only scholarly works be included in the collection?*
   Probably not. The bulk of the material in the collection will doubtless have permanent value, but some will not. In many cases, items will be both in the main collection and in the issues collection, and items of permanent value will certainly continue to be added to the permanent collection. The issues collection is a supplement, not a replacement.

19.
"A Plan for Battle"

• • • • • • • • • • • • • •

This was the year that Rhodes State College hired additional faculty, reorganized several high administrative posts, and increased its state funding considerably. Its library served a college of 5,000 undergraduates, 800 graduate students, most of whom were part-time, and 240 faculty members. Rhodes offered graduate degrees in eighteen fields in addition to a balanced undergraduate program. The sixty-three-year-old institution was part of a system of state colleges and universities administered by a board of regents whose primary responsibility was budgetary control. Their small executive staff limited itself to collecting data and assisting in budget preparation. The local campuses exercised a large measure of fiscal control, and the presidents were free to plan their budgets with considerable autonomy.

Three years earlier, Rhodes State College had begun to expand its curriculum. Once primarily a teacher training institution with a strong additional commitment to engineering and vocational education, it now had three schools: Education, Arts and Sciences, and Engineering and Vocational Education.

Sinat Library had a staff of twenty-three full-time people including eleven librarians and twelve clerical employees. While the collection of just over 225,000 volumes reflected a good many areas of strength, it did not adequately support the new and expanded mission that the college had defined for itself, nor did it adequately serve the needs of the students. The collection was uneven because it had been built as a result of the demands of particular faculty members to support their courses or research interests.

This was the context of the problem that faced Michael Rogers, recently appointed director of the Sinat Library. In his opinion, the library was grossly underfunded. Matters were made worse, in Rogers' view, by the fact that a faculty-allocated book budget did not allow the director and his staff freedom to plan the most effective use of the limited funds that were available.

Because he was determined to improve library support, Rogers devoted a great deal of time during his first months at Rhodes to a survey of expenditures among comparable publicly supported college libraries, and found that his book budget fell into the lowest quartile. He summarized his findings in a report to Paul Dekker, Academic Vice President, and he also pointed out that, while the college had rapidly expanded its course offerings and had established seven new graduate degree programs in the past few years, library support had not grown accordingly. In fact, it was currently only 3.7 percent of the total educational budget, a figure what had not changed much over the years.

To his surprise, these findings did not seem to alarm Vice President Dekker, nor did Rogers' arguments against the system of allocating book funds meet with any discernable success. In reply, Dekker explained that the low level of support was due to extensive commitments for equipment to support the School of Engineering and Vocational Education and the Instructional Media Center. This distorted the budget, or in Dekker's words, "made the college budget unusual in comparison with similar institutions." An information copy of Rogers' report, forwarded to the president of Rhodes State, elicited no response at all.

Now, in his second year as director, Rogers reflected on his lack of success so far in generating support for the project. He realized that he would have to devote more of his efforts in the coming year to the matter, and he began to formulate what he called "a plan for battle."

The first step was to enlist support from the library faculty. To this end, he called a meeting just after commencement to discuss library goals for the coming year and specifically the matter of allocation and funding.

He passed out copies of the proposed book and periodical budget (Appendix A) and asked for comments. Rogers had worked on this document during the spring months and discussed it with all department chairmen according to past procedure and tradition at Rhodes. Following review by the library faculty, it would be brought to the Library Committee for review and discussion. A flurry of questions from the librarians centered around the adequacy of the collection for each discipline, the extent of involvement of the faculty from the various departments in selecting books, and the problem of cost increases in certain fields. At length, several minor modifications were made.

Once the matter of the allocations was settled, Rogers moved on to the topics he was most interested in—the process of allocation and fiscal support. He said, "I am not at all convinced that the practice of annually allocating the book budget promotes adequate, long-term collection building. Some departments don't spend their allocated amounts, others surrender their allocations to the most aggressive member of the department so that he can advance his special interest, and a few are so tightly controlled by the chairman that funds are disbursed only to his supporters. Too much of our library consists of excellent collections in minor areas of a discipline. Often, the faculty member who wanted those books and who built that collection has moved on, and, while excellent, the books are used little or not at all. I must admit that there are departments that do a great job of selection, but I wonder how long they will function that way—resignations and promotions could change the makeup of those departments almost overnight. We need to set priorities for collection building against which faculty requests (based on allocations) can be judged. These priorities, set by the faculty themselves, could be used to reject requests in some instances."

Rogers paused, paged through his notes, cleared his throat, glanced around the room, and continued: "Now I want to go on to a related matter. The problems we encounter with the allocated budget are only part of what we're up against. What's even more serious is that we don't receive a large enough book budget to maintain an adequate level of current buying for the curriculum of this college. In other words, we're underfunded for book purchases, regardless of whether the book budget is allocated or not. We need a strategy for convincing budgetary officials and the president of our needs."

Lucile Schotten, head of reference for the past ten years, opened the discussion: "We've allocated the book budget to departments for at least twenty years. The Senate Constitution states that this must be done. We could refine the process—I know that some very detailed formulas for allocations have been written up. We could study these more detailed and sophisticated formulas for allocation, but we must allocate because we're required to."

"What about increasing the funding for book acquisitions?" Rogers asked.

"Perhaps you should speak to the president about it," Schotten replied.

"I had hoped," said Rogers, "to set up a program for identifying ten-year goals for building the collection. This might be done with the advice and assistance of departments and the Library Committee. I think we could formulate detailed goals that would tell us what areas of the collection need concentrated attention and, also, what level of completeness we require for each discipline. Obviously we would need faculty cooperation to project anticipated curricular additions and changes. Perhaps a simple questionnaire addressed to each department. . . ."

Before he could go on, Rogers was interrupted by the librarian with the longest tenure on the staff. "Our faculty resists questionnaires and surveys. They won't cooperate. That method will never work here, and we can't afford to lose face by sending out a questionnaire that won't be answered. We'd be the laughing stock of the college. Besides, even the members of academic departments won't agree among themselves. On top of that, the faculty has always done most of the book selection and done it well. After all, they are the authorities in their disciplines. They ought to know what they need."

As a whole, the library faculty was definitely dubious about the director's proposal, but because there was no question that some changes were necessary if ever the library was to improve, there was general agreement to attempt to develop a useable questionnaire.

Rogers and his staff worked on the document for the next six months. In the process, he managed to obtain the cooperation and assistance of the Library Committee. After one unsuccessful attempt, both the library faculty and the committee approved a survey document (Appendix B).

Rogers then asked the academic vice president for permission to send out the survey. Dekker had tight control of his faculty, especially the department chairmen, who either respected his leadership or feared him. Rogers persuaded Dekker to send the survey questionnaire to all departments with a memo directing the chairmen to meet with the members of their departments to discuss the questions and to formulate responses.

Much to everyone's surprise, including Rogers', all of the departments replied, and only a small amount of prodding proved necessary. For a while, Rogers despaired of the department of foreign language, but eventually its internal strife was settled by selecting a new chairman and its response, the last, was mailed to the vice president's office. Even more surprising was the fact that the instructions accompanying the document were followed. This made the task of compiling the responses an easy one. (Two examples are included as Appendixes C and D.)

The work of tabulating, reproducing, and assembling the survey was completed two months after the last departmental response was received. Copies were delivered to the president, the academic vice president, and members of the Library Committee, several of whom commended Rogers for his work.

A few weeks later, Rogers showed the report to the director of a neighboring state university, Dr. Clarence Doty, who had built an excellent collection in a rapidly growing university in a period of only ten years. Doty said that this kind of self-survey could indeed serve as the first step in determining collection goals, and told Rogers that the next logical step would be to engage a library consultant, who could confirm the findings of the survey and make a detailed cost analysis from this document.

A consultant's report would provide exactly the kind of evidence needed to persuade the president, vice president, and other budget officers to increase the book budget substantially. Rogers went to Dekker to request money to hire a consultant with the same kind of experience that Doty, the neighboring university library director, had. With him he took the concurrence of the Library Committee. Dekker's response was typically direct and brief. "Mike, in this state we don't usually hire consultants. Every time the regents authorize a consultant they get an authoritative report, which puts a gun to their heads. They look at it as a kind of blackmail, and they don't like it. I'd like to help you, but I don't see how I can. The request for a consultant just won't be approved. I'm afraid you'll have to live with your survey as it is, unless your staff can do the costing."

● ● ● ● ●

Based on the two examples (Appendixes C and D), which are typical of the other responses, do you feel the survey in its present form is authoritative? How could it be improved to strengthen it in the eyes of the faculty or the administration? Can Rogers utilize his staff as Dekker suggests? Are there aspects of such a survey a consultant can do that the library faculty cannot?

What is the value of the survey as it stands? What are its limitations? Can Rogers use it to accomplish his objectives? Should he have elected to improve the conventional book allocation system? If so, how?

What other strategies might have been employed to obtain better financial support for diminishing reliance on the allocated budget and for implementing a collection development program? Is allocation as important a problem as Rogers contends?

How are the problems of collection evaluation different at Rhodes as compared with Griffith University, described in case 26, "The Question Is 'How'?", and is it easier or more difficult for the librarians at Rhodes than for those at Griffith?

APPENDIX A
RHODES STATE COLLEGE BOOK AND PERIODICAL BUDGET

Serials, standing orders, back issues, and microfilm	$20,000.00
Binding	6,500.00
Periodical subscriptions	25,500.00
Library General Fund	5,500.00
Allocations to departments	40,000.00
	$97,500.00

Allocation of the departmental totals

I.	School of Education		
	A. Department of Curriculum and Teaching	5%	$2,000.00
	B. Department of Administration and School Services	3%	1,200.00
	C. Department of Psychology and Counselor Education	3%	1,200.00

D. Department of Health, Physical Education and		
Recreation	2%	800.00
II. School of Arts and Sciences		
A. Department of Art	4%	1,600.00
B. Department of Biology	6%	2,400.00
C. Department of Business Administration	7%	2,800.00
D. Department of Chemistry	6%	2,400.00
E. Department of English	10%	4,000.00
F. Department of Foreign Language	2%	800.00
G. Department of History	10%	4,000.00
H. Department of Home Economics	2%	800.00
I. Department of Mathematics	5%	2,000.00
J. Department of Military Science	1%	400.00
K. Department of Music	4%	1,600.00
L. Department of Physics	6%	2,400.00
M. Department of Social Science	10%	4,000.00
N. Department of Speech and Dramatic Art	3%	1,200.00
III. School of Engineering and Vocational Education		
A. Department of Mechanics and Materials Engi-		
neering	3%	$1,200.00
B. Department of Thermal-Fluid Engineering	2%	800.00
C. Department of Electrical and Electronics Engi-		
neering	4%	1,600.00
IV. Extension	2%	800.00
	100%	$40,000.00

These allocations are for books to be placed in the library for use of all faculty and students. Any departmental funds not spent or encumbered by March 1, revert to the Library General Fund.

The Library General Fund is used to meet the following needs:

1. Student recommendations.
2. Purchase of books for sectors of the library collection not supported by a department.
3. Retrospective purchasing and completion of sets and collections.
4. Recommendations of the library staff.
5. Book replacements, reference, library science and indexes.

APPENDIX B
LIBRARY SERVICES FOR RHODES STATE COLLEGE
Departmental Survey

The college library is considering the problem of constructing a fair and equitable policy, which will answer the needs of the college for the next ten years. In order to do this, we require your assistance in indicating the depth and extent of the library collection required for your discipline or field.

Please check on the following pages the kind of collection you believe necessary and appropriate for the subjects taught in your department. After each subject taught in your department, indicate by the numbers 1–4 the degree of depth required. A rating of "3" or "4" should be accompanied by a paragraph or two explaining the department's plans with regard to this area.

Level of Coverage in Specific Subject Areas

Needs and demands vary in the various subject areas. To indicate how far the college library should go in meeting these needs, we shall recognize the following degrees of intensity of acquisition effort which will be made within the limitations listed above:

1. *General Collection*
   A selective collection serving to introduce and define the subject and to indicate the varieties of information which are available elsewhere. It shall include textbooks, dictionaries, encyclopedias, selected editions of important works of major authors, historical surveys, biographies, basic periodicals, and serials for keeping in touch with current scholarship in the field.
2. *Instructional Collection*
   A good working collection designed to meet all instructional needs. It shall include a wide range of basic works, complete collections of the works of more important figures, both authors and critics, selections from the works of secondary writers, yearbooks, handbooks, representative journals, and the fundamental bibliographic apparatus pertaining to the subject.
3. *Comprehensive Research Collection*
   A comprehensive collection adequate for independent research by both graduate students and faculty, including all current publications of research value, and such retrospective publications as are deemed desirable by the faculty and are procurable. It shall include all the important or useful works, original editions of the classics in the field if such editions serve a scholarly purpose, and an extensive assemblage of critical and biographical works, contemporary pamphlets, published documents, and the fullest possible list of journal and serial sets and bibliographic tools.
4. *Exhaustive Research Collection*
   A collection including as far as possible all publications of research value, including marginal materials such as manuscripts, archives, and ephemera. Such collecting will be undertaken only in restricted areas, for example material about a single literary or historical personage.

APPENDIX C
BIOLOGY DEPARTMENT

Level of Coverage for Books, Serials, and Periodical Collections

2. Instructional Collection
   Premedical, predental, and preveterinary sciences
   Biology, general

   Botany, general
   Zoology, general
   Anatomy
   Histology
   Embryology
   Plant morphology
   Plant taxonomy
   Conservation (biological)

3. Comprehensive Research Collection
   Bacteriology, microbiology
   Mycology
   Parasitology
   Cytology
   Ecology
   Entomology
   Genetics
   Animal physiology
   Plant physiology
   Mammalogy
   Ornithology
   Ichthyology
   Limnology
   Invertebrate zoology

Comments and Explanations

The areas marked with a "3" priority are those in which we are qualified to direct research at the master's level. None of these areas are complete as far as journal holdings are concerned. Many journals to which we now subscribe need completing as far as a series is concerned.

In certain areas—entomology, invertebrate zoology, genetics, plant pathology and mycology—we must subscribe to additional journals if we are to be adequate.

Where reference books, other than journals, are concerned we feel that we are in good shape in our library as long as we can continue to purchase the new books as they become available.

We do not have any areas in which we feel that we should have library holdings which would be adequate for "Exhaustive Research."

APPENDIX D
HISTORY DEPARTMENT

Level of Coverage for Books, Serial, and Periodical Collections

1. General Collection
  European
   Balkans

       Scandinavia
       Diplomatic
    World
       General
       Australasia
       Canada
       Middle East

2. Instructional Collection
    American
       General
       Early Republic and Jacksonian Era, 1789–1850
       Progressive Era, 1900–1916
       Post–World War II to present
    European
       General
       Early, Egypt through Rome
       Medieval, 476–1250
       Renaissance and Reformation, 1250–1500
       Modern Europe, 1500 on
       France
       Russia, pre-Revolutionary
       Military
    World
       Africa
       Asia
       China and Japan
       Latin America
       Philosophy of history, historiography

3. Comprehensive Research Collection
    American
       Colonial and Revolutionary to 1789
       Civil War and Reconstruction, 1850–1877
       Post-War Industrial America, 1877–1900
       World War I and nineteen-twenties
       New Deal and World War II
       Diplomatic
       Economic
       Intellectual (including cultural and social)
       Military (including naval)
       Western expansion
    European
       England (including constitutional, political, and social)
       Germany
       Russia, Revolutionary and Soviet
    World
       India

Comments and Explanations

In deciding what areas of historical study required ratings of "3," this department considered (1) activities and interests of staff members, (2) interests of graduate students and thesis subjects over the past decade, and (3) probable future needs of both faculty and graduate students. Large increases in the number of graduate students in history in the past several years (14 master's degrees granted this past year alone and over 60 other students involved in various phases of graduate programs) strongly suggest the need to develop and maintain satisfactory levels of research materials.

In Colonial and Revolutionary American history, the research activities and interests of Professors James B. Frick and Robert K. Rating, coupled with widening interests of our graduate students, suggest the need to develop our holdings.

The activities, interests, and publications of the chairman, in addition to continuing graduate research in the Civil War period, require continued attention to that era.

Professor Alan C. Downs' several courses and independent research argue for continued acquisition of sound research materials in post-Civil War America. Graduate interests will develop further significant research in this period.

Professor Frederick B. Sott's courses and continuing research and publication in the area of World War I, the twenties, thirties, and World War II (with major emphasis on America diplomatic history) have led to the development of fairly popular graduate seminars requiring more and better resources.

Professor Thomas R. Kansten's interests, research, and graduate seminar offerings will require the steady acquisition of more research materials in both economic and Western American history.

Both Professor Downs and the chairman are active in military and naval history, and significant numbers of graduate students are following their lead in this field. The former's personal research in intellectual history, as well as his two senior–graduate courses (stimulating notable graduate research studies) urge that materials in these areas be augmented.

Professor Judith G. Nagar's offerings at the senior and senior–graduate levels, as well as her own research activities in English history, require the acquisition of more appropriate materials here.

Professor David A. Dawson's serious research in German history (twentieth century), as well as graduate student interest developed out of Gerlof D. Homan's research, publication, and course offerings, all argue for continued accumulation of important materials needed particularly for graduate seminars.

Professor Thomas Littlefield's own ongoing interests and activities, as well as his new course offerings (modern Far East and modern India), provide the basis for requesting continuing acquisition of research materials for both Indian and Russian history, particularly in the nineteenth and twentieth centuries.

If further elucidation, explanation, and/or justification be needed, I will happily attempt to provide them.

20.
"Maybe They'll Give Up Someday"

· · · · · · · · · · · · · ·

"Dammit!" muttered Robert Mora, as he laid down a memo from Henry Yellin, which described the latest move toward a joint acquisitions program among the state colleges and universities. As he leaned back in his chair, he thought to himself, "All they ever see is the fact that the six institutions spend over two and a quarter million dollars a year on acquisitions, and that somehow this can be cut down by eliminating duplicated research material. But none of our libraries has anywhere near what the Clapp/Jordan formula calls for. I can't figure out why they don't realize that our real problem isn't how to share, but how to get enough to provide adequately for the programs we're supporting now. They're completely unreasonable and the only way to handle them is to keep stalling—maybe they'll give up someday."

Mora lifted the receiver and rang his secretary. "Esther, I'd like you to make a photocopy of the *Summary Report.* I want to work on it this evening."

· · · · ·

After reading Appendixes A–C, how would you respond to Yellin's request? Do you feel Mora's attitude is justified? Describe the ways you think this system can cooperate more effectively. Do you feel centralized processing should also be considered? What arguments could be made for and against centralized processing? How would your response to these questions differ if you were the director of libraries at one of the other five institutions?

How would you evaluate the accomplishments to date in the area of collection building and utilization of the Council of State College and University Librarians?

Many librarians are concerned about cooperative acquisitions programs that force their libraries to rely on holdings of other institutions because it is often expensive and time-consuming to obtain material located on another campus or at a central storage facility. Should these considerations influence the recommendations of these six librarians? If so, how? In general, how would your recommendations modify present budgetary and staffing patterns at these institutions?

Is it reasonable for the state and the chancellor's office to expect an overall reduction in library costs if cooperative acquisitions programs are mandated for this system? If not, are there still advantages to a cooperative acquisitions program?

APPENDIX A

STATE UNIVERSITY AT MOFFIT
MEMO

To: Emma L. Beeler, State College at Lewiston (SCL)
      Joe W. Carioti, State University at Elkwood (SUE)
      Edward R. McCandless, State University at Greenhill (SUG)
      Robert Mora, State College at Bradley (SCB)
      Clifford Trathen, State College at Richfield (SCR)

From: Henry Yellin, Director of Libraries, State University at Moffit (SUM)

Subject: CSCUL Meeting

Early last week I received a call from Ernie Zorbaugh, Vice Chancellor for Academic Affairs, asking me as this year's chairman of the Council of State College and University Librarians to meet with him to discuss the matter of more effective cooperation among the libraries of state-supported institutions of higher education, primarily in the area of collection building and utilization. In order to bring him up to date, I hastily prepared a brief review of the activities of our group since its formation (see attachment).

At our meeting, he outlined the concerns of Chancellor Pauley and the regents. Basically, they are worried about such things as "the spiraling costs of libraries," "unnecessary duplicate purchases," and the like. The chancellor feels that we have been dragging our feet. Whether he is right or wrong, I do feel we have not made our case very effectively.

At the end of the meeting, Ernie asked us to develop a position paper containing a detailed analysis of the problem, together with our recommendations, by April 1. These will be discussed by the Council of State College and University Presidents later that month. Further revision might then be made, but the document will be scheduled for discussion by the regents at their June meeting.

We will have to devote our entire March meeting to preparing this paper. Even then, it will still be difficult and a second meeting may be necessary. Perhaps we can avoid this if each of us outlines his own ideas beforehand. Then if you will send copies of your own outline to each member of CSCUL at least a week before the meeting, we can study them carefully and be much better prepared to discuss the whole problem and hammer out a draft.

Ernie was vague about budgets, but I think he was saying that the chancellor would be willing to consider additional expenditures now if they would reduce costs of library service in the long run.

ATTACHMENT

PAST ACTIVITIES OF THE COUNCIL OF STATE COLLEGE AND UNIVERSITY LIBRARIANS (CSCUL) RELATING TO COOPERATIVE ACQUISITIONS

By Henry Yellin

This report will review briefly the major actions of CSCUL during the past five years as they relate to cooperative acquisitions. However, since any move toward cooperative acquisitions involves cooperation at other levels, I have reviewed and briefly described all discussions and actions relating to cooperation among the libraries of the six state-supported institutions of higher education.

The context for action is found in a report to the Council of State College and University Presidents on the objectives of CSCUL. A number of these relate to cooperative acquisitions. Specifically, these are:

1. To study and develop coordinated acquisitions policies that will rationalize the scope of materials acquired by each library.
2. To develop mechanisms for sharing library resources.
3. To study the feasibility of shared common storage facilities.
4. To develop rapid communications systems among state college and university libraries.
5. To study the development of compatible machine systems.
6. To develop a coordinated plan for long-range growth.

The balance of this report will review progress in each of these areas.

1. Coordinated acquisitions policies. Considerable discussion has resulted in two significant actions:
   (a) Acquisitions policies for each library are collected and summarized in the annual *Summary Report.*
   (b) It was agreed to discuss and share information regarding the purchase of expensive sets and other material.
2. Resource sharing. Members of CSCUL have devoted a considerable amount of time to studying means for sharing existing resources. As a beginning, and in order to generate better understanding on the part of staff members at each library, a program of formal visits was initiated. To date, interlibrary loan and circulation librarians have spent a day at each of the state institutions. In the future, this program will be extended to include serials, acquisitions, and special collections librarians, and perhaps others.

In order to stimulate greater use of existing resources, CSCUL inaugurated a direct borrowing program. This encourages faculty and students to go and use collections of other institutions themselves, thus reducing the administrative expense of traditional interlibrary loan. This policy has been in effect for two years with few problems.

Current discussion is concerned with efforts to develop a uniform borrower's card as well as uniform circulation policies.

Because interlibrary loan remains the heaviest mode of exchange of library resources, a decision was made to drop charges for Xerox copying services. No problems have been discovered in connection with this. Also under study is the possibility of extending interlibrary loan privileges to undergraduate students.

Most important, perhaps, is the development of a courier service. Twice-weekly service was established three years ago among all state institutions except Bradley because of its remote location.

CSCUL has also considered at length preparing documents to facilitate the use and exchange of materials among the institutions. This is especially important because resources cannot be easily shared unless users and librarians know what is available at other institutions. Developing a union list of serials had highest priority, but the matter was deferred indefinitely because of the cost of compiling and printing such a document. At the present time, printed serial lists from each university or college are distributed to the other institutions.

Preliminary discussion was inaugurated to review the possibility of centralized book processing as well as a union catalog located at Greenhill. It was proposed that each institution send a card for each title cataloged. However, because there are no additional funds, these proposals have not been pursued.

3. Shared storage facilities. A central facility to house seldom-used materials or special collections combined with a rapid delivery system could offer a number of benefits. This matter has not been pursued because of the cost and because of faculty objections.

4. Rapid communication. Libraries at Greenhill, Moffit, and Lewiston experimented briefly a year ago with the use of telefacsimile transmission. This was abandoned and further consideration has been rejected because hardware and telephone rates were still too expensive and the quality of the copy was poor. Eventually, as the costs are reduced and the quality improved, this matter should be restudied. Presently, telefacsimile transmission equipment links Shepard Library at Greenhill with the Medical Center Library. This appears to be working satisfactorily.

Teletype units are owned by all state college and university libraries and are used primarily for interlibrary loans.

5. Machine systems. An area of cooperative activity that appears to offer considerable potential is the application of various machine-assisted technologies to library operations. Studies were initiated with the aim of developing a large file of shared bibliographic information. The results of the study have been disappointing. A shelf-list conversion project at Moffit was halted because of lack of funds. Other problems are caused by lack of standardized cataloging among the institutions.

CSCUL favors the establishment of a central systems team, a concept endorsed by computer center directors at each institution. This has not materialized, however. For the present, efforts toward cooperation have been in the hands of librarians and computer center staff who are committed to other responsibilities.

Also under consideration is a project at Greenhill to develop an on-line serials control system. If this experiment proves successful, it may be possible to utilize these programs at the other state institutions and thus to develop a union list of serials.

7. Long-range planning. This aspect of CSCUL objectives has proven to be very difficult in light of the fact that available knowledge and information on the future is oriented toward the short term. Yearly changes in funding combined with a lack of planning and goal setting on the part of the institutions themselves has impeded progress in this area.

Observations

1. That the amount of material published continues to increase.
2. That no library in the state system can maintain control of the published output.
3. That by developing a common acquisitions policy, the rate of growth of library collections can perhaps be reduced.
4. That some duplication can be eliminated.
5. That joint action involving planning and acquiring library material offers opportunities to improve overall system effectiveness. By distributing specialties among state institutions to the degree that the institutions will permit, staff can be utilized more effectively.
6. That cooperative programs for library development can enhance the environment for better research opportunities for students and faculty members.

APPENDIX B
LIBRARY SERVICES

Summary Report of State College and University Libraries

Table 1
PUBLICS SERVED (FULL-TIME EQUIVALENT)

	SUG	SUM	SUE	SCL	SCB	SCR
Undergraduate students	15,432	13,406	10,467	6,417	4,912	3,512
Graduate students	6,584	3,123	1,698	1,131	606	471
Faculty	1,461	1,033	662	409	257	248
Research personnel	447	402	—	—	—	—

Table 2
CIRCULATION (ANNUAL)

	Volumes
SUG	942,225
SUM	391,737
SUE	256,682
SCL	224,114
SCB	173,918
SCR	74,880

Table 3
INTERLIBRARY LOANS (ANNUAL)

	Lending	Borrowing
SUG	8,172	4,690
SUM	6,079	4,168
SUE	1,749	2,924
SCL	527	1,030
SCB	847	1,408
SCR	388	754

Table 4
WEEKLY SERVICE

	Hours
SUG	93*
SUM	87.75
SUE	101.75
SCL	88.5
SCB	83.75
SCR	88.75

*Main library. Other hours vary.

Table 5
CATEGORIES OF COLLECTIONS

A = Present level of collection. B = Required level of the collection to support present curriculum.
The numbers assigned to the collection levels are from the Columbia University study (see definitions following this table).

The levels assigned are highly subjective and the collection is not necessarily fully adequate if the number assigned to "A" matches the number assigned to "B." There may be gaps in the various collections that need to be filled.

	SUG A	SUG B	SUM A	SUM B	SUE A	SUE B	SCB A	SCB B	SCL A	SCL B	SCR A	SCR B
Agriculture and Natural Resources	1	1	—	—	1	1	1	—	1	1	—	—
Agriculture, general	—	—	3	3	—	—	—	—	—	—	2	2
Agronomy	—	—	3	3	—	—	—	—	—	—	2	2
Soils science	—	—	3	4	—	—	—	—	—	—	2	2
Fish, game & wildlife management	—	—	3	3	—	—	—	—	—	—	2	2
Agricultural & farm management	—	—	3	4	—	—	—	—	—	—	1	2
Natural resources management	—	—	3	3	—	—	—	—	—	—	2	2
Range management	—	—	3	3	—	—	—	—	—	—	2	2
Architecture & Environmental Design	3	3	3	3	1	1	1	1	1	1	—	—
City, community, & regional planning	—	—	2	3	3	4	—	—	—	—	1	1
Area Studies												
Asian studies, general	1	2	1	1	1	2	—	—	—	—	—	—
East Asian studies	3	3	—	—	1	2	—	—	—	—	—	—
South Asian studies	—	1	2	2	1	1	—	—	—	—	—	—
Southeast Asian studies	—	1	1	1	1	1	—	—	—	—	—	—
African studies	2	3	—	—	—	—	—	—	—	—	—	—
Islamic studies	—	1	—	—	—	—	—	—	—	—	—	—

Table 5 (*continued*)

	SUG		SUM		SUE		SCB		SCL		SCR	
	A	B	A	B	A	B	A	B	A	B	A	B
Russian and Slavic studies	4	4	—	—	—	—	—	—	—	—	—	—
Latin American studies	3	4	—	—	2	2	—	—	—	—	—	—
Middle Eastern studies	1	1	—	—	—	—	—	—	—	—	—	—
European studies, general	2	3	—	—	—	—	—	—	—	—	—	—
Eastern European studies	2	3	—	—	—	—	—	—	—	—	—	—
West European studies	3	3	—	—	2	2	—	—	—	—	—	—
American studies	3	3	—	—	—	—	—	—	—	—	—	—
Pacific area studies	—	1	—	—	—	—	—	—	—	—	—	—
Biological Sciences	4	4	3	3	3	3	3	3	2	3	2	3
Business and Management	3	3	3	4	3	3	2	3	2	3	2	3
Communications	3	3	—	—	2	3	2	2	2	2	2	2
Journalism	—	—	3	3	2	3	—	—	—	—	—	—
Radio/television	—	—	1	2	3	3	—	—	—	—	—	—
Advertising	—	—	—	—	3	3	—	—	—	—	—	—
Communication media	—	—	—	—	3	3	—	—	—	—	—	—
Computer & Information Science	2	3	1	2	3	3	2	3	2	2	1	1
Education	3	4	3	3	3	3	3	4	—	—	3	3
Education, general	—	—	—	—	—	—	—	—	3	3	—	—
Elementary education, general	—	—	—	—	—	—	—	—	3	3	—	—
Secondary education, general	—	—	—	—	—	—	—	—	3	3	—	—
Junior high school education	—	—	—	—	—	—	—	—	3	3	—	—
Higher education, general	—	—	—	—	—	—	—	—	1	1	—	—
Junior & community college education	—	—	—	—	—	—	—	—	2	3	—	—
Adult & continuing education	—	—	—	—	—	—	—	—	2	2	—	—
Special education, general	—	—	—	—	—	—	—	—	2	3	—	—

Subject	1	2	3	4	5	6	7	8	9	10	11	12	13	14
Remedial education	—	—	—	—	—	—	—	—	—	—	3	3	3	—
Social foundations	—	—	—	—	—	—	—	—	—	—	3	2	3	—
Educational psychology	—	—	—	—	—	—	—	—	—	—	3	3	3	—
Educational statistics and research	—	—	—	—	—	—	—	—	—	—	3	3	3	—
Educational testing, evaluation & measurement	—	—	—	—	—	—	—	—	—	—	3	3	3	—
Student personnel	—	—	—	—	—	—	—	—	—	—	3	3	3	—
Educational administration	—	—	—	—	—	—	—	—	—	—	3	3	3	—
Curriculum & instruction	—	—	—	—	—	—	—	—	—	—	3	3	3	—
Industrial arts, vocational & technical education	—	—	—	—	—	—	—	—	—	—	3	3	3	—
Engineering	1	1	—	—	—	—	—	—	—	—	3	3	3	3
Engineering, general	—	—	—	—	—	—	—	3	3	3	3	3	3	—
Aerospace, aeronautical & astronautical engineering	—	—	—	—	—	—	—	3	3	3	3	4	3	—
Chemical engineering	—	—	—	—	—	—	—	3	3	3	3	1	1	—
Petroleum engineering	—	—	—	—	—	—	—	3	2	2	3	1	1	—
Electrical, electronics & communications engineering	—	—	—	—	—	—	—	3	3	3	3	3	3	—
Mechanical engineering	—	—	—	—	—	—	—	3	3	3	3	3	3	—
Industrial & management engineering	—	—	—	—	—	—	—	3	3	3	3	3	3	—
Fine and Applied Arts	—	—	—	—	—	—	—	—	2	2	—	—	—	3
Fine arts, general	2	2	2	3	3	3	3	—	—	—	—	—	—	—
Art (painting, drawing, sculpture)	2	2	2	3	3	3	3	—	—	—	—	4	—	—
Art history & appreciation	2	2	2	3	3	3	3	—	—	—	—	—	—	—
Music (performing, composition theory)	2	2	2	3	4	3	3	—	—	—	—	—	—	—
Music (liberal arts program)	2	2	2	2	2	2	3	—	—	—	—	—	—	—
Music (history & appreciation)	2	2	2	4	4	3	3	—	—	—	—	—	—	—
Dramatic arts	2	2	2	3	2	2	3	—	—	—	—	—	—	—
Dance	1	1	—	2	2	2	2	—	—	—	—	—	—	—
Applied design	2	2	2	3	2	2	2	—	—	—	—	—	—	—
Cinematography	1	1	—	1	—	1	1	—	—	—	—	—	—	—
Photography	2	2	2	2	2	2	1	—	—	—	—	—	—	—

Table 5 (*continued*)

	SUG		SUM		SUE		SCB		SCL		SCR	
	A	B	A	B	A	B	A	B	A	B	A	B
Foreign Languages												
French	3	4	1	2	2	2	2	2	2	2	2	2
German	3	4	1	2	2	2	3	3	2	2	2	2
Italian	1	3	—	—	2	2	1	1	1	1	—	3
Spanish	2	4	1	2	3	3	3	3	2	3	2	3
Russian	4	4	—	—	1	1	3	3	1	1	1	2
Chinese	2	3	—	—	1	1	3	3	—	—	—	—
Japanese	2	3	—	—	—	—	—	—	—	—	—	—
Latin	3	3	—	—	2	2	2	2	1	1	1	1
Greek, classical	2	3	—	—	2	2	2	2	1	1	—	—
Hebrew	—	1	—	—	—	—	—	—	—	—	—	—
Arabic	—	1	—	—	—	—	—	—	—	—	—	—
Indian (Asiatic)	1	1	1	1	—	—	—	—	—	—	—	—
Scandinavian languages	—	3	—	—	—	—	—	—	—	—	—	—
Slavic languages	2	3	—	—	1	1	—	—	—	—	—	—
African languages	—	2	—	—	—	—	—	—	—	—	—	—
Portuguese	1	1	—	—	1	1	—	—	—	—	—	—
Health Professions												
Health professions, general	—	—	—	—	2	2	—	—	—	—	1	1
Hospital & health care administration	—	—	—	—	2	3	—	—	—	—	—	—
Nursing	—	—	—	—	2	3	—	—	1	2	2	2
Medicine	4	4	3	4	2	3	—	—	—	—	—	—
Medicine, veterinary	—	—	—	—	2	—	—	—	—	—	—	—
Dental hygiene	—	—	2	2	2	3	—	—	—	—	—	—
Speech pathology & audiology	—	—	2	2	2	4	—	—	—	—	2	2

Field													
Medical laboratory technologies	—	—	—	—	—	—	2	2	—	—	—	—	3
Dental technologies	—	—	—	—	—	—	2	2	—	—	—	—	4
Home Economics	2	2	2	2	2	2	1	1	3	3	1	3	3
Law	—	—	1	1	1	1	—	—	1	1	4	—	—
Letters	—	—	—	—	—	—	—	—	—	—	—	—	—
English, general	4	4	3	3	3	3	3	3	3	3	3	4	4
Literature, English	4	4	4	4	3	3	3	3	3	3	2	3	3
Comparative literature	2	3	3	3	2	2	3	3	2	2	2	2	2
Classics	3	3	3	3	2	2	2	2	2	2	1	2	2
Linguistics	3	3	3	3	2	2	2	2	3	3	2	2	2
Speech, debate, & forensic science	2	2	2	2	3	3	2	2	3	3	2	2	2
Creative writing	1	—	2	2	2	2	2	2	2	2	1	1	2
Teaching of English as a foreign language	—	—	—	—	—	—	2	2	—	—	—	—	3
Philosophy	2	2	3	3	2	2	2	2	2	2	3	2	2
Religious studies	2	2	2	2	3	3	3	3	3	3	2	2	2
Literature, American	—	—	3	3	4	4	2	2	3	3	3	3	3
Library Science	3	3	2	2	1	1	2	2	4	4	2	2	2
Mathematics	4	4	3	3	3	3	3	3	3	3	3	2	3
Military Sciences	1	—	2	2	2	2	—	—	—	—	—	—	—
Military science (army)	—	—	—	—	—	—	2	2	2	2	—	—	—
Aerospace science (air force)	3	3	4	4	2	2	2	2	2	2	—	—	—
Physical Sciences	4	4	—	—	—	—	—	—	—	—	—	—	—
Physical sciences, general	—	—	—	—	—	—	3	3	3	3	3	2	3
Physics, general	—	—	—	—	—	—	3	3	3	3	2	2	2
Molecular physics	—	—	—	—	1	—	2	2	3	3	2	2	2
Nuclear physics	—	—	—	—	2	2	2	2	3	3	2	2	2
Chemistry, general	—	—	—	—	3	3	3	3	3	3	3	2	3
Inorganic chemistry	—	—	—	—	3	3	3	3	3	3	2	2	3
Organic chemistry	—	—	—	—	3	3	3	3	3	3	—	—	—
Physical chemistry	—	—	—	—	3	2	2	2	3	3	—	—	—

Table 5 *(continued)*

	SUG		SUM		SUE		SCB		SCL		SCR	
	A	B	A	B	A	B	A	B	A	B	A	B
Analytical chemistry	—	—	—	—	3	3	2	2	—	—	—	—
Pharmaceutical chemistry	—	—	—	—	1	1	1	1	—	—	—	1
Astronomy	—	—	—	—	1	1	1	1	2	2	1	1
Astrophysics	—	—	—	—	1	1	1	1	—	—	—	—
Atmospheric sciences & meteorology	—	—	—	—	2	2	1	1	2	2	2	3
Geology	—	—	—	—	3	3	1	2	2	2	2	—
Geochemistry	—	—	—	—	1	1	1	1	—	—	—	—
Geophysics & seismology	—	—	—	—	1	1	2	1	—	—	—	—
Earth sciences, general	—	—	—	—	2	2	2	2	2	2	2	3
Paleontology	—	—	—	—	3	3	2	2	—	—	—	—
Oceanography	—	—	—	—	1	3	1	1	—	—	—	—
Metallurgy	—	—	—	—	3	3	3	—	2	2	—	—
Psychology	3	4	3	4	3	3	3	3	2	3	3	3
Public Affairs & Services	3	3	3	3	3	3	3	—	2	2	1	1
Community services, general	—	—	—	—	1	1	1	1	—	—	—	—
Public administration	—	—	—	—	3	3	1	1	—	—	—	—
Social work & helping services	—	—	—	—	3	3	1	2	—	—	—	—
Law enforcement & corrections	—	—	—	—	3	4	1	1	—	—	—	—
Social Sciences												
Social sciences, general	2	3	2	3	3	3	3	3	3	3	2	3
Anthropology	3	4	1	2	2	3	2	3	2	2	1	2
Archaeology	2	3	—	—	1	1	1	2	2	2	1	2
Economics	4	4	2	3	3	3	2	3	2	2	2	3
History	3	4	2	3	2	3	3	3	2	3	2	3
Geography	3	4	2	2	2	2	2	2	2	2	2	2

Subject										
Political science & government	3	4	2	3	3	2	3	2	2	3
Sociology	3	4	2	3	3	2	3	2	2	3
Criminology	2	2	—	2	3	—	—	2	2	—
International relations	3	3	3	2	2	1	2	2	2	2
Afro-American (black culture) studies	2	3	2	2	1	2	2	1	1	2
American Indian cultural studies	1	—	1	1	1	2	2	1	2	2
Mexican-American cultural studies	—	2	1	1	2	2	1	—	2	1
Urban studies	3	3	2	2	3	1	1	—	1	1
Demography	2	3	3	3	1	1	2	1	1	1
Theology	1	—	—	1	—	—	1	—	—	1
General liberal arts & sciences	—	2	3	—	—	—	—	1	1	1
Biological & physical sciences	—	3	3	—	—	—	—	—	1	1
Humanities & social sciences	—	2	3	—	—	—	—	—	1	1

Collection Levels Used in Table 5*

1. A *Basic Information Collection* is one in a subject area which falls outside the scope of the Libraries, yet within which readers may need minimum service to aid their immediate understanding or use of material which is properly within scope. Such a collection consists of a dictionary, encyclopedia, handbook, or texts, or a combination of these, in the minimum number which will serve the purpose. It is not sufficiently intensive to support any courses in the subject area involved.

2. A *Working Collection* is one which is adequate to determine the current knowledge of a subject in broad outline, and the most important historical aspects of the area. It consists of one or more dictionaries, an encyclopedia, handbooks, yearbooks, a reasonable selection of monographs in the best editions, and several of the basic journals. Such a collection will support undergraduate courses in the subject.

3. A *General Research Collection* is one adequate for the needs of graduate students of the subject, and includes the major portion of materials required for dissertations and independent research. It includes dictionaries and encyclopedias, the most important handbooks, periodicals and journals, and other publications in the languages usually associated with

*Columbia University, President's Committee on the Educational Future of the University, Subcommittee on the University Libraries. *The Columbia University Libraries: A report on present and future needs* (New York, Columbia University Press, 1958), pp. 260–261.

Table 5 *(continued)*

the subject, and in the latest and best editions, as well as comprehensive bibliographies, and indexing and abstracting journals. Some weeding of obsolescent material may take place.

4. A *Comprehensive Collection* is a General Research Collection having all the material in the above category, plus a wider selection of books and periodicals having value for current research, and additional works for historical research in the subject, in all pertinent languages, though not necessarily in all editions, or in translation. Considerable documentary and original source material is included. Little or no weeding prehensive bibliographies, and indexing and abstracting journals is undertaken.

5. An *Exhaustive Collection* is one which endeavors, so far as is reasonably possible, to include everything written on the subject, in all languages of all time, in all editions and translations. Under prevailing conditions of library finance and the proliferation of publishing throughout the world, the responsibilities of an exhaustive collection can be assumed only in the most exceptional circumstances.

Table 6
STATISTICS OF COLLECTIONS

College or University	Books	Documents	Microfilm (Reels)	Other Microforms	Records	Periodical Titles
SUG	1,735,286	329,093	30,293	306,868	12,590	19,248
SUM	720,009	231,031	18,924	390,764	5,504	12,119
SUE	411,979	377,285	9,562	168,212	602	4,285
SCL	273,258	173,651	8,735	131,792	0	3,032
SCB	241,396	125,457	10,121	5,747	275	2,108
SCR	236,770	207,741	4,540	18,913	0	2,656

SUG Also has 151,091 maps (sheets), 2,651 manuscripts (linear ft.), 21,864 photographs.
SUM Also has 8,736 scores, 278 tapes, 4,128 slides.
SUE Also has 63 manuscripts (linear ft.), 371 tapes, 3,014 slides.

Table 7
MEASURES OF COLLECTION GROWTH
(Volumes added in one fiscal year)

	SUG	SUM	SUE	SCL	SCB	SCR
Books	70,694	43,503	25,168	18,145	9,823	9,261
Other	203,661	16,039	54,862	29,298	9,628	31,207

Table 8
MINIMUM STANDARDS FOR RESOURCES
(Washington State Formula)

	SUG					
A.	Basic collection	1	×	85,000	=	85,000
B.	FTE faculty	1,461	×	100	=	146,100
C.	FTE students	22,016	×	15	=	330,240
D.	Master's field (no doctorates)	31	×	6,100	=	189,100
E.	Master's field (doctorates)	63	×	3,050	=	192,150
F.	Doctorate field	67	×	24,500	=	1,641,500
G.	Total formula units					2,584,090
H.	Actual units held					1,803,937
	Percentage of formula					69.8%

	SUM					
A.	Basic collection	1	×	85,000	=	85,000
B.	FTE faculty	1,033	×	100	=	103,300
C.	FTE students	16,529	×	15	=	247,935
D.	Master's field (no doctorates)	37	×	6,100	=	225,700
E.	Master's field (doctorates)	30	×	3,050	=	91,500
F.	Doctorate field	32	×	24,500	=	784,000
G.	Total formula units					1,537,435
H.	Actual units held					787,778
	Percentage of formula					51.2%

	SUE					
A.	Basic collection	1	×	85,000	=	85,000
B.	FTE faculty	662	×	100	=	66,200
C.	FTE students	12,156	×	15	=	182,475
D.	Master's field (no doctorates)	37	×	6,100	=	225,700
E.	Master's field (doctorates)	4	×	3,050	=	12,200
F.	Doctorate field	4	×	24,500	=	98,000
G.	Total formula units					669,575
H.	Actual units held					442,569
	Percentage of formula					66.1%

	SCL					
A.	Basic collection	1	×	85,000	=	85,000
B.	FTE faculty	409	×	100	=	40,900
C.	FTE students	7,548	×	15	=	113,220
D.	Master's field (no doctorates)	29	×	6,100	=	176,020
E.	Total formula units					415,020
F.	Actual units held					298,467
	Percentage of formula					71.7%

Table 8 *(continued)*

	SCR						
A.	Basic collection	1	×	85,000	=	85,000
B.	FTE faculty	248	×	100	=	24,800
C.	FTE students	3,983	×	15	=	59,745
D.	Master's field (no doctorate)	26	×	6,100	=	158,600
E.	Total formula units					328,145
F.	Actual units held					243,674
	Percentage of formula					74.2%

	SCB						
A.	Basic collection	1	×	85,000	=	85,000
B.	FTE faculty	257	×	100	=	25,700
C.	FTE students	5,518	×	15	=	82,770
D.	Master's field (no doctorate)	27	×	6,100	=	164,700
E.	Total formula units					358,170
F.	Actual units held					242,235
	Percentage of formula					67.6%

Table 9
BIBLIOGRAPHIC UNITS
REPORTED PER FTE STUDENT AND FACULTY

	Units per Student	Units per Faculty
SUG	81.9	1,234.7
SUM	47.7	762.6
SUE	36.4	668.5
SCL	39.5	729.7
SCR	61.2	982.6
SCB	43.9	942.5

21.
"Instant Deadwood!"

• • • • • • • • • • • • • • •

Every morning Fredrick Hudson, Director of the Library at Mitchell State College, opened his mail carefully, letter by letter. The routine never varied. He slit each envelope down the side with a letter opener, blew into the partially opened envelope and finally pulled out the sheet inside. Most of the correspondence was routine and he set it aside to read later, but he stopped abruptly when he came to a letter (Appendix A), from the statewide dean of instruction, who served in the office of the chancellor of the ten institutions in the state college and university system.

The letter came as no surprise. It was another and predictable effort on the part of the chancellor to justify his role in coordinating these schools. His staff was funded by the state to serve the board of regents (Appendix B) on the assumption such an office would save the state a great deal of money. Two years ago, Chancellor Knight proposed centralized acquisitions and cataloging for all the institutions. His staff presented a detailed report outlining the anticipated savings. However, it met with a storm of protest from most of the library directors, which prompted the chancellor to call in a library consultant for a more detailed study. His report brought to light many considerations that the support staff in the chancellor's office had not recognized and caused the proposal to be shelved. Not content to abandon his pet project, however, the chancellor directed his staff to continue to seek ways to save money. A second proposal had been presented, but had also been set aside. Now came another.

After he finished reading the letter, Hudson frowned, scratched his nose nervously and called James Herrod at Fulton University, eighty miles away. He came right to the point. "Jim, have you seen Anderson's letter?"

"Yes, I have, and I think it's a great idea," Herrod replied. "As a matter of fact, I suggested the idea to him."

"Well, I'm not quite so enthusiastic. I'm going to be out your way next Tuesday. Could we get together and talk it over then?"

"Sure. Why don't you drop by my office at about 11:45 and we'll have lunch."

"Okay. I'll see you then."

As they sat down to lunch Herrod opened the conversation with a justification of his position. "For many years now I've felt that our system should be able to purchase used books at lower prices by pooling our resources and buying collections that are too large and too full of duplicates for any one of our libraries to handle by itself.

"Many of us have experienced the frustration of letting a good collection go because we couldn't justify buying all the duplicates we'd acquire in the collection. We've known this, but we haven't been able to find a way to cooperate except through outright gifts to one of the other institutions. Some small colleges have benefited from such gifts, but the larger institutions have always played the role of benefactor. That's why I proposed that we formalize a cooperative acquisitions program for used books. I think there would be a number of benefits. First, systematic and efficient development of the library resources system-wide. Second, maximum value for the least cost. Third, equalization of campus opportunities to obtain used and antiquarian materials. Fourth, optimal distribution of duplicate materials within the system."

"But how," Hudson asked, "can this be done economically?"

"I'm proposing that an ad hoc committee study the problems, and submit its recommendations to the library directors not later than October 1. This committee would consist of bibliographers, booksellers, professors, library directors, and perhaps a business manager, or if not all of these, at least their advice should be sought.

"The way I see it," Herrod continued, "a certain percentage, say 5 percent, of each library budget would be retained in the chancellor's office as a lump sum to be used for this purpose. The fund would be administered by a bibliographer whose chief responsibility would be to acquire and distribute collections of books and other printed materials for the ten libraries. The materials would be distributed to the various campuses according to these criteria:

"First choice for collections discovered and acquired by the system bibliographer would be given to the library with the greatest strength in the subjects included, as determined by the bibliographer. Subsequent choices would be given in the order of collection strength until all books had been distributed. Titles not needed by any of the libraries would be held for new campus libraries, or exchanged or sold for whatever could be obtained.

"A collection discovered by a librarian at one of the five libraries would give that library the right to first choice of materials from the collection. Other choices would be given in order of collection strength.

"Duplicates would also be distributed through the cooperative acquisitions system according to the principle of building to strength. The number of volumes accepted by each library should be recorded and reported monthly by the bibliographer. On the basis of this information and his judgment of the quality of the materials distributed to each library, the bibliographer should attempt to provide an equitable value to each library."

Herrod went on, "A system-wide bibliographer would have the rank of associate director, and would work under the general supervision of the associate chancellor for academic affairs. He would have an office at the library of his choosing, staffed with at least one clerical assistant, along with appropriate equipment, supplies, and storage space. He would also need a budget for travel and telephone. The basic cost for space, personnel, telephone, etc., would be about $32,000 a year. I hope you'll support me when we meet with the rest of the librarians."

Fredrick Hudson was by this time about to begin his dessert, a specialty of the restaurant, ice cream and a special chocolate sauce. He had just picked up his spoon, but laid it down carefully as he prepared to answer Herrod. "After considerable discussion with my staff, I've concluded that while the cooperative acquisition of current books by the five libraries might well be centralized advantageously, the cooperative acquisition of used books is in fact disadvantageous. I think the library directors should investigate acquiring and distributing current books, rather than used books.

"The principle espoused in building to strength favors two things: large libraries and esoteric collections. Specialized collections will be built at the expense of the collections we need to support basic instructional programs, and smaller libraries, without strengths to build to, would be left with the culls after the larger libraries select the best material for themselves. Also, if the 5 percent formula were followed, the bibliographer would be responsible for spending close to $300,000 of the system-wide book budget. This is a great deal of money to put beyond the control of the individual libraries, and I doubt that the libraries would realize as much on this investment as they would by spending it themselves."

Hudson paused, took a bite of his dessert that was already beginning to melt, and began again almost immediately, not allowing Herrod to begin a rebuttal. "Our book formulas are devised to permit the libraries to develop collections of materials needed to support instructional programs. These allocations aren't large, and spending must be directed toward meeting the needs of the academic programs offered by each college. The level of funding doesn't permit most of us to establish and maintain research collections, and money diverted to developing specialized research collections, that by definition are low-use collections, would be better spent on more basic materials. For all but the largest libraries the effect of spending money this way would be to deprive students of material they need for their studies.

"Furthermore, given the level of funding accorded our library, each title added to a given collection must be carefully evaluated on its own merit and selected on the basis of its appropriateness to the collection. That may not be true in your library, but we have to watch each volume. Evaluating current books is difficult, but not nearly as complex as evaluating retrospective material. We select current books by reading reviews or by going over the books themselves. The volume of current books is small in comparison to the vast amount of retrospective books. That's one reason why the evaluation and selection of new titles, while requiring the services of a competent staff of subject specialists, could be handled centrally. Retrospective material is another matter. We can afford to acquire only the very best of it. Screening must be much more carefully done, by people intimately familiar with our own needs. In other words, current acquisitions can be centralized with some savings from reductions in local acquisitions staff and bulk purchasing, but no saving would result from the centralized purchase of out-of-print material, and since decisions would have to be made on two levels, central and local, where they are now being made only locally, the creation of a central facility would simply increase the overhead costs.

"Storage is another problem. After each library has taken what it wants, what do you do with books that are left over? They could be sold, if anyone would buy them; they could be thrown away, if that were legal; or they could be stored and later inflicted on newly opened college or university libraries. To do that, the state would have to build or rent a facility to store the material until someone could be made to take it away. It's not likely that the state would welcome that prospect, when space for classrooms or expanded libraries is so badly needed. It's uneconomical to buy space to store material of doubtful quality on the assumption that someone may want it someday.

"Now, consider collectors and collections. Purchasing collections is a bad way to develop library holdings. At one time, scholars used to build good, sound collections for their own use, but now academic libraries have improved, book costs have risen, the rate of publishing has increased, and the paperback has developed. Good scholarly collections aren't being built much anymore. What exist now are mostly collector's collections, which tend to center around the esoteric and arcane. Such collections would fill our libraries with overspecialized material. Academic libraries already have too much of this. How many libraries have collections on the history of the book, or printing, or some obscure poet who was an alumnus or lived nearby? I couldn't begin to count them. We can't afford this kind of thing. In any case, research collections should be built only by libraries supporting doctoral programs, for which special funding is available, and then only in those areas directly related to doctoral research. Our libraries need breadth more than depth, and authoritative, scholarly bibliographies—which are essentially model collections—should be used as buying guides to develop the support collections needed.

"Finally, I doubt that when good collections do come on the market dealers would offer them to our system first. Dealers work for those institutions that spend the most money with them over the long term, and the universities that buy a lot of rare books will invariably be given first choice. Nor will individual collectors be likely to sell to us. They like to see their collections go to schools with distinguished reputations. And of course there is the possibility that we would be bidding against distinguished research libraries, running up the cost to no one's advantage but the dealer's. Private collectors often take a lower price if their collection will be kept together, and since we wouldn't do that we'd lose out there, too."

"Now take the system bibliographer," Hudson continued. "To do his job properly, he would need exhaustive knowledge of ten collections and ten academic programs—too much for one person to know. Moreover, he would need extensive knowledge of the informational needs of each discipline, which again is too much for one person to know. I, for one, won't ask our libraries to give one person a portion of their book funds and have him select books for them, for inevitably collections would be chosen on the basis of what's available and what it costs rather than on what books we need. The bibliographer's functions would be further complicated by being located on one campus, a condition that would lead to his favoring "his" library's needs. Your plan assumes that the participating libraries would get more for their money than they could get by themselves, and fair representation is a critical factor in the libraries' willingness to participate. A single bibliographer simply cannot respond to the needs of all the libraries equally. It's my feeling that while we might get more volumes because the bibliographer bought out some used-book stores at a good price, we'd only be filling our libraries with collections of instant deadwood!"

The lunch concluded immediately after Hudson made his last point. Herrod left for an appointment, and Hudson went on to his conference.

• • • • •

Do the arguments presented by Herrod and Hudson accurately present the pros and cons of this issue? If not, what other considerations should be brought to light? Can a single system-wide bibliographer represent all the ten libraries to the degree necessary to spend funds wisely? Could such a bibliographer save the state money?

If you were one of the ten library directors, how would you vote on this question at their meeting next month? Would the size of the library you represented (Appendix C) be an important factor in your decision? What other considerations would you have to take into account?

APPENDIX A

Dear Dr. Hudson:

The necessity for campus autonomy in the development of library resources is obvious to all who have a full understanding of the processes and goals of higher education. Until and unless all the state institutions of higher education have identical curricula, taught by faculty members from the same syllabi, and requiring the same supplementary readings, the building of identical libraries is not desirable if, indeed, feasible.

This is not to say, of course, that there is no overlap in collection goals and needs. Many thousands of volumes with the same titles are purchased by one or more of the state libraries each year. Even the older libraries, which are well established and have strong collections, buy some of the same books purchased by the younger, growing libraries. Chancellor Knight is aware of the possibility that a centralized purchasing unit could procure books at the lowest possible cost (by obtaining the greatest discounts from list prices), but that orders for a particular title would have to be held for a time to see if any other campus ordered the same book. Centralized selection would preclude such delays; however, the chancellor is aware that book selection is regarded as the prerogative of the librarians and faculty, a right zealously guarded when book budgets are small and great selectivity essential.

The library consultant hired by our office reported that insufficient savings would be realized when purchasing current titles centrally. True, there would be some savings, but charged against such savings would be staff to make selection judgements, to issue orders, to receive books, approve invoices and schedule the claims for payments, follow up books ordered but not received, correspond regarding errors, reorder books temporarily out of stock, maintain files of orders, and repack and reship the books received to the various campuses. A significant item would be the packing and postage for this reshipment (a cost now borne by the jobber). Any attempt to centralize the purchasing of current titles would involve a complex set of records showing which campus requested which titles.

The following statement by our library consultant should not be taken lightly:

"There should be a serious investigation of the feasibility, probable gains, and probable losses of a cooperative technical processing program. There is unquestionably a very substantial amount of material purchased in common by the libraries of the various colleges and universities, and it is possible that some substantial economies might—over a long period of time—be achieved in the utilization of personnel through a joint technical processing venture. On the other hand, it should be emphasized that this is not a simple problem and unless the economies are sizeable, they may easily be wiped out by the overhead costs of a joint operation. Real benefits are likely to be achieved, if at all, only after a rather elaborate systems and cost analysis. A large computer installation may also be necessary to carry out such an operation. By way of example, it is very doubtful that a simple joint purchasing operation (in contrast to full technical processing) would save as much money as it would cost."

While the chancellor agrees with this recommendation, he has asked me to request you and your colleagues to consider purchasing large collections of used books as they become available on the market and redistributing these books to the collections of the ten state institutions as you think appropriate. He feels that this could be done with one bibliographer and a clerk or two.

I hope you will consider this proposal next month when the library directors meet as a group. Savings and the acquisition of valuable out-of-print material may result from this arrangement.

Sincerely,
Norman Anderson
Associate Chancellor for Academic
Affairs

APPENDIX B

The Board of Regents is the statutory coordinating agency for the state system of higher education. The board consists of nine members appointed by the governor with the advice and consent of the senate. The members possess an interest in and knowledge of higher education. No member is a trustee, officer, or employee of any public or private college or university while serving as a member of the board. In addition to the members appointed by the governor, the chairmen of the education committees of the senate and the assembly are ex officio members of the board without a vote. Appointed members serve overlapping terms of eight years.

The board appoints a chancellor to serve at its pleasure and prescribes his duties. The chancellor is the administrative officer of the board, and is responsible for appointing all employees and staff members, subject to board approval. The chancellor must be qualified by training and experience to understand the problems and needs of the state in the field of higher education and to devise programs, plans, and methods of solving its problems and meeting its needs.

Specific powers of the Board of Regents are delineated in the law. It (1) makes studies of state policy in the field of higher education and formulates a master plan for higher education for the state, considering the needs of the people, the needs of the state, and the role of individual public and private institutions within the state in meeting these needs; (2) reports annually to the governor and the legislature on the findings from its studies; (3) approves the establishment of new branches or academic centers of state colleges and universities; (4) recommends the nature of the programs (undergraduate, graduate, professional), state-financed research, and public services to be offered by the state colleges and universities in order to utilize to the best advantage their facilities and personnel; (5) makes recommendations to the governor and legislature concerning the development of state-financed capital plans for higher education and the establishment of new programs at the existing state colleges and universities; (6) reviews budget requests of the state colleges and universities and submits its recommendations in regard to the biennial higher education appropriation for the state, including appropriations for the individual state colleges and universities; and (7) approves all new degrees and new degree programs at all state colleges and universities.

APPENDIX C

SUMMARY DATA
STATE COLLEGE AND UNIVERSITY LIBRARY ACQUISITIONS

	Vols. Added during Year	Vols. Held at Year End	Periodical Titles
Allegan SC	8,020	91,474	1,216
Central SU	24,621	245,093	3,768
Fulton U	75,419	1,260,049	6,793
Garwood SC	26,157	372,735	2,453
Houghton U	91,598	1,986,753	13,410
Mitchell SC	11,270	111,582	1,869
Northern SU	66,215	761,965	4,763
Rolland Cunningham SC	8,964	123,644	766
Webster SC	12,344	105,488	1,459
Westwood SU	31,489	374,788	3,907

22.
An Election Year
· · · · · · · · · · · ·

Governor Moore was fighting for his political future. In his bid for reelection to a second term, he was being challenged by State Attorney General Sillers. Sillers had been especially critical of the governor's spending during his first term. Seeking to blunt this attack, Moore announced that he would hold the line on spending, and that he would veto any budget necessitating higher taxes. Some increases in state spending such as merit salary increases for civil service personnel and price increases for supplies, equipment, and construction were unavoidable. These increases necessitated budget cuts in other areas, which triggered a bitter fight in the legislature and delayed passage of the budget bill far beyond its normal date.

Throughout May and early June, anxious administrators at state agencies awaited news from the legislature. At State University there was special concern, because a number of legislators had made no secret of the fact that they wanted that institution to absorb a substantial percentage of the cuts. Public support for this position was surprisingly strong, largely as a result of several narcotics raids on student dormitories led personally by the ambitious attorney general. While the raids netted more publicity than drugs, they strengthened the hand of those who opposed higher education. The importance of this election was clear to most faculty and administrators at State University. If Governor Moore lost, the institution would be faced with at least four years of stringent budgets.

A land-grant institution in the middle west, State University was founded in the populist tradition. Size was its most distinctive feature. Situated on a vast campus, with a full-time equivalent student body of 40,000, it had more than ninety departments and offered the doctorate in almost every field except mortuary science. It had grown a great deal over the last decade, which left it short of classroom space, laboratories, and library resources. While Governor Moore had been able to increase the budget for the university considerably, it was never enough. Reflecting this problem, the library held only forty-one volumes per FTE student, and the university spent just under 3 percent of its budget for the library.

Even more than most groups on campus, the librarians were concerned about the budget because cuts typically hit libraries hardest. Continued budget support was necessary if they were to catch up with growth generally and specifically to bring the collection to a level of adequacy. Thus, even though the director of libraries was out of town attending a conference on computer-based reference service, he had alerted Associate Director Craig Stinson to expect a call from Vice Chancellor Zeilinski as soon as the budget had passed and the top administration of the university had allocated funds to the various instructional and operating units. As he returned from lunch on Tuesday, the director's secretary told Stinson that the vice chancellor had called. Immediately he returned the call, and Zeilinski told him that the book and periodical budget had been reduced to $1,265,000, and that later on a reduction in staff would be made to reflect the decline in acquisitions.

As soon as he hung up, Stinson called the Assistant Directors for Technical Service and Public Service, Betty Viers and Robert Liebetreu, Assistant Director for Collection Development Charles Davis, and Ivan Kirkwood, Head of the Acquisitions Department.

Stinson opened the meeting by saying, "Just a few minutes ago Zeilinski gave me next year's budget, and it looks pretty bad. We've been cut down to $1,265,000. There'll also be some staff cuts, but I don't have the specifics right now. I'll be working on this thing over the next week. I've got to put together a report for the director by then. He wants recommendations about how to deal with the budget cuts. In other words, where do we cut? Right now, I'd like your thinking."

As he concluded, he stood up and passed out copies of the current year's acquisitions budget (Appendix A). Then he went on, "Now let's take a look at our ongoing commitments. First, we're spending $238,000 on current imprints. Figure that about two-thirds of the area programs budget, or roughly $40,000, also goes for current materials. Serials come to $662,000, and microfilm subscriptions add another $25,000. A lot of the money allocated to the colleges and subject specialists goes for current things that don't come in on approval—symposia, societal publications, art exhibit catalogs, scores, and so on. I'd guess that comes to about $100,000. Then you've got to add in replacements and duplicates for reserve. There's another $16,500.

"That all adds up to $1,082,000. Figure in roughly 10 percent for price increases, and you're up to $1,190,000. That leaves only $75,000 for the rest.

"That's it. I don't need to say anything more. The figures speak for themselves. Now I'd like to hear what you think. How should we handle it?"

Liebetreu opened the discussion by saying, "If you want to know what I think, the real problem is all those branch libraries. I know the campus is spread out, and I know we have a lot of faculty who want their stuff right near by for research, but it's time we asked ourselves how much does this cost and is it worth it? We've got twenty-four branch libraries and the duplication is fantastic. Could we consolidate some of these into larger units? For example, the engineering libraries could be merged. Most of the science libraries could be brought together, and some of the very small ones belong in the main library.

"About a month ago when we began to worry about the budget, I started thinking about this and I found that if the four engineering libraries merged, we could cancel thirty journal subscriptions and save quite a bit on books we wouldn't have to duplicate.

"Now at the same time, we're going ahead with the undergraduate library, and it will be several years before we finish the core collection for that. They're all duplicates. What I'm saying is that we ought to take a look at the whole setup. We just can't afford the luxury of all these separate libraries and all this duplication anymore."

"I can't argue with you, Bob," Betty Viers replied, "but that just isn't very realistic. You've been around here long enough to know that at the rate this place moves, it'll take five study committees, a couple of task forces, some consultants, and a few retirements before we get off the ground on that one. You know it'll take ten years to consolidate the branches, and our problem is right now.

"Craig tells us the staff will be cut too, and that has to be taken into consideration when we decide how to spend the budget. I've got to keep the flow of work moving. One possibility would be to cut back on periodical subscriptions. We've got something over 20,000. But as sure as we go off and cancel a lot of periodical and serial subscriptions, we'll be trying to pick them up next year, or sometime in the future when the budget picture looks brighter. A lot of time would be wasted writing the vendors to cancel this year and then turning right around next year and reordering the very same material. I'd cut back on the o.p. material, the microform subscriptions, and the undergraduate collection."

"Okay, but that still won't do it," Stinson said. "We're going to have to cut out a lot more than just those things."

"That's right," Kirkwood added, "and cutting back on the o.p. titles will create a lot of problems for us. We send out want-lists. Cancelling these is like cancelling subscriptions, except it takes a lot more time. It also screws up our relations with booksellers. Most of them advertise for titles, and that's expensive. A lot of them also send lists out to their own scouts. They've got a great deal of time and money tied up in those lists. We may be in a bind now, but we're going to need those people again one of these days and I don't think it's a good idea to get them too upset. They're a pretty touchy lot.

"I think we could chop some deadwood out of the current stuff. We could cut back on a lot of blanket orders. I don't think it would be too tough to reduce current spending by, say, $50,000."

"Hold on a minute," broke in the assistant director for collection development. "I know with the reduced budget that the bibliographers and subject specialists will spend a lot less time on retrospective material, but those blanket orders really save us a great deal of work. We can't possibly go back to checking each title individually. We simply don't have the time.

"Maybe there's no solution to this mess, but I do feel we must continue to get the current output. If we don't do that, our whole effort goes down the drain. Break the level of maintenance we've kept up for many years and we'll never pick it up again. That's what happened to a lot of libraries during the thirties and they'll always be weak in publications for that period.

"Maybe we can pare off a little here and there from current buying, but not a helluva lot. No more than say, seven or eight thousand. That's it. Anything more would either undermine our level of effort or require so much time that we wouldn't get anything else done."

As Davis paused for a moment, Stinson commented, "Except for Ivan, it looks like most of you are saying hold on to our standing orders and new books, and cut the o.p. orders."

"That's what I was leading up to," Davis went on to say. "There just isn't any solution. On the one hand, it would be wrong to abandon our level of acquisition for new books, yet we just can't afford to stop retrospective buying. Ivan explained the o.p. problem from his point of view, but there's more to it. Even though we've been adding at a pretty substantial rate recently, it seems we aren't any better off than we were five years ago. Cut off o.p. buying and you'll send a lot of faculty members into orbit. They don't care at all about the new books. They don't mind if we get them, but only if there's enough money for what they want. They don't believe a book is important until they want it—then we're supposed to buy it right away.

"I just know a lot of faculty will fight like hell if the choice is between current and retrospective books. I guess the only way to avoid a fight would be to junk what we've been doing for the past five years and throw it all up for grabs—let the faculty order whatever they want and let us try to fill in with whatever is left over. But that's no way to build a library."

"Seriously," Liebetrau added, "I just don't see why we couldn't cancel duplicate subscriptions to periodicals and serials. I'll bet we'd have over a hundred. In fact, I would go even farther and say that I think before we start cutting, we ought to hit the branch and departmental collections pretty hard. We just don't have that kind of money this year and, if Moore loses, we won't have it for a long time to come."

• • • • •

Were all the factors that should be taken into consideration brought out in this meeting? If not, what should Stinson do to supplement the information his staff provided?

What would your recommendations be?

APPENDIX A

STATE UNIVERSITY LIBRARIES
ACQUISITIONS DEPARTMENT
ALLOCATION OF FUNDS

Allocation to colleges	$ 353,250
Current imprints	238,000
International area programs	61,150
Library	97,700
Subject specialists	17,500
Sets	25,000
Undergraduate library	14,500
Serials	719,500
Total	$1,526,600

ALLOCATION TO COLLEGES

Administrative science	$ 18,700
Agriculture & home economics	9,100
Arts	25,900
Biological science	12,975
Dentistry	1,400
Education	13,625
Engineering	24,300
Graduate school	11,000
Humanities	106,950
Law	42,250
Mathematics & physical science	18,350
Medicine	19,800
Optometry	1,400
Pharmacy	4,100
Social & behavioral science	37,900
Veterinary medicine	5,500
Total	$353,250

CURRENT IMPRINTS

U.S. & Commonwealth	$212,500
Western Europe	25,500
Total	$238,000

APPENDIX A *(continued)*

INTERNATIONAL AREA PROGRAMS

East Asia	$ 9,500
Middle East—Arabic	2,750
Middle East—Hebrew	1,900
Slavic	31,000
Latin America	16,000
Total	$61,150

LIBRARY

Bibliography collection	$ 4,000
Browsing	750
Dormitory	2,000
General	20,000
Documents	1,500
International G. & E.	2,000
Library science	500
Map library	300
Modern authors	2,500
Microfilm subscriptions	25,000
Rare books	12,000
Reference	4,500
Replacements (ex circ)	5,000
Circulation department	6,150
Special collections	11,500
Total	$97,700

SUBJECT SPECIALISTS

Agriculture librarian	$ 500
Biomedical librarian	1,300
Black studies librarian	1,800
Botany & zoology librarian	600
Business librarian	650
Chemistry librarian	550
English librarian	1,775
Fine arts librarian	1,000
Foreign language librarian	1,150
Geology librarian	825
History librarian	1,180
Home economics librarian	725
Journalism librarian	450
Mathematics librarian	850
Microbiology librarian	775

APPENDIX A *(continued)*

Music librarian	850
Pharmacy librarian	400
Physics librarian	500
Slavic librarian	600
Social work librarian	475
Veterinary librarian	545

	Total	$17,500

PERIODICALS/SERIALS

Serial renewals	$662,000
Fill-ins	52,000
Replacements	5,500

	Total	$719,500

23.
A Balanced Collection

· · · · · · · · · · · · · ·

Charles Westvere, the young and brilliant collection development officer at San Pedro University, was angry. Over five years of marriage, Mary Westvere had learned to judge his moods by the way he threw the ice cubes into the glass for his before-dinner scotch and water. After he had filled the glass and taken a sip, which seemed to diminish slightly the sharp anger Charles was nursing, Mary hazarded a question, "It's 'Cluck' again, isn't it?"

"You're damn right it's 'Cluck'." Charles replied. "If he's a librarian I'm a- a- a," Charles stammered. He was at a loss for words, a rare occurrence for the young bibliographer who was definitely gifted with the ability to express himself. "Cluck" was, in fact, Clark Bakker, University Librarian.

"I've been shafted again!" he continued.

"The roast isn't done yet, so you might as well let me have the latest episode in the saga of 'Cluck' and the 'Rising Boy Librarian'," Mary said, hoping that her attempted humor might help ease the tension and reduce the emotion that would be unloaded directly on her.

" 'Cluck' was drinking with his buddies at the Faculty Club, and he promised Crane in the School of Business that the library would order $10,000 worth of books and periodicals on wine over the next three years. Crane, you know, worked in the regents' office for three or four years and then came back to San Pedro. Wine is his hobby, a subject he teaches once in a while in extension and what he loves most in this world. Another branch of the state university specializes in wine cultivation and chemistry, but Crane teaches the manufacturing and distribution of wine, and the history of the wine industry. The School of Business is grateful for many special services Crane has performed, and for the special knowledge he gained while at the regents' office, so they let him teach pretty much what he wants to. Now along comes 'Cluck' in his cups and commits all these funds for that one course."

"Why did he do that?" Mary inquired solicitously. "Liquor usually makes him amorous, not generous with money or books."

"I wish I knew," Charles said as he got up and poured himself a second drink. Mary was relieved to hear the ice cubes go in a little more softly.

"When old 'Cluck' called us in at 9:00 today and broke the news to me, I didn't even let him finish. 'But you know the annual schedule of collection building allows for no such sum,' I said. 'In fact, his own department wouldn't let him get away with that kind of order. You know the policy I drafted. It was approved by the Library Administrative Council, by you as university librarian, and by the Library Committee. I don't see how you can just set it aside.'

"Then he got that look of an old Indian warrior who had just caught a 15-year old brave bragging about how he stole two lame horses and a one-eyed cow. 'We are not fulfilling Crane's request because of our collection strategy,' he said, 'but to pay him off for the help he gave us in getting last year's book formula approved by the regents' office. We're $100,000 richer because of it. He helped with the report and took it personally to his old friend, the vice-provost for instruction. I think that deserves something. We're changing wine into money right here in the library.'

"By now Bakker had given up his old warrior look and changed it for a wheedling Fagin. I didn't give a damn for his tired line or his theatrics, and I told him so. 'If we have a program for building a collection, and it is approved at every level, how can you spend $10,000 for Crane because he is alleged to have helped the library? I won't order them,' I said.

"Bakker became patient and kind. 'You better take a few hours off, West-vere,' he said, 'and think this whole thing over. Your role in selecting books at San Pedro is an important one and your career is just beginning. I hope you will thoughtfully consider this problem.'

"I went back to my office and told my secretary to take messages for any calls that came through. By that time I couldn't control my frustration and I decided to walk as far as the Engineering Building. I often walk to think over my problems and search for decisions that seem to elude me in the office. But no solution came, and I couldn't seem to rid myself of thinking I would have to do what Bakker wanted.

"I just can't seem to get across to him that a university library is maintained to serve the informational and research needs of the students and faculty and that one of our prime responsibilities is to develop and maintain a balanced collection of materials that encompass the significant writings of the major disciplines—particularly those represented in the curriculum—and a broad representation of source materials related to these disciplines. The size of the library is determined by formula and depends basically on student enrollment. As we develop our collection toward the number of volumes provided under the growth formula, funds will be reduced to the point where we'll have to slow down the rate of acquisitions. It should be clear to everyone, and above all else to the university librarian, that we have to develop a carefully constructed and lean collection if we are going to meet this responsibility. But no. To him it's all a game of politics.

"I appreciate what Crane has done for the library, but a few extension courses on wine hardly justify a $10,000 commitment!"

• • • • •

Can the university librarian be justified in using the book budget to pay off political debts? Do favors rendered warrant deviating from the collection building plan?

Is Westvere's concept of a balanced collection a valid one? If so, to what degree is it possible to achieve? Have most university libraries collections been developed with this in mind? Under such a policy, what is the role of the teaching faculty and the librarian?

What books and journals might be appropriate for San Pedro University to support Professor Crane's course? What modification would need to be made in the library's current annual schedule of collection building (see Appendix A) in order to accommodate the special purchase of materials on wine, if Bakker is determined to honor his commitment to Professor Crane?

APPENDIX A

COLLECTION STRATEGY REQUIREMENTS
SAN PEDRO STATE UNIVERSITY

By Charles Westvere

Section I: Introduction

One of the major functions of the library is to develop and maintain a collection of materials which encompass the significant writings of the major disciplines—particularly those represented in the curriculum—and a broad representation of the source materials related to these disciplines. In addition, significant new materials are acquired as published. The collection is designed to reflect the current status of these disciplines, provide adequate interpretation of their findings, foster understanding, and promote further research investigation by advanced students and faculty.

Basic to this objective is the concept of a balanced collection. By a balanced collection, we mean a collection built by assessing the information and research needs of the students and faculty and the subject requirements for library materials. Needs of students and faculty may be assessed by examining course proposals, course offerings in the catalog, departmental enrollments, and the type of library use peculiar to each discipline. Subject requirements are in part a reflection of recent scholarly publications that deal with the theoretical concerns, current interests, and history of these disciplines.

The size of San Pedro's library is determined by formula and depends basically on student enrollments. As the collection approaches the point when building stops and maintenance begins, it becomes clearer that we must have a carefully constructed and lean collection. Ideally, each subject area in which undergraduate degrees are offered should have a working collection of books and other materials to support the courses and reflect the concerns of that subject. Graduate degrees should have additional specialized resources or research packages, such as ERIC or the Human Relations Area Files. A first step in building such basic research collections consists in determining which subjects require them. The physical sciences, for example, by virtue of the emphasis that they place on laboratory research, probably do not require as extensive a library research collection as do some other disciplines. Research collections, either in microform or in hard copy, must be constructed by collection developers in the subject areas which require them.

It is the job of the collection developer in a given subject area to assess the adequacy of our approval plan and to assess the felt wants of the teaching faculty within his subject area. He also must consider the requirements of the Acquisitions Department for smooth operation, and must achieve a level of current bibliographic control within his subject field that meets all these needs.

Retrospective bibliographic control is somewhat different. For our purposes, this includes titles which are out-of-print, not current (published prior to the current fiscal year), or reprint editions. Any member of the teaching faculty can recommend retrospective titles to the library for purchase. Collection developers evaluate the request for appropriateness. For other retrospective books we must use other measures of desirability. We assume that the quality of out-of-print and noncurrent books is to some extent assessed by those who compile bibliographies; bibliographies that are a part of a scholarly monograph are assumed to contain listings of high-quality works. These bibliographies generally should be quite reliable in identifying important research works which we may wish to acquire.

Comprehensive bibliographies should be consulted if they have a rather narrowly defined coverage. This type of bibliography is probably most useful in a subject that has had less developmental buying than have most of our traditional academic disciplines. It is useful for those areas in which we wish to develop basic research collections, and may also be used in filling out our coverage of subjects if applied selectively.

Comprehensive bibliographies with wide scope have, at this point in the development of our collection, only limited utility. *Books for College Libraries* has been entirely checked, and the lacks ordered. Several other lists have been checked, and *Books for Junior College Libraries* was used for a duplication project. Our library now holds such a high percentage of the books listed in these works that it no longer seems productive to use them as buying guides.

Dealer catalogs are another way of selecting retrospective titles for the collection. Catalogs, unlike bibliographies, do not assess the quality of books, and this is their major difficulty. What a book dealer offers for sale and what we need do not necessarily match. If the catalog can be handily checked against a scholarly bibliography on the same subject, it may prove useful. Catalog orders should usually be dealt with promptly since other libraries also know what is available, and if we are to get the best of what is offered, we must do so quickly.

Section II: Current Books

The library at San Pedro University should acquire all recently published books and serials relevant to the instructional program. Selection practices and the acquisitions rate should be such that an even level of qualitative and quantitative support for the collection is maintained.

All books suitable for the collection should be acquired and cataloged as soon after publication as possible. Books and journals supporting doctoral programs will receive priority.

Allocations for the following accounts are based on the anticipated rate of publication and the projected cost per unit. Generally, libraries assume that the publication rate increase and the unit cost increase combine to require a 12 to 15 percent increase in current book funding each year if selection practices and the acquisitions rate (in terms of the percentage of books published) are to remain constant. As the following comparison shows, we have increased our allocations for current spending by only 5 percent. This has been done for several reasons.

First, by establishing a number of new approval programs for foreign language materials, we will be buying proportionately more of our foreign materials from specialized vendors who generally sell these materials at a lower cost than vendors we have used previously. Second, in previous years, we have bought very large quantities of reprint materials from current funds. This practice, which we still follow, in effect transfers a portion of development buying to current funds. Our savings result from the fact that as the collection grows, developmental spending declines overall. That portion of our current spending given over to reprints declines as well, since the library each year requires fewer developmental books to fill out its collection. Reprint materials have a relatively high unit cost, and by buying fewer reprints, the library realizes relatively high savings. Third, the library in fact will buy a smaller proportion of the total publishing output in the coming year than before. This reduction is due to the fact that whereas the total publishing output increases at a rate of about 5 to 7 percent annually, the number of quality books that the library needs to support the instructional program remains about the same, so that by applying the same selection criteria from year to year, we quite naturally buy a smaller proportion of each year's publishing output. In summary, an increase of 5 percent is entirely adequate to support current buying requirements.

Account No.	Account Name	Allocation
0001	Current books	87,620
0002	Approval—French language	5,500
0003	Approval—German language	3,900
0004	Approval—Russian language	1,600
0006	Approval—Spanish language	7,350
0009	Approval—English language	245,000
0010	Current art gallery and museum publications	3,400
0020	Standing orders	17,000
0021	Continuations	131,000
	Total	502,370

0001 Current Books: This account is a general fund used to buy materials not covered by the various approval programs. It is reduced from last year's level because new approval programs have been developed or, in some cases, listed as separate accounts for the first time.

0002 Approval—French Language: A new program to provide the Library with French language publications. The allocation is a best guess, since no data have yet been generated to provide unit costs and publication rate data for projections.

0003 Approval—German Language: Listed as separate account for the first time, this year-old program provides German language materials in language and literature and several other fields. The spending pattern is well enough established to indicate that the allocation is adequate. The apparent difference between French books and German books reflects two things: French needs are greater because the graduate program in French is the strongest among all the foreign languages, and French book costs are considerably higher than German books. (Actually, French paper bounds sell for about the same as bound German books—the difference is largely the price we pay the French dealer for binding the books.)

0004 Approval—Russian Language: A new approval program developed to provide the library with Russian language materials. This figure represents a best guess.

0006 Approval—Spanish Language: This involves two programs. First, a new approval program developed to provide the library with Spanish books on language and literature (excluding Latin American university press books.) This is a best-guess figure. Second, a selective blanket order program to provide the library with scholarly publications by Latin American university presses.

0009 Approval—English Language: This is our primary approval program, and we have funded it at an increase over the previous year. This increase reflects increased unit costs as well as increased coverage of the total publishing output by the vendor. Increased spending here represents a decrease in the general current account (0001), since the dealer now supplies certain material that we previously bought direct from publishers.

0010 Current Art Gallery and Museum Publications: A new standing order program with a specialist dealer designed to provide the library with art gallery and museum publications. The bibliographic control of these publications is extremely bad, but the material is valuable. Often these publications represent the only systematic studies of the work of individual artists, and consequently must be acquired for art history and design students. As with all art materials, the cost is high, largely because of limited printing runs and the cost of color reproduction. We are not entirely happy with this dealer's selection practices, but his coverage is good—far better than we could do by ourselves—and we are working closely with him to refine his selection practices. In any case, our acquisition of this kind of material is much more systematic and comprehensive than in the past.

0020 Standing Orders: This account represents anticipated expenditures for materials placed on standing order with publishers and dealers, such as sequentially published sets. The account has been separated from the general current fund (0001) for the first time this year, and the allocation is a best guess.

0021 Continuations: This fund, which has been increased over the previous year's allocation, is for current serials acquisitions. The increase should take care of increased unit costs and increased costs generated by the addition of new serial titles last year. Like periodicals, serial titles have to be selected carefully, since each new title has the effect of encumbering funds for not only the current year, but all future years as well.

Section III: Retrospective Books

Last year, $91,250.00 was budgeted for retrospective books/collection development. For the coming year, this allocation should be increased slightly to $94,650.00. Retrospective book monies are used to purchase both in-print and out-of-print books published prior to the current year. Funds are allocated to various subject areas on the basis of recommendations made by the subject bibliographers, who design specific collection development programs in accordance with the university's informational needs. In designing such programs, the bibliographers analyze the academic program, discuss informational needs and instructional methods with faculty, and evaluate the library's holdings against standards and scholarly bibliographies. Lacks that appear in these evaluations are programmed for buying over a period of time that depends on availability of material, costs, quantity desired, and similar considerations. Allocations are summarized in the attached table, and the bibliographers' subject-by-subject analysis of materials needed follows.

The statements that follow in support of these allocations were prepared by subject bibliographers on the basis of information from a variety of sources. Besides discussions with members of the university community, the bibliographers have conducted numerous studies of the library's present holdings and matched these holdings against anticipated needs. Needs are determined through reviews of the academic sector plan, analysis of circulation statistics, reports student FTE by discipline, and the bibliographers' own subject expertise. We believe that the recommended distribution of monies is an equitable one, and while we would like to be able to accelerate retrospective buying in all of the subject areas, funds simply do not permit it and the best we can do is assure that one area of the collection does not grow at the expense of another.

Afro-American Studies (see Ethnic Studies). The library has been particularly aggressive in developing the areas of the collection relevant to this program. The retrospective books listed in a large number of bibliographies have been compared with the library's holdings and the lacks ordered. Examples include *Blacks in America: Bibliographic Essays,* Miller's *The Negro in America: A Bibliography,* New York Public Library's *Negro in the United States: A List of Significant Books.* Other bibliographies checked include Work's *Bibliography of the Negro in Africa and America* and Welsch's *The Negro in the United States: A Research Guide,* both of which were used as selective buying guides. Important lacks discovered in the above surveys have been placed on order.

0041 Anthropology (see also Linguistics) $3,000: Initially, retrospective titles were selected from *Books for College Libraries (BCL),* Onstott's *Six Hundred Titles in Teaching of Anthropology,* and Beckham's list in Mandelbaum's *Resources for the Teaching of Anthropology,* and purchase of these completed. Buying is still proceeding from the *International Encyclopedia of the Social Science (IESS),* but in addition, we have moved to more specialized bibliographies. Our subscription to the Human Relations Area Files (HRAF) provides us with basic research materials on cultures throughout the world. The subscription to this resource has greatly increased our research capacity in ethnography and cultural anthropology. Our monographic buying emphasis should consequently shift to reflect this strength. Theoretical anthropology, archaeology, folklore, linguistics, and physical anthropology should receive emphasis. Toward this end, the bibliographies from the following works have recently been used as buying guides: Robert Haizer's *Guide to Field Methods in Archaeology;* Otto Von Hering's *Anthropology and the Behavioral Sciences;* Martin Harris' *The Rise of Anthropological Theory;* Robert A. George's *Folklore and Mythology;* Richard A. Ruess' *Folklore in Paperback;* Felix M. Kessing's *Culture Change;* and Bruno Natti's *Reference Materials in Ethnomusicology.* The extensive geographic and theoretical scope of anthropology as well as the scattered publication pattern makes it difficult to secure books while they are current and indicates a relatively substantial allocation.

0061 Art $6,000: The Art Department has reorganized into four separate departments: Art—History, Art—General Studies, Art—Two Dimensional Media, and Art—Three Dimensional Media. The department now offers a master's degree and has indicated a desire to offer the M.F.A. and the M.A. in art history. Although recommendations on these programs have been deferred temporarily, the department continues to expand in these directions. There are 952 FTE students and 63 faculty. With an eye toward the eventual M.A. in art history, a growing in-depth approach is evident; e.g., senior pro-seminars in art history are offered and a course in bibliography and connoisseurship is planned for the near future.

To augment these developments and future goals, the collection has been developed both currently and retrospectively. Foreign publications and art exhibit catalogs are selectively purchased. Retrospective needs have been studied and concerted efforts made to support the art program in all four areas. A comprehensive survey of the art collection has been made by the library, and lacks are systematically being acquired. Both Lucas and Chamberlin have been checked for lacks and carded for purchase. Bibliographies in the Pelican History of Art series are in the process of being checked and carded for lacks, with selective buying planned to extend over the next few years.

Courses in art education have large enrollments, and are required for art majors and minors planning to teach, as well as candidates for the standard elementary credential. Lowenfeld's *Creative and Mental Growth* has been checked and lacks added to the collection. However, needs engendered by art education courses must be studied and further projects initiated in this area. Studio art courses in both two dimensional and three dimensional fields also need further support. Identification of specific needs in studio fields is difficult for the library: currently, our efforts are directed toward the acquisition of show catalogs illustrating contemporary work and techniques and technical information in book form. Art slide funding is discussed in Section VI.

Astronomy (see Physics and Astronomy)

0081 Biology $2,000: The Biology Department offers both the B.A. and the M.S., with options in chemical biology, genetics, environment and ecology, and structural and systematic biology. Retrospective titles remain important to biology, and bibliographic control in the field is good. The Council on Undergraduate Education in the Biological Sciences publishes a list of suggested titles for libraries, which is updated periodically and which is used as a guide in purchasing retrospective titles. The *Quarterly Review of Biology* is useful for both serial and monographic works, current and retrospective. Areas which need particular attention in the future include those aspects of biology basic to ecological studies, and background material in the structural and systematic areas, particularly mammalogy.

0150 Business $3,000: The School of Business Administration and Economics enrolls about 11 percent of the university's FTE. A B.S., M.S., and M.B.A. are offered in business administration, and a B.A. in business education. Because of the size of the school and diversity of the course offerings (seven options are available in the business administration bachelor's and master's degree programs), increased duplication of core titles should probably be undertaken by the library. A complete check of the 4,000-title *Core Collection* of the Baker Library, Harvard Business School, indicated that our basic business collection was a relatively strong one. It suggested, too, that more book selection from business journal reviews was needed.

0200 Chemistry $1,000: Fortunately, bibliographic control in chemistry is excellent. As far as retrospective titles are concerned, the Advisory Council on College Chemistry's *Guidelines and Suggested Titles List for Undergraduate Chemistry Libraries* has been useful in evaluating our collection. Because undergraduate research exists in this department, a strong retrospective collection is especially needed. One particular lack is a complete set of reference spectra. These should be purchased in five-volume groups, due to their high cost, and should have special monies set aside for them as funds permit.

Child Development: A committee representing the departments of home economics, music, physical education, recreation and the School of Education has established an interdisciplinary major in childhood development, focusing on the biological, social, psychological, and educational foundations of child behavior and development. Surveys have been made of the bibliographies of Pollard's *Growing Child in Contemporary Society* and Alexander's *Children and Adolescents; a Biocultural Approach to Psychological Development* and the lacks purchased. The results of these and future surveys will enable us to evaluate our collection and develop buying programs oriented toward child development in the fields upon which the major is based. No separate fund has been established for purchasing these materials; the bulk of them will be purchased from the expanded education allotment.

Chinese (see Foreign Languages and Literatures)

0220 Classics $400: Course offerings in classics are limited to basic grammar courses in Latin and Greek, a few upper division courses in Roman literature, and an upper division course in Greek and Roman mythology taught in English. There is no major in classics (there is a Latin minor); enrollment is very small, and development of a degree program is unlikely.

The library's holdings in classics are very strong in relation to the program's needs. We have the complete Loeb Classical Library, most of the Oxford texts, and have acquired the most important variant scholarly and critical editions. Other aspects of the general subject—mythology, archaeology, art, and history—are covered by developmental buying in other disciplines. *BCL* has been surveyed, most lacks and wanted duplicates purchased.

0240 Communications and Journalism $500: A B.A. and an M.A. (mass communications) are offered by the Journalism Department and a B.A. is offered by the Radio-TV-Film Department. A graduate program in Radio-TV-Film is being developed, and last year the humanities bibliographer submitted copy for the library section of the Request for Approval of a New Degree Program. Extensive developmental programs have taken place in this subject area. The National Association of Broadcasters' *Radio and Television Bibliography* has been carded and bought. Hansen's *Mass Communications: A Research Bibliography* was used selectively (but extensively). Price's *An Annotated Journalism Bibliography* and Emery's *Histories of Journalism* have been checked for selective purchasing. *BCL*'s limited listings have been done. Some appropriate material was selected from the radio-TV sections of the *Theatre Arts Bibliography, 1953–57*. Future projects should include:

1. A careful reuse of the Price bibliography for journalism materials.
2. Continued buying of microfilmed newspapers.
3. A survey, and a possible buying program, in the technical/production aspects of radio-TV. (To support the M.A. program in this area. It may be that the collection is in good shape as a result of earlier projects, but until the collection can be surveyed, a final judgment cannot be made.)

Computer Science: The interdisciplinary B.S. in computer science is made up of courses now existing in business, mathematics, engineering, physics, and philosophy plus a core of new courses in computer sciences. Since relevant courses are offered by several departments, the library has been providing support for these in the appropriate funds.

Retrospective buying has been aided by the bibliographies suggested in the guidelines set up by the Association for Computing Machinery and published in the *Communications of the ACM*. Karen Quinn's "A Brief Bibliographic Guide to Information Sources on Computers" (in *Scientific Information Notes*, 1:290–7) has also been used as a buying guide. A separate retrospective fund in this area is unnecessary: materials in computer science will continue to come primarily from the Math, Engineering, and Business funds, depending on their emphasis.

0260 Drama $1,000: The Drama Department offers the B.A. and the M.A. The department has indicated a desire to offer the B.F.A. in drama, but a recommendation on this proposal has been deferred pending a long-awaited special study. Implementation of a B.F.A. program should not, however, significantly affect the library-use pattern of drama students, as such a program may be expected to utilize almost exclusively existing performance courses. In fact, since students in the M.A. program have a choice of writing a thesis or doing a project, such as directing a play, from a practical standpoint an M.F.A. program is already in effect.

The needs of drama students are wide-ranging, but there appears to be no immediate need for comprehensive surveys and developmental projects in dramatic works, materials on the history of the drama, or on dramatic criticism. Surveys in *BCL* and in related disciplines, such as English and history, have largely taken care of these areas. There is some interest on the part of the department in primary source materials on the history of drama, and collections of such materials that appear on the market should be carefully considered.

Future developmental buying should be mainly directed toward materials on acting, directing, and the technical aspects of drama productions. *Theatre Arts Bibliography* and supplements have been used as a buying guide in the past.

Earth Science (see Geology and Geography)

0280 Economics $3,000: Economics and business, while combined in one school in the university, have significant differences as far as library resources are concerned. Economics is more historically oriented and thus relies much more on retrospective material. In addition, it depends more than business on statistical data published by various national, state, and local governments, international organizations, and large corporate research departments.

The collection has been developed using *Cumulative Bibliography of Economics Books (Economics Library Selections I and II)* and *BCL*. A primary source for older titles has been the *International Encyclopedia of the Social Sciences.* Many titles still required to complete a basic collection will be identified by the use of the very substantial bibliographies in Henry W. Spiegel's *The Growth of Economic Thought.*

0290 Education $4,000: General bibliographies of retrospective materials continue to be useful in education. *BCL,* the *Encyclopedia of Educational Research,* and Marks' *NYU List of Books in Education* have been used in the past. Richmond's *The Literature of Education* is being used. Our retrospective collection of education books is supplemented by two major microfiche collections. ERIC (Educational Research Information Center) lists and reproduces the most important documents for educational research and expands our collection by more than 23,000 resumes. An additional microfiche collection with considerable education holdings, the Library of American Civilization, was acquired by the library recently. This collection should serve to meet some of the need for older titles in American education.

In addition to the general bibliographies used to purchase retrospective books, specialized bibliographies have been and will continue to be used in those areas that are experiencing growth, projecting new programs or modifications. Administration and supervision, reading improvement, early childhood education, the education of non-English-speaking students, and special education seem, at present, to be those areas.

0440 Engineering $2,000: Bibliographic control of retrospective titles in engineering is difficult, but science librarians are hopeful that a new national society for the communication of engineering information will be chartered soon. At present, the School of Engineering is placing emphasis on oceanography, urban studies, biomedical engineering, and environmental engineering. Some attention should be paid to buying in the last area, since the new proposed interdisciplinary engineering major will possibly stress environmental technology. Initial purchases in this area should be non-technical in nature so they may also be utilized by students in other disciplines who are interested in the subject.

0460 English (see also Linguistics) $13,000: The English Department offers both the B.A. and the M.A. and enrolls about 6 percent of the FTE at the university. Until recently, the department's course list was a fairly traditional one—with perhaps a bit more emphasis on linguistics than is common—and the needs of students enrolled in the programs could be taken care of using standard bibliographies as buying guides. *BCL* was used and the *Concise CBEL* was used selectively. The buying of duplicates should continue (although *Books for Junior College Libraries* has already been used, along with *BCL,* on duplication projects). The linguistics collection is in good shape, and no developmental projects need to be scheduled for that area in the near future. Two developments may change English majors' library use patterns. First, the department has developed an "open" major that permits students to take more or less what they want instead of requiring specific courses. It is unlikely that FTE shift to more popular courses will result in the removal of less popular ones from the course list (no area, in other words, can be completely neglected from the standpoint of collection development), but it is almost certain that the more popular courses will require some modifications in the duplicate buying program, and perhaps some modification of the depth to which certain areas of the collection are developed. FTE and library use should be watched closely for trends.

The development is a drift from a critical approach to literature to a more interdisciplinary approach that considers the broad social context, the cultural milieu, that spawns creative writing. Biographies, histories, and second-level literature will be used more heavily by students than in the past and developmental projects should consider this phenomenon.

0470 Ethnic Studies (see also Afro-American Studies and Mexican-American Studies) $3,000.

Foreign Languages and Literatures (see also Classics, French, German, Italian, Spanish, and Russian). Various instructional programs in foreign languages continue to be offered: Hebrew, Portuguese, Chinese, Japanese, and Swahili. Except for Portuguese, which was included in part of the *BCL* Spanish survey, no developmental projects have been mounted in these languages. However, it seems highly unlikely that any of these programs will advance beyond the basic grammar and literature survey courses, particularly with the present deemphasis of foreign language requirements. The buying program should focus particularly on classic literary works and examples of genre as well as basic dictionaries and grammars. Due to the modest needs of these programs, no special allocations need be made.

0480 French $1,000: Both a B.A. and an M.A. in French are offered and, although the number of students enrolled in these programs is not large, our holdings are moderately strong. Retrospective book needs have been identified and buying programs initiated. Brereton's *A Short History of French Literature* was checked and all lacks purchased. Cabeen's *A Critical Bibliography of French Literature* was used for selective buying as was the Modern Language Association's *French XX Bibliography: Critical and Biographical References for the Study of French Literature since 1885.* *BCL* has also been surveyed, and lacks selectively carded. A concentrated effort has been made to provide support in the area of medieval French literature, one of the weakest areas of the collection, with selective purchases of reprints of classic studies.

0520 Geography $3,000: The Geography Department has built a high-quality program leading to both the B.A. and the M.A., and was the first department on campus to propose a doctoral program. This program has been shelved for an indefinite period due to the absence of guaranteed funding.

The course list of the department is long relative to the number of faculty members and students it has. Very specialized courses appearing in the catalog and the schedule of classes appear to require specialized support materials. The problem of providing adequate coverage is increased by the considerable amount of individual attention given students enrolled in these courses (because of the way the courses are structured and taught), which tends to encourage independent study. Fortunately, the bulk of material now needed by geography students falls into the current book category. Retrospective needs are fairly well satisfied, and although there are some gaps in the collection, monies spent in past years have provided a solid base on which to build the level of research holdings needed by the department.

0540 Geology $2,000: The older literature in geology often remains of considerable interest; in this field published material is outdated much less rapidly than in many other sciences. As far as retrospective buying aids are concerned, several small surveys of the geology collection have been made: bibliographies entitled *Sources of Mineralogic Information* and the *Great Books List for Sedimentary Petrology* have been used. Some lacks from these lists have been filled, and the remaining ones, along with faculty requests, should make up the bulk of retrospective buying for the next few years. A new master's degree program is beginning this fall.

0560 German $1,000: The basic support collection is by now in fairly good shape. A four-to-five-year program of filling in lacunae is being initiated this year. It will begin with a thorough review of the shelf list, a copy of which has been made available to the German Department. (It should be noted also that a much better than average gift situation has existed during past years, compared to French and Spanish, due to the large number of German residents who were refugees from Nazi Germany. The retrospective German collection is about equal in size to French and Spanish as a result, even though it has received less support.) The allocation of $500.00 should suffice.

0580 Health Science $2,000: Bibliographic control in health science is excellent, although because the department's interests are interdisciplinary, many different tools have to be used to maintain this control. For retrospective buying the following have been used as guides: the State of California's *Suggested Books and Periodicals for Health Department Libraries*; Henrik Blum's *Health Planning 1969 Bibliography*; Brandon's "Selected List of Books and Journals for the Small Medical Library"; and Stearns and Ratcliff's "An Integrated Health-Science Core Library." Two new lists of public health materials, recently published in the *Bulletin of the Medical Library Association*, are in the process of being checked.

Hebrew (see Foreign Languages and Literatures)

0600 History $15,000: This is one of the most library-dependent disciplines, and a substantial part of the historical literature will never become obsolete in spite of more recent studies. The library must thus continue to acquire older books, as well as keep up with current publications in history. Progress has been made, but we are still relatively weak in titles published prior to the inauguration of the approval buying program.

BCL has been checked and all appropriate titles acquired or ordered. Two other major sources, the American Historical Association's *Guide to Historical Literature* and the *Harvard Guide to American History*, Arthur S. Link, editor, continue to be valuable in strengthening the collection in this area. A program of buying selected materials from the National Archives, initiated last year, will be continued. Our holdings of British Parliamentary records will be extended from the Microform (2040) account. Other lists of more limited scope have been and are being checked, particularly for Latin America, Africa, and the Middle East.

0620 Home Economics $1,000: Developmental efforts in the area of foods and nutrition have improved the collection greatly, and it now may be considered quite adequate. Retrospective titles have been purchased with the aid of such general tools as *Books for College Libraries*. Since the literature of home economics is scattered, much material used by home economics students is purchased from other funds.

0640 Italian $750: No degree program is offered in Italian at this time. Foreign language FTE generally is generated by students who plan to teach in secondary schools, and Italian is taught by few schools. However, students majoring in another language or in art history might find it an acceptable minor. Nevertheless, the program is likely to remain small, with the focus on basic grammar and literature survey courses.

Japanese (see Foreign Languages and Literatures)

Journalism (see Communications and Journalism)

Linguistics: An M.A. is offered in linguistics and a B.A. is scheduled for implementation. Two years ago the collection was surveyed, and wanted lacks were want-listed or purchased. Bibliographies used in the survey include Hughes' *Science of Language*, Allen's *Linguistics and English Linguistics*, Hammer and Rise's *Bibliography of Contrastive Linguistics*, Rice's *Information Sources in Linguistics*, and Rice's *Study Aids on Critical Languages*. Course offerings in the existing and in the scheduled program are drawn principally from the lists of the Anthropology and English Departments, although Foreign Languages, Speech, and other departments participate in this interdisciplinary program as well. The collection appears to be in good shape; no developmental buying programs are contemplated. Needs that do arise can be handled by augmenting the base allocations of the appropriate parent disciplines.

0660 Mathematics $2,000: The Committee on the Undergraduate Program in Mathematics has published a *Basic Library List* which has aided retrospective buying considerably. A current emphasis on the history of mathematics will need greater support.

Mexican-American Studies (see Ethnic Studies): Chicano studies not only encompasses the Chicano experience in the United States, but also includes studies of conditions and influences from outside the United States that have contributed to the existence of "Chicanismo." The struggle to establish a proud identity and a vital role in contemporary society is revealed through the literature generated during the long experience of the Mexican in the United States. Literature on the Chicano is not well developed. Bibliographic control has improved, but much material is still difficult to identify through conventional publishers or the usual bibliographia channels. Format of many items also presents problems in acquisitions, cataloging, and circulation.

The publication of the *Selected Bibliography of Resources for Chicano Studies* and *La Raza: A Selective Bibliography of Library Resources* is part of the library's effort toward an identification of the literature of the field. Toward this end, a number of other bibliographies have been checked and the lacks purchased: *A Concise Bibliographical Guide on Mexicans and Mexican-Americans*; *Chicano—A Selected Bibliography of Materials By and About Mexico and Mexican-Americans*; *Bibliografi de Aztlán: An Annotated Chicano Bibliography*.

If the field is viewed in a broader sense, literature, history, sociology, and anthropology all serve to support the degree program. An active effort to identify and purchase the relevant retrospective literature will continue to be made.

0680 Music $4,000: The Music Department offers both the B.A. and the M.A., with a slight emphasis on performance skills. New courses are being added to the curriculum, and plans are in process to add the B.M. degree; probably this will lead to an increased emphasis on performance. The prospect of a doctoral program, once probable, now seems remote.

A thorough coverage of *Gesamtausgaben* is essential for any good music library; comparison of our holdings against a checklist prepared for this purpose by SUNY Buffalo shows considerable lacunae. A spot check of Heyer's *Historical Sets, Collected Editions and Monuments of Music* indicates gaps in our coverage. Until recently, many of these works were out-of-print and unavailable, but now we are in the age of reprints and these works are rapidly becoming available. Old music periodicals, of which we have very few, are also available in reprint. Duckles' *Music Reference and Research Materials* has been checked, and items should be selectively purchased from it. In the past, collection development emphasis was placed on English language publications. Many graduate students are prepared to utilize foreign language materials; therefore publications in French and German should receive more emphasis in the future.

0700 Philosophy $2,000: The Philosophy Department, with 450 FTE students, seventeen full-time faculty and two part-time faculty, currently offers B.A. and M.A. degrees. As the department tends to focus on contemporary analytic philosophy, the library's acquisition program reflects this interest. In the history of Western philosophy, the collection has been well developed in the past and should be maintained at its present level.

With the growing interest in the philosophies of Asia, the library should be alert to both current and retrospective works in this field in addition to filling the lacunae in the history of Western philosophy. For retrospective bibliographic purposes the works currently being checked include DeGeorge's *A Guide to Philosophical Bibliography and Research*, Koren's *Research in Philosophy*, and Plott and Mays' *Sarva-Darsana-Sangraha, A Bilbiographical Guide to the Global History of Philosophy*.

Physical Education: Retrospectively *BCL* has been bought, and more recent buying has used specialized bibliographies. Marlin M. Mackenzie's *Toward a New Curriculum in Physical Education*, Kirchner's *Introduction to Movement Education*, John Loy's *Sport, Culture and Society*, and John E. Nixon's *An Introduction to Physical Education* were checked and the lacks purchased. The needs of physical education graduate students appear to have been met with the purchase of a well-rounded private collection that was strong in historical materials, and a subscription to the complete microcard texts of all current theses and dissertations in physical education brought the library over 2,000 items. Our present collection is small, but well balanced. Future buying should stress kinesiology and concern itself with duplication of basic works. No separate allocation will be made for physical education. Our efforts to conform to the HEGIS accounting categories necessitated that its allocation be combined with that of Education.

Physical Science (see Chemistry and *Physics*)

0740 Political Science $5,000: The information needs of this discipline are great, and include a substantial amount of retrospective literature, government documents, filmed collections of personal documents, large sets, newspaper backfiles, and periodicals. Retrospective material should be selectively purchased as lacks are identified in such tools as the *London Bibliography of the Social Sciences*, the *International Bibliography of Political Science*, and bibliographies from the *International Encyclopedia of the Social Sciences*. In areas heavily used, increased duplication is called for. Specializations such as international law, African studies, European studies, and Communist-party states may require additional development due to greater emphasis and expanded programs.

0780 Psychology $3,000: In addition to the B.A., the Psychology Department offers an M.A. in any one of five areas of specialization: general psychology (area of specialization determined by student), human factors; psychobiology; psychological services; and social psychology. The department also offers a state credential for school psychologists, which requires supplementary course work.

Several buying guides have been used to build the retrospective book collection in psychology. *Books for College Libraries*, the *Harvard List of Books in Psychology* and the *IESS* have been particularly useful. Specialized bibliographies are being consulted to build up the collection in specific areas; relative weaknesses have been identified in industrial psychology, physiological and psychobiological areas, and social psychology.

Radio-TV-Film (see Communications and Journalism)

0800 Recreation $500: Retrospective needs for this discipline are modest due to the interdisciplinary character of the field. Retrospective projects in education, public administration, psychology, and physical education provide materials useful to recreation. A basic recreation collection was established with purchases from *Books for College Libraries*. This base has been augmented with the purchase of lacks from the more specialized *Guide to Books in Recreation*. Departmental interest in library holdings centers on duplication of heavily used materials.

0810 Religious Studies $3,000: The recently established Religious Studies Department enrolled 224 FTE students and numbered nine full-time and six part-time faculty members in the last academic year. The collection had many weaknesses, which needed rapid attention in order to meet the needs of this expanding department. The M.A. is probably four or five years away. Special attention should continue to be given to both current and retrospective works in Biblical studies, Asian religions (especially Hinduism, as a new professor in this field will join the faculty in the fall), and major religious thinkers of the West. The department also plans to develop courses for high school and elementary teachers of religious studies in the city schools. For retrospective buying C. J. Adams, *A Reader's Guide to the Great Religions*, and R. P. Morris, *A Theological Book List*, are most helpful.

0820 Russian $500: Although the B.A. in Russian has been phased out, courses are still offered in the language and buying should continue. Bearing in mind that retrospective o.p. items are usually more costly, we should continue attempting to fill gaps in the existing collection. We still lack items of earliest literature, some lesser authors of the eighteenth and nineteenth centuries and many early twentieth-century authors. These materials are becoming available through reprints, but the unit cost is invariably high. Infrequently, we obtain retrospective items through scanning dealers' lists from abroad. The unit cost is less than for reprints but higher than for current materials.

0840 Sociology $3,000: Retrospectively, general bibliographies continue to be useful. *Books for College Libraries* has been purchased. Selections have been made from Faris' *Handbook of Modern Sociology*, and *IESS* is still being used. In addition, more specialized bibliographies have been used to identify and fill collection gaps. This list exemplifies recent surveys: Michael Argyle, *Social Interaction*; Peter Buckman, *The Limits of Protest*; Robert Friedrichs, *A Sociology of Sociology*; Holland and Steur, *Mathematical Sociology*; Peter Maida, *The Poor: A Selected Bibliography*; Hans Zetterburg, *Sociology in the United States of America*.

0860 Spanish $1,000: Both the B.A. and M.A. in Spanish are offered, and Spanish has the largest FTE of any of the foreign languages taught. Since the literatures of many countries are involved in this field, book needs are high, although unit cost per volume is relatively low. It should be noted that Latin American literature is emphasized on our campus and a survey should be done to eliminate weaknesses in the collection. In the retrospective area, all *BCL* lacks have been purchased. The formidable Simon-Diaz *Manual de la literatura española* has been surveyed, carded and a selective buying program planned to span the next several years.

0870 Speech Communication and Communicative Disorders $2,000: Both the B.A. and the M.A. are offered in speech. Undergraduate speech majors have choice of three tracks in the major: rhetoric and public address; communication theory; and speech therapy. *Books for College Libraries* has been surveyed for every area pertinent to speech. Rhetoric and public address holdings were surveyed using Cleary's *Rhetoric and Public Address: A Bibliography*. Future surveys in this area should utilize the updates to Cleary provided by the annual bibliography in *Speech Monographs*. Needs in the area of communication theory are largely taken care of by developmental projects in psychology, and although no thorough evaluation of this part of the collection has ever been done, the general feeling is that the collection is in good shape. When this area of the collection is surveyed, the survey should be done from multiple points of view encompassing as many interested areas as possible: speech, education, psychology, possibly radio-tv-film, journalism, and political science. No comprehensive bibliography of the speech therapy area has been located to be used as a buying guide, and of all areas in speech, this one probably shows the effects of unsystematic growth the most. Faculty in this area are quite good about recommending titles, however, and it is unlikely that the library lacks any of the basic materials needed by students.

Swahili (see Foreign Languages and Literatures)

Urban Studies: Urban studies courses are offered in a variety of departments, such as Biology, Geography, Psychology, Business, Economics, Political Science, and Sociology; and a few courses are offered under the aegis of the Urban Studies program. Even though the interdisciplinary degree in urban studies is new, the library has been providing support for these related courses so that a core of basic material is already in the collection. Branch's *Comprehensive Urban Planning* has been checked against our holdings, and lacks purchased. Developmental efforts should be directed to filling gaps in our coverage of such areas as urban economics, urban environment, and the behaviorally oriented studies. Separate allocation is not being made to the program; funding will come from the many contributing disciplines.

Section IV: Miscellaneous Developmental and Special Accounts

This section of the report deals with those accounts that do not fit exactly into other sections. Each of the accounts is explained below.

0900 Duplicates and Replacements $35,000: This fund is used for two purposes. First, it is used to purchase added copies for the Reserve Book Room; second, it is used to replace titles that have been lost.

0920 Library and General Development $12,000: This small contingency fund is designed to meet informational needs that suddenly appear and that do not seem to fit into the developmental accounts listed in Section III: Retrospective Books. The initial purchases of ethnic studies materials and religious studies materials came from this fund. However, much-improved communications between the several schools and the library have enabled the bibliographers to anticipate new degree programs and course offerings, and have almost obviated the need for the fund.

0930 Core Duplication $50,000: Last year, $35,000 was set aside to purchase duplicate copies of heavily used materials in the permanent collection. The project was funded late in the year, however, and other problems intruded to make completion of the project impossible. Only about $15,000 was spent, and the rest of the money was distributed into the other developmental accounts. A sum of $50,000 has been allocated to complete the project.

0940 Reference Development $38,000: This fund is used by the Reference Department to acquire standard reference sets. A slight decline in funding is actually a larger reduction than it appears to be, when considered in the light of increasing book costs. The decrease reflects the fact that we have made substantial progress in developing our reference collection, and consequently need to spend less money on sets. We expect that expenditures on reference serials, however, which are supplied by other funds, will increase.

0943 Recreational Reading $2,150: This small fund is used by the Reference Department to purchase about twenty popular books each month for a recreational reading display. Some of the books are later added to the permanent collection, but the program is primarily intended to provide students with material they want to read, but in which the library has no long-term interest, and has the added advantage of making some major works available without the delays incurred in cataloging and processing. The fund remains the same because it was slightly over-allocated over last year.

0945 Sets and Backfiles $11,500: Traditionally, this account has not been funded at the beginning of the academic year. While the greatest need is in monographs, and we attempt during the course of the year to spend as much of our budget as possible on monograph material, a number of important sets have been identified. The allocation reflects these needs, and as the fiscal year comes to a close, what is left over from reserves and savings will be added to this account to buy large, expensive sets, such as standard sets of works by individuals and collections in various subject areas. In the coming year we expect this to be in the neighborhood of $40,000.

0950 Periodical Backfiles $60,000: This allocation is used to purchase back runs of periodical titles, and has been reduced from $90,000. The reduction represents three things. First, we have fewer backfile requirements each year, and this fund follows the pattern of the other developmental accounts in declining as needs decrease. Second, the reduction represents the availability of materials in the market. The titles we most want to buy get harder and harder to find each year. Finally, for several reasons we feel that it is best to purchase older periodical volumes in microform rather than in bound form. First of all, material that is not available in bound form often is available in microform, and we are faced with a choice of getting the material now, or waiting in hopes of getting it later. Second, the material costs much less in microform, and since older periodical volumes tend to be low-use material, we feel that it is more economical to provide the material in this way, both in terms of expenditures and space. Third, the state university book formulas impose a ceiling on collection development, and we are concerned that if we fill the collection with quantities of low-use material, we may be cheating ourselves of much more desirable material we will want later on.

0955 Serial Backfile $20,000: Used to purchase backfiles of serial titles—yearbooks, abstracts, and so on—this allocation has been decreasing over the past few years. The reductions represent both a decreasing need, and the scarcity of materials in the market. One special note here: Ceased periodical titles are purchased from the periodical backfile fund, as are back runs of current periodicals. But ceased serial titles are purchased from the 0945 Sets and Backfile fund, and only back runs of current serials are purchased from the serial backfile fund. The two are handled differently because the library handles the purchasing responsibility and processing of the materials differently.

0960 Reserve $43,921: This fund provides for overexpenditures in the various accounts, and permits the library to take advantage of special purchasing opportunities that occasionally arise. Too, the bulk of what is eventually spent on sets and backfiles at the end of the year comes from this allocation.

Section V: Periodical Subscriptions

This fund provides for the maintenance of periodical subscriptions, both new and continuing. Periodical backfile acquisitions are funded separately, and are discussed in a later portion of this report.

Last year, the library allocated $175,000 for periodical subscriptions. The allocation was low, and actual expenditures (although the year is not yet completed) will be about $185,750. The overspending, which was intentional, was easily absorbed by reserves.

Periodicals present a special problem to the library in that each subscription represents expenditures for both the current year and for following years. The book formula under which we are funded does not provide for maintenance allocations after the collection reaches a certain size, and until these formulas are revised we cannot determine what the level of maintenance funding will be. Consequently, we have been reluctant to subscribe to large numbers of periodicals, since we do not know at all how many subscriptions we will eventually be able to support.

Generally, we feel that we should be spending more money on periodicals, for in terms of our size and the size of the student body, we subscribe to relatively fewer titles than do comparable institutions. But again, without any knowledge of what kind of maintenance funding can be anticipated, we are reluctant to commit ourselves too heavily. At the rate of 13.5 percent increase annually, we can expect that in about eight years, periodicals will require over half of the total budget.

The bibliographers have attempted to determine the minimum number of new titles we should acquire each year. These estimates, which total about 350 new periodical titles annually, appear in a separate report.

We estimate, considering increasing costs and the addition of 350 new titles, that we need to increase funding. Thus, we have allocated $223,076 for periodical subscriptions.

Section VI: Nonbook Materials

The budget allocation for nonbook items last year was $68,451.00. This year, $38,560.00 has been allocated for this purpose. Monies for nonbook materials are derived from the library's operating expenses budget, and are not funds given to the organization specifically for the purchase of library materials. In a very real sense, the monies that we are able to divert to library materials reflect, in any given year, our ability to keep operating expenses down. The difficulty in holding expenses down this year stems from the new library building. We expect to be moving into the new building during an overlap period in the coming year, and since we have not been able to secure supplementary funds during either fiscal year to cover the cost of the move, the expenses will have to be paid out of operating. The reduction will be taken care of principally by deferring the purchase of most microform materials.

2000 Archives $100: A small fund has been established to enable the library to purchase materials published on campus that cannot be obtained free.

2001 Art Prints $600: Art prints are heavily used by students in a number of disciplines—art history, drama (for costumes and sets), and education (especially students who are practice teaching)—and in the absence of a large, comprehensive slide collection and supporting equipment constitute an important information resource. The fund has been increased from $400 for two reasons: first, because of some increase in Reference Department personnel, who maintain the collection, we expect to be able to survey the collection and fill in more gaps; second, the age of the collection is beginning to require the purchase of replacement prints.

2010 Books—Supplies $600: This account is used to purchase reference books for use by the library staff. Dictionaries, professional reports, bibliographies for use in analyzing the collection, and similar materials come from this fund. Materials that are of more than limited interest are, of course, duplicated from other funds and made available to the public.

2015 Curriculum $600: This allocation is unchanged and is used to purchase model elementary and secondary school curriculum guides from various school districts. This fund is only three years old; school districts used to supply the material free but no longer do so.

2020 Documents $1,400: This allocation is the same as last year's and is used for the purchase of state and federal documents. The library receives the bulk of its collection free or on deposit, and this fund is used to replace missing items, purchase duplicates of very important and heavily used materials, and acquire nondepository items of interest.

2040 Microform $500: This fund is used to purchase back runs of periodical and serial titles available on microform and collections of microform material used for basic research. Many important collections that extend the research capabilities of the library have been acquired from this fund. This is a minimal allocation and it is anticipated that the reduction is for one year only.

2050 Microform Subscriptions $25,760: This amount is needed to support subscriptions to microform collections such as *ERIC* and *HRAF*; newspaper and periodical subscriptions; and subscriptions to microfilm projects such as the *STC* books.

2060 Music Scores $2,000: The library collects only study scores; performing scores are collected by the Music Department. The allocation is unchanged and will enable us to continue a program of purchasing scores to complement the phonorecord collection and to purchase definitive collections as they become available.

2100 Pamphlets $500: The allocation has been doubled from the year before. The Reference Department maintains this collection and, as with art prints, staff increases will enable the department to fill in lacks in the collection. The pamphlet file contains ephemeral material of short-term interest that is not quite important enough to add to the permanent collection, but which is of great interest to students. Although the file covers a wide range of subjects, it is particularly useful for "hot topics," such as environmental studies or the various liberation movements, where the first information available tends to be published in an undisciplined fashion. Subsequently, of course, the best material is codified into more disciplined and scholarly works and is added to the permanent collection.

2110 Phonorecords $1,500: The allocation is unchanged and will enable the library to purchase important new releases as well as replace worn-out materials. The collection is not yet as complete as we would like, but considerable attention has been devoted to it in the past and we feel that it does an adequate job of supporting the music program at the university. In the future, we intend to explore the possibility of obtaining more spoken recordings (plays, poetry readings, and documentaries), but we prefer at this point to wait until certain technical aspects of the collecting question become clearer, principally the role of the tape cassette. This question will be considered as we plan Phase II of the new library building, which we expect will have extensive AV capabilities.

2120 Unbound Periodicals $4,000: This fund is used to purchase single issues of periodicals to complete bindable units. Although a few such issues are used simply to adjust subscription time periods, the bulk of the funds goes to replace issues that are missing from the collection. The library's loss and mutilation rate has remained fairly constant over the past several years.

2145 Slides $400: An unchanged allocation has been made to this account. The library has wanted for some time to develop a collection of slides, principally art slides. Difficulties in processing the material (cataloging, mounting, marking, etc.) as well as the lack of space for good viewing facilities have made a large-scale program unfeasible at present. The allocation will enable us to continue a low-level acquisitions program against the time when the material can be more fully utilized.

2150 Video Cassettes $600: An unchanged allocation has been made for the purchase of information available in this format.

Section VII: Detailed Line Sum

0001 Current books	$ 87,620	0780 Psychology	3,000
0002 Approval—French language	5,500	0800 Recreation	500
0003 Approval—German language	3,900	0810 Religious Studies	3,000
0004 Approval—Russian language	1,600	0820 Russian	500
0006 Approval—Spanish language	7,350	0840 Sociology	3,000
0009 Approval—English language		0860 Spanish	1,000
	245,000	0870 Speech	2,000
0010 Current art gallery and		0900 Duplicates and replacements	35,000
museum publications	3,400	0920 Library and general	
0020 Standing orders	17,000	development	12,000
0021 Continuations	131,000	0935 Core duplication	50,000
0041 Anthropology	3,000	0940 Reference development	38,000
0061 Art	6,000	0943 Recreational reading	2,150
0081 Biology	2,000	0945 Sets and back files	11,500
0150 Business	3,000	0950 Periodical back files	60,000
0200 Chemistry	1,000	0955 Serial back file	20,000
0220 Classics	400	0960 Reserve	43,921
0240 Communications & Journalism	500	1001 Periodical subscriptions	223,076
0260 Drama	1,000		
0280 Economics	3,000	Total Book	$1,092,667
0290 Education	4,000		
0440 Engineering	2,000	2000 Archives	$ 100
0460 English	13,000	2001 Art prints	600
0470 Ethnic Studies	3,000	2010 Books—supplies	600
0480 French	1,000	2015 Curriculum	600
0520 Geography	3,000	2020 Documents	1,400
0540 Geology	2,000	2040 Microform	500
0560 German	1,000	2050 Microform subscriptions	25,760
0580 Health Science	2,000	2060 Music stores	2,000
0600 History	15,000	2100 Pamphlets	500
0620 Home Economics	1,000	2110 Phonorecords	1,500
0640 Italian	750	2120 Unbound periodicals	4,000
0660 Mathematics	2,000	2145 Slides	400
0680 Music	4,000	2150 Video cassettes	600
0700 Philosophy	2,000		
0740 Physics	1,000	Total Nonbook	$38,560
0760 Political Science	5,000	Grand Total	$1,131,227

24.
"Sometimes I Wonder
Whether It Was Worth It"

· · · · · · · · · · · · · · · · · · ·

The history of Carson University could be traced back to the year 1783, when Miguel Jimenes, a soldier in the service of Charles III of Spain, was assigned to the remote presidio of Santa Gertudis. Upon retirement, he received a large grant of land, which became known as Rancho Las Posas. It was one of the few old land grants that remained in the hands of the original owners after the American conquest. In time, the once remote rancho was encircled by suburbia. Recognizing the potential Rancho Las Posas offered for residential as well as business and industrial development, and partly to attract firms that depended on highly trained personnel, the family offered the state a parcel of land on which to build a branch of the state university.

After careful study, state officials concluded that there was need for an institution in that area, and accepted the property. The regents then established a committee to study and define the role of the future university. The committee called for an institution that would develop innovative programs, with special emphasis on undergraduate education. Only later would master's and doctoral programs be added. The promise of a new approach to education combined with a beautiful setting attracted a number of outstanding scholars to the new institution.

A full year before the first students were enrolled, Bruce Simmons was appointed university librarian. He held a Ph.D. in English as well as a degree in librarianship, and for the last eleven years had been curator of special collections at a prestigious Eastern private college. Simmons enjoyed a national reputation as a bibliophile and scholar. His record of success in building special collections made him the ideal candidate in the new president's mind.

The original plan projected the growth of the library to 500,000 volumes over a fifteen-year period. In the first two years, the library was allocated funds to develop a basic collection of 75,000 volumes. In the third year, the budget was $305,460, which seemed to Simmons generous for a campus with only 750 students. Of this, $125,460 was allocated to the various departments, $80,000 for current books, $85,000 for periodicals and serial subscriptions, and $15,000 was left in reserve. These figures had been agreed to by the Library Committee. While the committee's role was officially advisory, the faculty was vitally interested in the book budget. Developing library resources was especially important because the collection was small, many faculty members were research oriented, and many sought to involve undergraduates in the research process.

Simmons held that the best way to develop a university library was to acquire collections en bloc. He spent much of his time ferreting out good material at reasonable cost. He traveled a great deal, avidly pursuing leads on collections, and he had already acquired several important private collections.

His future prospects included the collection of Roy Vernon, a local bookseller. Years ago, Vernon abandoned his big-city bookstore and purchased a ranch in the hills near the northern edge of Rancho Las Posas, where he built a large adobe book room to house his stock. As the years went by, Vernon became increasingly interested in regional history and he gradually shifted the emphasis of his business from literature, belles lettres, and rare books to this field. Simmons had visited Vernon on several occasions. He guessed that Vernon had about 25,000 volumes and that this was probably the best collection of regional and local history that would ever be assembled, for many of the volumes were so scarce that they might never again appear on the market.

Vernon often spoke of giving up his business and Simmons was anxious to purchase his entire stock. However, he hoped Vernon would not sell out for a few years, until the library budget was large enough to absorb the cost without damaging other acquisitions programs. As luck would have it, however, Vernon suffered a near-fatal heart attack that spring. No longer able to continue his business, Vernon approached Simmons about selling it. However, he told Simmons that he had also contacted a wealthy private collector and a couple of booksellers. Vernon explained that while he would like to see his books in one place, medical expenses would be high over the coming years and he had no other source of income. He would have to sell his books for the best price he could possibly get. Therefore, he decided that prospective buyers could go over the collection and submit their offers. The highest one would be accepted.

Simmons wasted no time in asking David Ross of the history department and Joel Sutton, a reference librarian with a master's degree in history, to join him in inspecting and evaluating the collection. All three concluded that the collection was even better than originally described. Ross, in fact, wrote a letter (Appendix A) to the chairman of the Library Committee urging the committee to recommend purchase.

The high spots of the collection included a handful of manuscripts, among them a diary of a journey from Boston to San Francisco written by a New Englander who sailed around Cape Horn to the gold mines in 1850; some very scarce county histories; quite a few rare early local imprints; seven gold field maps; and almost three hundred printed narratives of overland journeys and exploring expeditions. While there were also some rare books, mostly first editions, and two incunabula, the bulk of Vernon's stock consisted of standard literary and historical works, sometimes in two or three copies. The three estimated its retail value at nearly $225,000.

The Vernon collection was much larger than any Simmons had acquired during his tenure at Carson. He realized that because the library currently held barely 100,000 volumes the purchase would be hard to justify. Moreover, faculty from disciplines that would not benefit from the collection would be likely to oppose it. While he had routinely sought and received approval from the Library Committee for all large purchases, he was especially anxious for its support of this acquisition. The minutes (Appendix B) hardly reflected the stormy nature of the meeting. Predictably, representatives from disciplines that would benefit supported Simmons' proposal while those that would not, opposed it. For over an hour the debate continued. By a vote of 6 to 5 Simmons was authorized to negotiate purchase of Vernon's books with the stipulation that no action was to be taken until the Library Committee was called into special session to authorize purchase at a specific price.

Two weeks after the meeting, Vernon announced that he would accept bids through July 31. In order to determine how much to bid, Simmons consulted separately with several bookmen who were familiar with the contents of Vernon's book room and the book market generally. They all felt it would bring around $90,000. With this information, Simmons called a special meeting of the Library Committee for July 12. At this time of the year, several members were out of town. Fortunately for Simmons, two of the strongest opponents were away while those who stood to benefit most from the collection were still on campus. The committee authorized Simmons by a 4 to 2 vote (Appendix C) to purchase the collection for no more than $90,000 on condition that $40,000 come from the president's contingency funds. Then the committee went on to reallocate funds for the fiscal year.

Armed with this backing, Simmons went to the president, who expressed considerable interest in the collection, but said that he could not provide more than $10,000 so early in the fiscal year. Discretionary funds had to be held, he explained, at least until after the fall semester was underway to determine whether enrollment projections had been met. Before submitting his bid, Simmons talked again with Vernon, who told him that there was greater interest in the collection than he originally anticipated, intimating that the selling price would probably be well over $100,000. Simmons finally decided to ask Vernon whether it would be possible to defer part of the payment until the following year. Vernon readily agreed.

With only a week left, Simmons pondered the question of exactly how much to offer. The more he thought about it, the more determined he became to acquire the collection, and he submitted a bid of $121,000, of which $31,000 would be paid at the beginning of the following fiscal year.

Simmons anxiously awaited word from Vernon and was elated to learn that his was the highest bid. He immediately set about making arrangements for the monumental task of bringing the volumes to the campus. Since the new library building was only partially filled, the material was stored in the basement on temporary shelving. Only a handful of the rarest items were processed immediately. Because no additional staffing was available, it took the better part of the year for the Acquisitions Department simply to card the collection and add it to the already existing backlog of nearly 20,000 volumes in the basement. Cards for the backlog were filed in the acquisitions department by title. A few faculty members knew of this file and checked it. Any book requested would be rush cataloged and made available within 24 hours. The file was also checked by acquisitions clerks to avoid duplicate purchases and by a library assistant in interlibrary loan. Routine bibliographic checking of the backlog before the books were sent to the catalog department was done as time permitted.

Simmons' elation was short lived. Less than a week after the sale, he was summoned to the office of President James Walling. As he entered, Walling brushed his hair back from his forehead, did something peculiar with his nose that looked very much like screwing it on a bit tighter, and pushed his glasses back. Friends and colleagues of Dr. Walling knew that this particular set of exercises indicated that he was distressed. Next, he kicked the corner of his desk and scowled out the window. None of this seem to give relief so he looked down at his desk and pushed two letters (Appendixes D and E) to Simmons as the secretary carefully closed the door.

Walling broke the silence. "Needless to say, I'm concerned about this situation and not at all happy about this anonymous letter going to the state people. Bruce, tell me this, can you justify this purchase?"

Simmons outlined the steps that led to the purchase and concluded, "The Vernon collection really was a rare opportunity—one that is not likely to occur again for a long time, if ever. What some critics don't understand is that the actual purchase price is less than half the collection's true value. We didn't realize until we began moving it that it is much larger than we originally thought. It looked like about 25,000 volumes at first, but it's going to be more than 30,000. That means that the cost is just about $4.00 per volume, and that's a bargain."

Walling looked down again at the letters, shook his head, and said, "Well, it's pretty hard to argue with those figures. That represents quite a saving. I'll support you, but, Bruce, stay away from auctions for a while, will you?"

It was far more difficult to convince the faculty. News of the purchase spread gradually as the start of the fall semester drew near. Two men in particular, William McFarland of the biology department, and Stephen Reed in chemistry, both members of the Library Committee, voiced their anger. McFarland bitterly resented the assessment of $1,000 against the biology department's allocation because the Vernon collection contained a number of books on cacti. "No one," he fumed, at the first meeting of the committee that fall, "now or in the foreseeable future will have any interest whatsoever in those books. Most of them are popular works, which belong with all that local history junk. They have no more value for a biologist than books on barbed wire do for a college of engineering. Charge history; they wanted this damn thing!"

Reed was equally outspoken. While his allocation was not directly affected, the $10,000 cut in the continuations budget effectively meant that there would be no new periodical subscriptions that year. At the same meeting of the committee, he said, "Journals are the only material that have any real value to us. The current book program doesn't provide much of anything we want. We're handicapped here because there is no large research library close at hand. Interlibrary loan is too slow and undependable. Without periodicals, we are unable to do our research."

Both had opposed the purchase when it was first proposed, and were especially angry that the Library Committee had approved it at $90,000 in their absence. They echoed the thinking of a large number of the faculty. A group of about a dozen, particularly in the sciences, led a move to restrict Simmons' future freedom of action by a resolution, which was approved by the Faculty Senate, prohibiting the university librarian from making any purchase over $500 without the express approval of a majority of the total membership of the Library Committee. Simmons declared that he would ignore this resolution, which in itself increased the hostility between him and the faculty because it left many with an even greater sense of bitterness and frustration.

A heated battle developed in the Library Committee during the following fiscal year as it was necessary to reduce departmental allocations in order to pay the remaining $31,000. The brunt was born by the history department because most members of the committee felt it had benefited most from the purchase. What is more, for a number of years afterward, the Library Committee held allocations to that department well below what they had been before the Vernon purchase. This, in turn, caused resentment on the part of some of Simmons' original supporters, especially Professor Raymond Berg, who was on the Library Committee at the time the Vernon collection was under discussion. A noted scholar whose research interests lay in the history of science, Berg came to feel that his research work had been crippled as a result of the Vernon purchase.

In spite of these difficulties, the Vernon Collection brought a measure of distinction to the university library. It was well publicized, and attracted gifts from private collectors. The most valuable was a collection of 241 maps from the estate of Robert Knowles. Over a period of forty years, Knowles had built the finest private collection of maps of the region ever assembled. Only the collection at the State Historical Society was better. Other gifts included ten manuscript letters from Josiah Gregg to his brother John concerning business and trade, and a diary of J. Rhett Mott, an Army surgeon, covering his tour of duty in the Indian Territory in 1843. The library also received thirteen travel narratives and several county histories.

Work on cataloging the collection moved slowly. Five years after the collection was acquired, nearly two thirds of it had been cataloged, but it was not until two years later that Clyde Danner, Chief of Technical Service, handed Simmons his final report (Appendix F). Simmons looked up, smiled and said, "Thanks, Clyde. It really is a great collection, but sometimes I wonder whether it was worth it."

• • • • •

Do you think it was worth it?

In general, do you agree with Simmons' approach to acquisitions? Specifically, do you think the Vernon purchase was a good idea? How should the number of volumes in the library have affected Simmons' decision to purchase the Vernon collection? What other factors ought he to have considered?

Regardless of the quality of the collection, should Simmons have purchased it knowing that this would anger many faculty members and create ill-will?

Were there ways Simmons might have acquired the collection without upsetting the faculty?

What impact do purchases of this sort have on the acquisitions staff? Are they likely to save time?

APPENDIX A

Dear Professor Van Norman:

Recently Dr. Simmons, a member of his staff, and I inspected the book room of Roy Vernon, an antiquarian bookseller who has been forced out of business for reasons of health. In order to liquidate his business, his book stock will be offered for sale to the highest bidder within the next few months.

I understand that Dr. Simmons intends to discuss this with the committee and seek approval to purchase Vernon's entire stock. I would like to endorse this purchase without reservation. Over a period of twenty-five years, Vernon has developed a superb library of books on regional history. An outstanding feature of this library is the number of county histories, diaries of explorers and pioneers, and reminiscences of early settlers. There is some valuable "boomer" literature from various periods, but especially the 1880s. There are several account books of pioneer merchants, some photographs, a few letters, and a manuscript gold rush diary.

This is not to say that Vernon's stock is of value only to historians. He has an excellent general stock and a substantial majority of the volumes would be important for other departments such as English, art, biology, philosophy, and economics.

Let me stress again that this is a unique opportunity for the university to acquire in a single purchase a library that would take a collector a lifetime to assemble.

> Sincerely,
> David Ross, Associate Professor
> Department of History

APPENDIX B

LIBRARY
CARSON UNIVERSITY

Library Committee Minutes
April 16

Present: Berg, Buss, Cook, Garcia, McFarland, Reed, Shelden, Slay, Simmons, Van Norman (Chairman), Wiebe.

Vernon Collection

Dr. Simmons described to the committee the collection of Roy Vernon, which is being offered for sale. The collection is particularly strong in western history, but has many volumes pertaining to other areas of history as well as social sciences. The collection is reputed to be one of the best known to be available for purchase. It is considered, in some areas, to be the equal of the holdings of a number of long-established universities. The details of the sale of this collection are not known at present, but it appears that it is feasible to purchase the collection to augment the resources of this library. The major problem is whether it would be appropriate to invest a large segment of the budget for next year in the purchase of this collection should it be available to us. After much discussion of the ways and means of purchasing the collection, the committee passed the following motion: That the university librarian be authorized to take preliminary action to secure the Vernon collection with the stipulation that before specific action is taken, the Library Committee be called into special session for authorization.

APPENDIX C

Library
Carson University

Library Committee Meeting
July 12

Present: Berg, Cook, Garcia, Simmons, Van Norman (Chairman), Wiebe

Vernon Collection

The committee discussed proposed revisions of the book budget. No objections were raised about the amount of assessment to departmental accounts. After some discussion it was moved, seconded, and passed that the university librarian be authorized to purchase the Vernon collection at no more than $90,000, and only if $40,000 were funded from discretionary funds. It was further moved, seconded, and passed that if the purchase price should be less than anticipated, or if additional funds should become available, these funds shall be used to restore the departmental fund accounts to the initial allotments. After that motion was adopted, it was moved, seconded, and passed to accept the university librarian's proposed budget revision as amended.

PROPOSED BUDGET REVISION AS AMENDED

Account	Initial Allotment	Vernon Assessment	Balance
Current books	$ 80,000	$10,000	$ 70,000
Departmental allocations	125,469	25,000	100,469
Continuations	85,000	10,000	75,000
Reserve	15,000	5,000	10,000
	$305,469	$50,000	$255,469

ASSESSMENTS FOR
VERNON COLLECTION

Anthropology	$ 1,500
Art	1,000
Biology	1,000
Economics	1,500
English	6,500
History	12,000
Philosophy	750
Political Science	750
	$25,000

APPENDIX D

Dear President Walling:

As a member of the faculty at Carson University I feel it is my duty to inform you of a commitment by the university librarian to purchase the Vernon collection of some 40,000 volumes at a price of $121,000. The Senate Library Committee was originally informed that no more than $90,000 would be paid for the collection. The nature of the collection is so specialized that it cannot possibly serve the general needs of our curriculum for which even the present book budget is too limited.

I suggest that your office investigate this matter with a view toward recommending a reconsideration in light of the fact that the university librarian acted without proper authority.

                                              Very truly yours,
                                              Paul H. Warren
                                              Professor of Physics

APPENDIX E

State Purchasing Officer
State Building

Dear Sir:

It has just come to my attention that the librarian of Carson University has committed the university to purchase a collection of books (about 25,000 volumes) at auction for about $125,000. Various members of the faculty were told that nothing in excess of $90,000 would be spent for the collection, since it answers only a relatively few needs of the curriculum at a time when we need every dollar to round out the collection to meet the coming accreditation survey. The library has a pitifully small science collection and this collection will add little to it.

The faculty all feel that the purchase at this time was most unwise and represents a breach of faith. Since the university is having great difficulty in raising the purchase price, it is not too late for your office to start an investigation, if it is undertaken immediately.

                                              Very truly yours,
                                              A faculty member
                                              c: Dr. James Walling

APPENDIX F

ANALYSIS OF VERNON COLLECTION

Subject	Volumes Acquired	Volumes Added to the Collection
Ancient history	353	262
Bibliography	857	621
Botany	621	496
British history	1,057	560
European history	1,796	988
Far East	515	380
Fine arts	1,007	637
Historiography	262	211
Law	134	43
Literature	6,014	3,813
Philosophy and religion	417	221
Political science and economics	595	324
Psychology and medicine	609	315
U.S. history	4,563	2,428
Western Americana (includes Indian life, lore, and linguistics)	9,656	7,124
Miscellaneous	5,307	1,506
Total	33,763	19,929

25.
"It Looks Like We Need to Make Some Changes"

· ·

It was a beautiful spring morning and Harold Fashing, University Librarian at Barker State University, could not keep from glancing out his window. Unable to concentrate, he finally decided that he ought to find some excuse to get outside. Then he remembered that last fall he had promised to look at the geology department's map collection, which had outgrown the room that had housed it for the last eighteen years. The chairman of the department had requested an additional room, but he was informed that no more space could be diverted from classroom use. Faced with the need to find some solution, he called Fashing to tell him that the geology department might possibly be willing to let the library assume responsibility for the maps if it would maintain the collection and continue to develop it.

When the chairman first called Fashing, he was busy and promised to call back in a couple of weeks. By that time, the weather had turned cold and Fashing kept putting it off until it finally slipped his mind entirely.

An appointment was made for 2:00 P.M. On his way back to the office after the meeting, Fashing ran into Clifton Lewis, Dean of the new College of Allied Medical Professions. The college was in the process of developing programs in dental hygiene, physical therapy, medical records administration, nursing, respiratory technology, medical technology, and medical dietetics, along with a physician's assistant program. All these fields were entirely new to BSU, and library holdings until recently were minimal. Thus, the library was under pressure to build a collection rapidly. To this end, the president had made a special allocation at the beginning of the fiscal year of $22,500 to acquire books, periodicals, and other material. Fashing requested an additional position for a biomedical librarian, but this was rejected on the grounds that such a librarian could not be justified this year with only six full-time faculty and ninety-eight students in the new college. However, the president did promise to reconsider Fashing's request next year.

For the present, therefore, Fashing had to rely on his existing staff. He assigned the responsibility for selecting material for the new college to Sally Boyer, a reference librarian who held a bachelor's degree in biology. She agreed to help, but pointed out that her normal responsibilities were more than enough to keep her busy. She began by studying the basic planning document that had resulted in the establishment of the college. From this she learned that the present faculty was expected to grow in the next five years to a full-time equivalent of forty-two and the student body to nearly 900. While programs were selected initially on the basis of greatest need, the college did plan to add more programs in the future, including medical illustration, health services administration, occupational therapy, and radiologic technology. Boyer then met with Dean Lewis and the two agreed, in principle, that the best approach would be to acquire a basic collection of books and periodicals. They also agreed that back issues of periodicals should be acquired only for key titles and only for five years. Boyer added that even though the basic core collection would more than expend the $22,500 allocation, she would try to talk with all the faculty members now in the college about their individual needs. Lewis concluded by asking her to notify him of the titles added, and accordingly, she arranged to have a copy of the order slip sent as soon as each book was cataloged.

Since that time, Boyer had managed to see four of the six faculty members, and received a number of requests for specific books from them. Soon after the first of the year, she tried twice to make an appointment with Lewis to review progress. He spoke with her once on the phone and apologized for not seeing her because he was too busy writing grant proposals. He told her that he hadn't noticed any problems. "No need to worry," she thought, and she made no further efforts to see him.

As they exchanged greetings, Fashing suggested, hoping to delay the inevitable return to his office for a few minutes, that they stop at the commons for some coffee. Fashing asked about the library's efforts to serve the new college. Lewis did not hesitate a moment in expressing his dissatisfaction.

He reported recently having received a batch of about 300 slips, representing several month's acquisitions. While reviewing them the previous evening, he found five that upset him considerably. One was a six-year-old book on cancer prevention. The other four dealt with hospital administration, and were from five to eight years old. Lewis continued, "I don't want what I say to reflect in any way on Sally Boyer. I greatly appreciate what she's doing but this special allocation is just for our college, and it's not nearly adequate. I have a responsibility to see that it's used properly, and I'm very disturbed about buying things that are dated. It looks like we need to make some changes. Specifically, we need to develop a better way of deciding what to purchase with funds allocated for the enrichment of our college. All purchasing should be suspended until a College of Allied Medical Professions Library Committee is established to review acquisitions."

"We can't do that, at least not right now," Fashing explained. "We're getting toward the end of our budget year, and there's not much time left to encumber the funds. I'll certainly take a close look at this, and get back to you as fast as I can."

Back in his office, Fashing asked his secretary to call Sally Boyer. While waiting for her, he shook his head as he thought about the grant proposals Lewis had written, and how the director of sponsored grants complained at having to rework them because they were so sloppy.

As soon as Boyer came in, Fashing explained the problem and asked her to outline specifically how she had gone about spending the money. Boyer first apologized for not having told him more about what she was doing. She went on to say, "I guess I haven't talked with Dean Lewis as much as I should, but he's always busy, and I thought everything was okay. It's almost impossible even to get him on the phone. He worries about every single detail and probably works about sixteen hours a day, but I hear he doesn't get much done. I know he's interested in libraries. As a matter of fact, he was on the library committee at St. Luke's Hospital for many years. That has probably influenced his thinking a lot. Those physicians make every single decision about which books to buy and they can do it because the budgets are so low. But this is a much different operation.

"I used the standard bibliographies for basic medical collections. Brandon's list of books and periodicals for small medical libraries was in the *Bulletin of the Medical Library Association*. Stearns and Ratcliff published two lists, a general one that includes the allied health fields and another dealing with nursing. There was another list on nursing in *Nursing Outlook* not too long ago. I used Mapp's *Books for Occupational Education Programs*, Blake's *Medical Reference Works*, and *Subject Guide to Books in Print*, along with Austin Medical Library's monthly accession list. I also scan about half a dozen journals—*Journal of the American Medical Association, Bulletin of the Medical Library Association, Library Journal, Annals of Internal Medicine*, and the *New England Journal of Medicine*.

"I'm sure a few out-of-date things slipped in. Naturally, I looked over the lists and eliminated some titles, but I couldn't catch everything and neither could anyone else, given the amount of time I could spend on this project.

"If all he can come up with is five questionable items, we're doing a pretty good job. The idea of having a committee review all of the acquisitions bothers me. It's not a matter of not wanting to talk with them, but I just don't have enough time now to check with a committee every time we want to order a book."

• • • • •

In general, do you feel Boyer's approach and the specific sources she used represented the best way to spend the special allocation? What changes, if any, would you have made? Do you feel Boyer's relationships with the dean and the faculty of the College of Allied Medical Professions were the best that could be expected under the circumstances? What changes, if any, would you have made?

Would you favor a committee, consisting of members of the College of Allied Medical Professions faculty combined with one or more librarians? What could such a committee accomplish and what would its limitations be?

How do you feel Fashing should handle this situation?

What are some of the special problems of crash acquisitions programs? What special considerations face librarians working with faculty in this particular kind of situation?

26

"The Question Is 'How?'"

. . . .

Over the last ten years, the major emphasis at Nelson Library had been on developing resources to support a number of new or expanding area study programs at Griffith University. In view of the difficulties in identifying and acquiring materials from these areas, the library found it expedient to follow the lead of other, more aggressive university libraries in appointing bibliographers, in this case, for each of six areas—Africa, Hispanic America, East Europe, West Europe, Southeast Asia, and East Asia. By a combination of hard work and a great deal of money, they had, for the most part, done an outstanding job. Each bibliographer carefully scanned national bibliographies and other sources that identified needed material. Sometimes these were routed to the teaching faculty for consideration; sometimes the bibliographers made selections themselves. In addition, each bibliographer had made at least one overseas buying trip in order to acquire government documents, trade books, and other important publications from government agencies, booksellers, and educational institutions, and several had set up exchange programs.

Successful as these acquisitions programs were, they created a number of problems. First, because large amounts of money were needed to acquire retrospective material to bring the area collections to the desired level of strength, spending was cut in the traditional fields of study on the assumption that existing holdings were generally adequate to support instruction and research. While that was true at the time, a number of changes had subsequently taken place. New faculty members and new courses had been added in these disciplines and each created pressure for more library resources. Second, the university administration found it no longer possible to support the library as it had in past years. Ten years ago, Nelson Library had received a relatively high 5.8 percent of the educational budget. However, this percentage had slowly declined to a current level of 4.1 percent. The book budget had increased an average of just over 5 percent per year, which did not keep up with increases in cost and the rate of publication. The result was that Nelson Library had slipped behind a number of other large ARL libraries in terms of its total volume count, and no longer ranked among the top ten academic libraries in the nation.

Because this situation developed slowly, the Director of Libraries, Richard Borland, had ample time to think it over. He knew that changes would be necessary. Two things, in particular, bothered him. First, while the acquisitions rate was declining, faculty were besieging him as never before with demands for more material. Second, in talking with his staff, he was unable to develop much precise information about specific strengths and weaknesses of the collection to help him judge the merits of these demands for more material. Each of the six bibliographers knew his own field well, and could assess strengths and weaknesses in these areas. However, none of them knew very much about other fields. The head of acquisitions was largely absorbed in administrative responsibilities. While he was familiar with the kind of requests the faculty submitted, he could not judge their importance to the collection. Only a few members of the Reference Department were able to offer any help, and that was too fragmentary to give a clear picture of the problem. Several reference librarians were familiar with specific areas of collection, mostly because of their contacts with individual faculty members.

As Borland continued to think about this matter from time to time, he gradually reached the conclusion that in years past, with enough money for almost every need, systematic evaluation of the collection and coordination of its growth were not a problem. Now things had changed, and the best solution seemed to be a broad detailed analysis of the collection. He considered a number of approaches. Some institutions relied heavily on the teaching faculty for this purpose. Others depended more on librarians. Borland decided that, however this was to be done, it should be coordinated by a librarian and that it should be the beginning of an ongoing program for developing the collection systematically. Therefore, it would be necessary to appoint someone to assume this responsibility on a full-time basis.

He approached the provost, who explained that he could not fund a new position, but that he would raise the salary of an existing position vacated by resignation or retirement to the level of assistant director. Soon after, a vacancy occurred and Borland announced the creation of the new position, Assistant Director for Collection Development. A job description accompanied the memo and described the position as involving responsibility for coordinating the growth of the collection, including supervision of the six area bibliographers who formerly reported to the head of acquisitions. Several applications were received. He chose John O'Connell, who had been assistant head of reference, over the rest, including one of the bibliographers, because

O'Connell seemed to have a broader view of the problems than the others. After announcing his decision, Borland set up a meeting with O'Connell and Associate Director Thomas Kabalin.

As Kabalin entered the office, Borland waved him to a chair. "Sit down, Tom. John's been here a couple of minutes and we've already started talking a little about what he'll be doing in the next year. I want the three of us to go over this carefully because there are quite a few questions we need to answer."

"Right," Kabalin replied. "I think we know what we need to do; top priority should go to systematic evaluation of the collection, subject by subject—periodicals, back files, books, microfilms, whatever. The question is 'how?' How do we go about it? I've talked with you some about this, John, and I know you have been thinking more about it."

"Yes, I have. For one thing, we're lucky in that we can draw on the experience of a lot of other libraries. I've tried to find out everything I can about what they've been doing. I agree that systematic evaluation, I guess I'd call it a kind of inventory of resource requirements, is what we should really do first. I think about the best way to do it would be to appoint and use several bibliographers for, say, social sciences, humanities, and behavioral sciences. We may need someone else, but the rest of the fields like science, education, engineering, business, art and music, are covered pretty well by the branch libraries. Probably we should try to coordinate what they're doing with the bibliographers' work. At any rate, the kind of people I have in mind for the new bibliographers would be different from those we have now; they'd be more like generalists even though they should have graduate degrees in some area of their responsibility."

"One thing bothers me," Kabalin said. "Can't you use some of the people in reference who are subject specialists? A lot of libraries do. And you're perfectly willing to use branch librarians."

"Oh, there are a couple of good reasons, I think. The branch librarians are different. They're more subject oriented and they're used to being involved in book selection. Reference librarians aren't, and many libraries have found out that they don't work out too well. Collection development is really an added responsibility; some like it, some don't. The result is uneven quality, and that's exactly the thing we're trying to do away with now. Smaller colleges and universities use reference librarians because they have to, but we don't. I really think this is a full-time job."

Still not convinced, the associate director continued, "John, we've got a good bunch of people in reference. A number have graduate degrees and some have developed good relations with faculty. It just seems to me as though they're the logical ones to do this. Any good reference librarian should accept it as part of his job."

"I agree. But like I said, it doesn't work out that way. If you want me to do a good job, you've got to give me people to do it."

"We don't have to settle this today," Kabalin conceded, "but there's another problem. We can't simply pull new positions out of a hat. We'd have to do it by attrition; that may take some time."

"I think this deserves more thought," the director added. "It's important that we do it right. But, at this point, I'd like to focus on something else. We all agree on the importance of taking a systematic look at our holdings, and I liked what you said, John, about an 'inventory of resource requirements.' I want to get something down on paper. Lots of libraries have formal acquisitions policies; we don't, but I'd like to see you move in that direction. We need some guidelines or an outline for developing the collection, not just for ourselves, but also to justify budget requests and for working with faculty."

"I agree. But whatever we do will take a long time."

"Yes," Borland concluded, "and I think everybody will learn a great deal in the process. We're committing a lot of staff time to it, and I want to get something worthwhile out of it. To make sure we do, I want to give the whole matter more thought. Take a look at what others are doing, think it over, and then outline what you want such a document to say, and how you plan to go about doing it. This also involves Tom's concern about whether we use reference people or full-time bibliographers. It might be best to list the advantages and disadvantages of each. I don't need a formal memo, but I do want you to think this out carefully. Then let's talk it over again in about a week or ten days, and plan to make a firm decision."

• • • • •

Outline, as Borland has requested, in as much detail as possible, the specific steps for planning and conducting an "inventory of resource requirements" for Nelson Library and subsequently for developing a sound overall acquisitions policy.

27.
"Everybody's Going to Have to Justify His Existence"

. . . .

As the acquisitions librarians gathered first thing Monday morning in his office, James Ramsey, Assistant University Librarian for Acquisitions, handed out copies of a draft document describing the functions of the order and collection development departments (Appendix A). As soon as all had arrived, he closed the door and began.

"I worked most of the weekend on this, and now I'd like each of you to go over it and tear it apart because it's very important to our future. We don't have much time, because it has to be in the director's office by Wednesday noon. But before I go any further, let me back up and explain what this is all about. All of you know as well as I do what the university's fiscal problems are, and I think we all suspect that's really why President Hansen retired.

"It certainly looks like President Gleisner isn't going to waste any time getting things straightened out. Last Friday, after just five days on campus, he directed each unit to submit a mission statement. Personally, I think this is just a first step, and that everybody's going to have to justify his existence. I'm also sure that he'll be moving into program budgeting.

"Now I think we are doing a pretty good job. In fact, I think we're doing an outstanding job. But, does President Gleisner realize it? Of course not. In fact, he may not even know what acquisitions is. So we're going to have to do a good job of selling him on what we're doing.

"I'm certain he'll go over these mission statements pretty carefully and that he'll use them to decide where to start looking for places to make budget cuts. We all know that libraries and especially book budgets usually get hit pretty hard in any budget crisis. That's why I am determined that this is going to be the best document we have ever put out.

"I'd like each of you to go over this, and, as I said before, tear it apart. Get your comments back to me as soon as possible. There's no hard and fast deadline like noon or five this afternoon, but we will meet again first thing to-morrow. Just don't get involved with anything else until you're finished with your response. Again, I can't emphasize too much the importance of this report. I think it is no exaggeration to call it a life or death matter."

Ramsey concluded by asking for questions, but it was pointed out that no one had had a chance to read the statement in advance. Recognizing that questions might come later, Ramsey urged them to come in and talk over anything relating to the report, although he cautioned that he would be out of the department quite a bit going through the literature to see if he could find ways to improve the statement.

• • • • •

Assuming Ramsey's draft document accurately reflects the work of the order and collection development departments, as a member of one of the departments, what suggestions would you make to improve this statement in light of the purpose for which it is intended?

APPENDIX A

Draft: The Function and Organization of Acquisitions

Acquisitions is responsible for the development of the library's collection. To ac-complish this, it is divided into two departments, responsible for collection devel-opment and ordering. The function of the first is to select books and evaluate requests submitted from the various departments, while the function of the second is to order this material. Book selection involves identifying the optimum amount and character of the literature required to support academic programs on this campus. Responsibil-ity for the entire collection is divided among four bibliographers who select material in the (1) humanities, (2) social sciences, (3) behavioral sciences, and (4) sciences. In addition, other librarians with specialized knowledge may be used for specific selec-tion projects. Bibliographers are recruited on the basis of academic preparation in the fields for which they are responsible, their ability to work effectively with members of the academic community, and their capacity to plan programs for developing library resources. In order to insure the uniform development of the collection, this effort must be carefully coordinated and the bibliographers must be able to work together as a team.

Two basic problems face the bibliographers: (1) selectivity and (2) communica-tions. Academic libraries often equate size with greatness. However, size alone does not ensure greatness. Two factors are equally important: (1) the quality of selections; and (2) the degree to which they reflect the needs of the institution. Selectivity based on an organized plan for developing holdings is the best guarantee of quality. Such an approach serves two functions: (1) to develop a collection that reflects needs; and (2) to provide a basis for mutual understanding of library goals between the library and teaching faculties. Bibliographers serve as a liaison between the library and the rest of the academic community in collection building. They evaluate statements by the teaching faculty with regard to library needs and translate them into library terms. They also prepare reports on the status of the collection, explain library policies and procedures connected with collection building, and attempt to stimulate interest on the part of the teaching faculty in the library and its use.

Developing a systematic program for collection building involves the following steps: (1) formulating collecting goals; (2) identifying specific needs; and (3) determining dollar requirements. The library is responsible for supporting the educational objectives of the college. Therefore, bibliographers must be involved in academic planning in order to understand the educational objectives of the university, the type of students being trained, the degree programs, specific course offerings, instructional methods, as well as research needs and objectives of students and teaching faculty. Although there are an infinite number of levels of collecting, for planning purposes they may be divided roughly into four groups: (1) a core collection of books, which the library should have regardless of its educational programs; (2) collections to support undergraduate instruction; (3) basic research collections to support graduate programs; and (4) comprehensive research collections to support specialized research.

Once needs have been evaluated and the appropriate level defined for each segment of the collection, the bibliographers must establish specific requirements for building or maintaining holdings at the desired level. Three steps are involved in this process: (1) determining the nature of the literature for each field and the relative importance of monographic, serial, periodical, and other material; (2) evaluating existing holdings for adequacy; and (3) selecting specific titles. Often all three steps can be accomplished at the same time by utilizing selective, authoritative bibliographies, which approximate the desired level of adequacy. Frequently, however, such tools do not exist and the bibliographer must rely on other resources such as comprehensive bibliographies, national bibliographies, book catalogs, accessions lists, citations, review media, or booksellers' catalogs.

The final step is to translate identified needs into specific dollar amounts, and to establish priorities to insure the balanced growth of the collection.

The second major division is the order department, which is responsible for acquiring books that have been requested by the bibliographers, librarians, teaching faculty, and students. The objectives of this department are twofold: (1) to get the material to the user as quicky as possible; and (2) to do this as economically as possible. Acquisitions librarians require considerable knowledge and background in: (1) management theory; (2) organization theory; and (3) human relations. They are concerned with the organization and flow of work, with identifying problems and reviewing them with the staff, and with developing solutions. This requires individuals who are thoroughly familiar with all the details of the work of the department, and who can utilize this knowledge for problem solving, work simplification, and improved work flow.

Day-to-day supervision is the responsibility of highly trained subprofessional assistants, who are encouraged to assume as much responsibility as they can. This policy is also extended to the clerical staff, who are encouraged to work as independently as possible so that their potential for higher level assignments can be evaluated. They must be able to identify problems and refer them to their supervisors. All members of the staff are encouraged to contribute toward developing solutions to problems related to the organization of work.

The activities of the acquisitions departments are described in the following reports:

1. *Workload Statistics, Acquisitions*, a monthly statistical report covering the amount of staff and the output for a number of selected activities.

2. *Acquisitions Monthly Report*, which describes: (1) important meetings with members of the teaching faculty in connection with accreditation visits, new degree programs, course offerings, or other factors that may affect library needs; (2) new exchange programs or important gifts; (3) the results of bibliographic surveys and research; and (4) significant activities, changes, and improvements in the checking, ordering, receiving, and accounting.

3. *Library Budget Recommendations* are prepared in April of each year. They summarize development of the collection subject-by-subject, project future needs, and contain estimates for allocation of library funds.

APPENDIX B

DATA SHEET
Baudette University

Students	14,178	
Faculty	2,406	
Volumes (books, bound periodicals,		
bound government documents)		1,009,422
Library budget		$3,641,287
Book & periodical budget		1,205,279
Staffing		
Librarians	57.5	
Clerical	142.6	
Student assistants	50.2	
Total staff	250.3	

APPENDIX C

BAUDETTE UNIVERSITY LIBRARY ORGANIZATION CHART

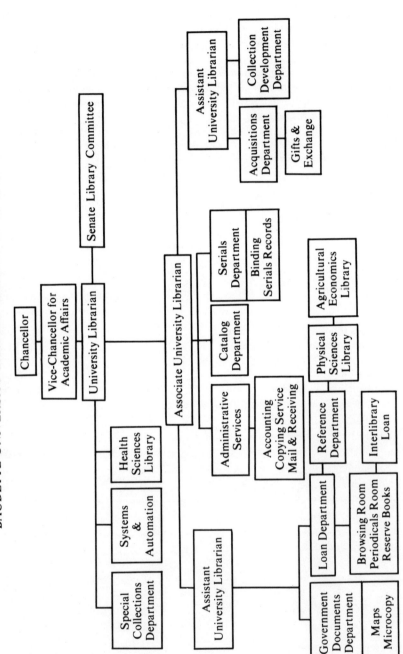

28.
"We've Got to Put Things in Perspective"

· · · · · · · · · · · · · · · · · · · ·

"Since I'm the only librarian on the selection committee," Hans Schmiedler began, "I'll really be representing all of you. I know everyone doesn't agree on what the new university librarian ought to be, and that's one reason I called this meeting. If we can talk some of the questions out, maybe we can agree on at least some points, and that would give me more leverage in the committee."

With that, he invited the librarians to express their ideas and threw the meeting open to discussion. While many were openly sarcastic about the failure of the administration to involve the librarians more actively in the selection process, they were, nevertheless, vitally interested in the outcome. In fact, only three of the forty-two librarians had not come to the meeting. Moreover, it was generally recognized that even one librarian on the committee would have been unheard of five years ago. When the president asked them to elect a representative, they chose Schmiedler, Near Eastern Studies Librarian, because they knew he would do his best to protect the interests of the library and because he was not identified with any particular faction among the librarians themselves.

Feelings were strong and there was no lack of discussion. Even though many different views were expressed, the librarians agreed on two points. First, they wanted the committee to act rapidly because they resented the fact that Theodore Phelps, professor of economics and chairman of the Senate Library Committee, had been named acting university librarian. Second, they expressed concern for better communication and staff involvement in the affairs of the library. For years, the former university librarian, Horace McDiarmid, had run the library with a dictatorial, though usually benevolent hand.

After about fifteen minutes of discussion, Iris Hibbard, a reference librarian, raised her hand and was recognized. "What I'm worried about are our priorities. By that, I mean what is really most important for the library. But before I go into that, let me say to those of you who don't know me too well, that I came here four years ago from Cunningham University. Even though it's very similar to Kirkland, the libraries are quite different. I find myself always making comparisons, and some of them bother me. Specifically, I think Dr. McDiarmid's priorities were wrong with respect to acquisitions. In other words, he put too much money in collection building at the expense of services."

She moved to the blackboard in the conference room and wrote out a table (Table 1).

Table 1

	Cunningham	Kirkland
Faculty	828	818
FTE students	9,193	8,162
Bachelor's degrees awarded	1,725	1,244
Master's degrees	1,031	532
Doctorates	225	219

"I thought these figures would be helpful in illustrating what I'm getting at. As you can see, there are a number of similarities. Cunningham has more students and more doctoral programs. We have doctorates in architecture and oriental studies, on the one hand, but they have business, education, law, medicine, and dentistry. Also they have eleven branch libraries, including medicine, law and dentistry, and we have nineteen. So, with more students and programs, they should be spending more than we do on acquisitions and their collection ought to be quite a bit larger than ours. But here's the way it looks."

Again Hibbard went to the blackboard and wrote out another table (Table 2).

Table 2

	Cunningham	%	Kirkland	%
Collections	2,601,192		2,545,755	
Budget				
Salaries	$2,109,941	61.3	$2,039,713	55.1
Books	916,548	26.6	1,460,660	39.5
Operating Expenses	415,330	12.1	199,471	5.4
Total	$3,441,819		$3,699,844	

"I think that sums it up pretty well; we're spending way too much on acquisitions. I'm not saying that collections aren't important, but we've got to put things in perspective. I don't have accurate staffing figures because the two libraries are organized differently, but I do know that they've got more people in public services at Cunningham and they're spending well over $100,000 a year on automation. They've got an on-line circulation system—the whole thing. That's service!"

An immediate response came from Dick Wilson, Preparations Department head, "I've worked here many years, Iris, and I'd say that Dr. McDiarmid was on the right track. I, for one, want a successor who would continue his policies. Remember that in the last analysis, the real guts of the library is the collection.

"But still I think you don't really understand what Dr. McDiarmid accomplished. For example, look at your second table. Salaries are a little more at Cunningham, but not that much. So there are only two real differences. One is automation. Now a lot of people may disagree with me, but I'd put $100,000 into books any day. Sure, a computer can file a whole lot of records rapidly, but it doesn't save any money doing it. About all an automated circulation system does, as far as I can see, is save students from filling out charge cards. If they can't do that, they don't belong in college. So the real difference is in the book budget.

"Dr. McDiarmid got more from the administration for books than Cunningham does. It's obvious; McDiarmid had a much better support from the administration than they do, and I, for one, don't want to see us lose that. But that's not all. We've got a distinguished faculty here and we can't hold them unless we give them first-rate libraries."

"Oh, I think the faculty at Cunningham is just as distinguished as ours, if not more so," Hibbard said. "As you can see, I spent some time collecting data for this afternoon, but, Dick, I never thought to count Nobel laureates. I'd guess our ratio is about like theirs. The 'distinguished faculty' argument isn't good enough. Anyway, that's really beside the point. What I'm saying is that as librarians I think we have some important professional responsibilities and one of them is service. Some studies have shown that actually only a small percent of most library collections is ever used very much. That's why I say it's important to place a little more emphasis on helping people to use whatever percent they use rather than on building huge repositories. What I'm saying is that Dr. McDiarmid's emphasis on collection building was unrealistic."

"The hell it was!" broke in Edwin Cowle, head of Circulation. "That's the way he kept his job—buy anything the faculty wants—no questions. He didn't even spend a fraction of what this library should be spending on binding. Lots of periodicals and most of the unbound material never have and never will be bound; the stacks are a mess! My people just can't keep them in good shape."

"That's ridiculous!" Wilson shot back.

"Look," Hibbard said, "I don't want this to degenerate into a brawl. I simply think we have a responsibility to consider a couple of points pretty carefully. I mentioned service, but let me elaborate a little and then go on to a related matter. Again, I don't have exact figures, but our reference staff is spread a lot thinner than the reference staff was at Cunningham, because there are so many people here working in technical services. The result is that we don't have time to do other things—important things. Before I came here, I had a lot more time to spend with faculty—time to let them know when new books came in, to help them with bibliographies and library exercises for their classes, or even to give a few lectures or tours. Again, I can't give you exact figures, but I know our circulation figures are below Cunningham's. I question the whole philosophy of merely putting books on shelves just in case someone might want them someday. Service, and that includes the circulation system, does make a difference. This kind of service has been completely out of the question here.

"There's another dimension to this problem, too. Our salaries are low. Turnover is high; almost a third of the staff leaves every year. All of you know that. My question is whether it's fair to pay us this way and whether it's economical for the university to keep training new people every year."

What Hibbard was thinking, but did not say for fear of offending others, was that better salaries might also attract better librarians. She was dismayed at the lack of professionalism on the part of many of her colleagues. Too many of the faculty and administration did not regard librarians as truly professional. However, she believed that a new director could do a lot to improve the image of librarians as well as their salaries.

"I've said my piece," she concluded, "and I'll be quiet now, but I do want to emphasize that I think our library should be something more than a big warehouse full of books."

In response, Wilson said, "All of you know that we have built a number of outstanding collections over the years. We've got some of the best collections in the country—no one equals us in the French Revolution or Victorian literature. Our African holdings are excellent and so is our East Asian collection. The Latin American, Slavic, and Near Eastern holdings aren't quite as good, but we're getting stronger. These collections aren't cheap, but they lend considerable prestige to our institution. I doubt that our faculty would tolerate any change that would reduce the quality of these collections and I personally would fight anything like that as hard as I could.

"We're not a small college, or even a small university. Our responsibilities are different. If we expect to continue to recruit top-notch faculty and graduate students, the library is an important drawing card."

• • • • •

To what extent is Wilson's argument that a large university's collection development program cannot be compared with smaller institutions valid? How can a university like Kirkland strike a reasonable balance between resources and services?

If you were Schmiedler, seeking to represent all interests within the library fairly, how would you relate the views expressed at the meeting to the process of selecting a new director?

If you were the newly appointed university librarian at Kirkland University, and the various opinions expressed by members of the staff were brought to your attention, how would you evaluate them and what action, if any, would you take?

29

"They Both Look Good"

• • • • • • • • • • • • • • • • •

Spring was always a busy time for Gail Bogadz, Assistant Director for Personnel and Budget at Warrington State University Library. However, this year seemed worse than ever before. Between budget preparation and recruiting, she'd hardly had a free moment in the last four weeks.

Among the several vacancies at Warrington for the coming year was the position of assistant acquisitions librarian. Bogadz sent letters announcing this position, together with a job description (Appendix A), to a number of library schools. As the applications came in, she reviewed them and checked references. Then she set up a meeting of the director, the associate director, the head acquisitions librarian, and herself, to narrow the list of applicants to two, because the budget allowed for bringing only that number of candidates to Warrington for interview. The group selected June Dillworth and Paul Witt. Dillworth, twenty-three years old, had graduated last year from a large university with a social science major and gone on the library school at the same institution. Both as an undergraduate and while in library school she had worked as a student assistant in the Acquisitions Department and in the director's office. On her resume, she described her work as follows:

"I perform various secretarial duties, including typing letters, graphs, collecting statistics, etc. I have also done preorder work, order typing, and bibliographic and duplicate searching. I have helped prepare bindery shipments and done preliminary work toward withdrawing books. While in this position, I have become familiar with basic bibliographic tools: *LC Catalog, National Union Catalog, Ulrich's, Union List of Serials*, etc."

Witt was older. He had graduated with a degree in German from an eastern university. Following that, he served as an Air Force officer for five years. During that period, he had several assignments, which he described as follows:

"Officer in charge of the Target Materials Library. Responsible for supervising seventeen airmen in the acquisition, storage, and retrieval of over one million classified maps, charts, and frames of aerial photography.

"Involved in editing intelligence briefs and personal presentation of these to the commander and key members of his staff."

After he was released from active duty, he took a master's degree in international relations and then went on to library school.

Bogadz scheduled interviews for both Dillworth and Witt. Each candidate met first with Gary Rosecrans, Head Acquisitions Librarian, who began by presenting an overview of the department. He reviewed the budget and explained that the rate of acquisitions had stabilized at about 51,000 volumes a year. Then he went on to say that the department was organized into five sections—bibliographic checking under a librarian, ordering under a library assistant, serials under a librarian, accounting under an accounting clerk, and binding and labeling under a library assistant. Next, Rosecrans discussed the bibliographic checking unit in greater detail, since the vacancy was for the supervisor of that section. There were six full-time civil service personnel—two library assistants, four clerks—and about sixty student hours. The section was responsible for all bibliographic checking and for maintenance of both an LC proof-slip file and a collection of publishers' catalogs.

After that, Rosecrans talked with each of the applicants about their own interests and experience. Then, he showed them through the department and introduced them to the section heads and to some of the bibliographic checkers. In the afternoon, they met with Bogadz and with the associate director, and the day concluded with a half-hour interview with the Director of Libraries, Roger Traxler.

June Dillworth was the first to be interviewed. Traxler began by asking her, "Tell me, Miss Dillworth, what interests you specifically about this job?"

"I've worked for quite some time as a student assistant in the director's office. In that kind of job, you get to know a lot about what's going on in the whole library. This experience has colored my whole view of librarianship. I see it largely as a set of problems—problems that we haven't solved, but we really need to solve. Things like making our work truly professional, making sure we operate as efficiently as possible. There are many others, too, but we're talking about acquisitions. Probably I know more about acquisitions than anything else because before I went to the director's office, I worked in acquisitions for a year doing a lot of the same things I'd be involved in with this job."

"What kind of job do you want ultimately?"

"Administration," Dillworth answered. "I guess my job in the director's office got me interested in it. I saw all the reports coming in from the various departments and watched the way things were being done. And to be very honest, I think there's a lot of wasted effort and that a lot of librarians are doing things that aren't very professional. As I said, I'd like to work with those kinds of problems."

"Now, you spent most of the morning in acquisitions. At this point I'd like to know what your reactions are, and whether you have any questions."

"A couple of things bothered me a little. I asked Mr. Rosecrans some questions, and frankly I thought his answers were a little vague. In the first place, I wanted to know something about training. I mean, how would I be trained? He said he would train me for a while in bibliographic checking until I could take over the section. But I think the clerks in the checking section are pretty competent. They can work with major foreign languages and they know the rules of entry pretty well. I talked with a couple of them. I honestly wonder whether they need a full-time supervisor in that area. Maybe I could contribute more if my assignment were a little broader."

"How do you mean?" Traxler asked.

"Well, at this point only the serials section is supervised by a librarian. I sort of think I could do more if I spent some of my time working with the other sections such as ordering and binding."

"What sort of things did you have in mind doing?"

"I think Mr. Rosecrans is pretty busy. In fact, he may be too busy to dig into some of the more complicated problems. Maybe I could help him by working on some of them. I'm thinking of file maintenance, work flow, and perhaps vendor evaluation. Some of those things take an awful lot of time. But, as I said, I don't feel he always has enough time to really dig in where it's necessary."

"What did he think?"

Dillworth paused for a moment to choose her words carefully, and then began, "I believe he doesn't see the problem. To be very honest, I believe he is too tied up with organizational charts."

"Sorry, I'm not sure I know what you mean."

"I mean he views the department as a series of boxes. Everybody is in one of those boxes, and that's where you stay. Sure, I know you have to have an organizational structure, but I sometimes feel you can carry it a little too far."

Later that same week, Paul Witt was also interviewed. Traxler began with the question, "What got you into librarianship?"

"While I was in the Air Force, I worked with a large volume of documents—intelligence reports and the like. I got interested in the problem of organizing materials and later, when I went back to work on my master's, I got to thinking about the same problem in the context of academic libraries."

"Why did you apply for this particular position?"

"I'm interested in administration and I think acquisitions is the best place to learn. This position would give me an opportunity to supervise people, to work with the budget, to work with the business office, and to get involved in a lot of other things that are important in administration. Acquisitions seems to be pretty much at the heart of things, or at least as close as I can expect to get in a beginning position."

"What got you interested in administration?"

"The Air Force," Witt replied. "I ran a small unit and I enjoyed getting people organized to do a job effectively. I just like it, I guess. And I think I'd do a good job. This job looks good because it would give me some administrative responsibility right away while at the same time I could be learning more about libraries. I've never really had any library experience. That's what I need most right now."

"Now, after you've had a chance to see the department and talk with Rosecrans, I'd like to know if you have any questions or comments."

"I don't think I have any questions, really. Gary explained things pretty well. It's clear enough to me. That's one good thing, I think. It looks like he's pretty well organized himself. In fact, everything seems to be running smoothly."

"I think so, too, and that makes me wonder. If your real interest is administration, wouldn't you get bored pretty fast there?"

"No," Witt said. "I like a well-run organization. I wouldn't want to work in one that wasn't. But I think the real question is how long it would take me to learn as much as I can about that job. That's the point at which I'll be ready for something else. But I'll stay for at least two years."

The following day, the same group that reviewed the original applications met again to discuss Dillworth and Witt. Traxler began by asking Rosecrans to summarize his reactions to the two candidates.

"Quite honestly, I'm not sure I can decide. Witt looks awfully good. I think he's a real administrator, and he'll go a long way. But I'm not sure he'll stay around too long. Dillworth's good also. She'll probably stay a lot longer, but she's not quite as mature. That's what worries me about her. She has some ideas about not just working with bibliographic checking."

"Why don't you go into that a little?" Traxler said, "I'm not sure I understand what bothers you."

"I'm afraid she just wouldn't have enough time for her own job, and that she's get involved in too many other things to do well. But I guess what really worries me is that I'm afraid this kind of arrangement will confuse the people in the department. If she goes off to work in different sections, it might get confusing and the staff might get to wondering who's the boss. That bothers me.

"At any rate, I think they're about equal. They're quite different, but they both look good. It's a lot different from the time we replaced Marilyn Bodiker as serials librarian. I had a pretty strong feeling about that one and we had quite an argument. But this time I'll be glad to take either—whichever you prefer."

• • • • •

If you were Traxler, which candidate would you recommend for this position? Why?

APPENDIX A

Position: Assistant Acquisitions Librarian

Classification: Librarian I or II

Definition:
Under the direction of the head acquisitions librarian, to perform the following
  duties:

Duties:
To supervise the day-to-day operations of the Bibliographic Checking Section.
To perform complex bibliographic checking and rechecking.
To review the work of the bibliographic checkers for completeness and accuracy.
To develop and prepare procedure manuals describing the operation of the sec-
  tion.
To train new staff members in learning their assignments.
To study and analyze the various operations of the Bibliographic Checking Sec-
  tion.
To develop and recommend programs designed to improve the overall efficiency
  of the section and to increase the effective utilization of the staff.
To conduct special studies for the department as directed by the head acquisitions
  librarian.

Minimum Qualification:
Graduation from an ALA-accredited library school.

Desirable Qualifications:
Experience in business and/or the book trade.

30.
"I Wonder What We're Really Looking For?"

· ·

HUMANITIES BIBLIOGRAPHER Blountsville State University. Responsible for collection development, library/faculty liaison in the following areas: English, French, German, Spanish, and Russian literatures; history, philosophy, fine arts, journalism, speech, and telecommunicative arts. University of 20,000 enrollment, doctoral programs offered in English and history. Appointment to the rank of instructor or assistant professor depending on qualifications. Minimum salary $11,000. TIAA, month vacation, other excellent fringe benefits. Apply to Hugh Baxley, Dean of Library Services, Blountsville State University.

Six weeks after the ad appeared, Baxley looked over the applications he had received and set aside ten which for one reason or another looked promising to him. He sent these on to Barbara King, Chief of Technical Services, to whom the bibliographers reported, with a memo asking her to review them and explaining that it would be necessary to narrow down the list of candidates. The memo went on to say that he would like her to set aside and rank in order of preference those she would be interested in interviewing, and then he would write for their references. After these had been returned, they could decide on which ones to select. As King read the documents over, she made the following notes in her mind:

William Eccles, 34. Bachelor's and master's degrees in English followed by the M.L.S. Master's degree in history six years later and since that time has been working on a Ph.D. in library science, which is expected this June. Experience includes three years of high school teaching (English and Spanish); after library school worked two years as a foreign language cataloger and in special collections. While in the doctoral program worked part-time in a public library. Has published some reviews, contributed to and edited a college literary magazine as an undergraduate.

Phyllis Stern. For the last three years a reference and humanities librarian at a similar university library noted for its low pay. During the same period working on doctorate in American literature. All course work completed; plans a bibliographic dissertation. B.A. and M.A. in English. Phi Beta Kappa. M.L.S. three years ago. Served on university-wide Commission on the Status of Women.

Patrick Crowley. Began college as an economics major. Dropped out and returned. Graduated with philosophy major and minors in history and English four years ago. One year of graduate work in doctoral program in philosophy, followed by two years experience in a large book shop buying used and rare books. Also taught music and performed professionally. M.L.S. expected in June.

Sylvia Liao, 22. Attended a medium-sized college with a four-year scholarship. Majored in history and humanities, minored in German. Served for two years as student member of library committee and self-study committee for reaccreditation. Received an award for the member of the graduating class with the highest standing in history. Went directly to library school with a state scholarship; served as a student representative to the curriculum committee of the library school. Throughout college worked part-time and as an undergraduate was a member of the women's intercollegiate volleyball team.

Sherrie Faber. Bachelor's degree thirteen years ago with major in history and minors in English and philosophy, Ph.D. four years ago in modern European history with minors in French and English. Dissertation on the concept of the ideal prince in the literature of the French Enlightenment. Teaching assistant while doctoral student. Since receiving doctorate, worked mostly part-time as a secretary and in various office jobs through temporary agencies, although received one-year appointment as a lecturer in the Department of History at a state college as temporary replacement. Presently in library school; M.L.S. expected in August. All A's received in first semester of library school. No library experience.

Anne Meeker, 27. Bachelor's in history with minors in political science and Russian. National Merit Scholar. M.A. two years later from Cunningham University, emphasized Russian history and peasant studies. Received tuition scholarship. Reading knowledge of French and Russian. Since receiving master's, worked as research assistant for a popular science magazine for six months and as a clerical assistant in a law library for similar length of time. Currently in library school. Degree expected in June.

Curtis Holm, 29. Bachelor's *cum laude* in English, minor in philosophy from a small college. M.A. same field two years after from large midwestern university. Reading knowledge of French, German, middle and old English. After master's taught English two years in small midwestern college.

Courses included both beginning and advanced subjects including literary criticisms, Shakespeare, literature of the Renaissance, and eighteenth century. Following that spent two years working on Ph.D. and teaching freshman English. Switched to library school at the same institution; M.L.S. expected in August.

Thomas Hill. Graduated two years ago *cum laude* from a major eastern university with a major in English and American literature and a minor in American history. During this period worked three years as a student assistant in the circulation department of the library. Has a reading knowledge of Spanish. Stayed on and went to library school part-time while working full-time in the documents and microtext department of the library. Work involved selection, acquisitions, and reference with regard to government publications of all nations and some international organizations. Has traveled widely throughout Latin America and has reading and speaking knowledge of Spanish.

Jerri Kinzer, 24. Bachelor's with major in art, but a broad background in humanities including English, music, theatre, philosophy, and languages. M.L.S. last year followed by one year's experience as a reference librarian at a similar institution. While an undergraduate, worked as a student assistant mostly in circulation. Fluent knowledge of French, reading knowledge of Spanish, Portuguese, Italian, German, Russian, and Latin.

Gregory Foster, 32. B.A. in French with English minor. Overall undergraduate grade point average 3.0. M.A. in Slavic languages and literature. Overall grade point average 3.1. In addition to French and Russian, has reading knowledge of Spanish, German, Polish, and Latin. Two years' experience as instructor in foreign languages (Russian and French) at small college. Left because doctorate was required for tenure. One year as a sales representative for publisher. Now in library school. M.L.S. expected in August. Special interests include literature, theatre, fine arts, films and filmmaking, and travel.

After she finished reading over the applications and resumes, she set them down and thought to herself how difficult it is to make any reasonable decision on the basis of a one-page resume. Then as she began to face the task at hand, she asked herself, "I wonder what we're really looking for?"

● ● ● ● ●

What qualities would you consider most important in selecting a humanities bibliographer at Blountsville State University? How would these differ at a larger or smaller university? Which candidates would you want to interview and why?